Cross-National Policy Convergence

Causes, Concepts and Empirical Findings

Edited by Christoph Knill

LONDON AND NEW YORK

First published 2006 by Routledge
2 Park Square, Milton Park, Abingdon, Oxfordshire OX14 4RN

Simultaneously published in the USA and Canada
by Routledge
711 Third Avenue, New York, NY 10017, USA

First issued in paperback 2016

Routledge is an imprint of the Taylor and Francis Group, an informa business

© 2006 Taylor and Francis

Typeset in Agaramond by Techset Composition Limited

All rights reserved. No part of this book may be reprinted or reproduced or utilised in any form or by any electronic, mechanical, or other means, now known or hereafter invented, including photocopying and recording, or in any information storage or retrieval system, without permission in writing from the publishers.

British Library Cataloguing in Publication Data
A catalogue record for this book is available from the British Library

Library of Congress Cataloging in Publication Data
A catalog record for this title has been requested

ISBN 13: 978-1-138-96702-1 (pbk)
ISBN 13: 978-0-415-37491-0 (hbk)

Cross-National Policy Convergence

A fresh analysis of policy convergences across nations, which identifies their key driving forces.

To what extent and in which direction can we empirically observe a convergence of national policies? In which areas and for which patterns of policy is convergence more or less pronounced? This text addresses these central questions with clarity and rigour.

With growing economic and institutional interlinkages between nation states, it is often assumed that there is an overall trend towards increasingly similar policies across countries. Comparative research on the domestic impact of globalization and European integration, however, reveals that policy convergence can hardly be considered as a dominant and uniform tendency which can be taken for granted. Although a number of factors have been suggested in order to account for the rather mixed empirical picture, we still have limited knowledge about the causes and conditions of cross-national policy convergence. In particular, the central mechanisms and conditions affecting both degree and level of cross-national policy convergence are yet not well understood.

This book will be of great interest to all students and scholars of the European Union, European politics, and international relations. This is a special issue of the leading *Journal of European Public Policy.*

Christoph Knill is professor of political and administrative science at the University of Konstanz, Germany.

Journal of European Public Policy Series

Series Editor: Jeremy Richardson is a Professor at Nuffield College, Oxford University

This series seeks to bring together some of the finest edited works on European Public Policy. Reprinting from Special Issues of the 'Journal of European Public Policy', the focus is on using a wide range of social sciences approaches, both qualitative and quantitative, to gain a comprehensive and definitive understanding of Public Policy in Europe.

Towards a Federal Europe
Edited by Alexander H. Trechsel

The Disparity of European Integration
Edited by Tanja A. Börzel

Contents

Preface

This book is the outcome of several activities. Many chapters have been written in the context of the European research project 'Environmental governance in Europe: the impact of international institutions and trade on policy convergence (ENVIPOLCON)', which is carried out by the Universities of Konstanz, Nijmegen, Hamburg, Berlin (FU) and Salzburg. The financial support of the European Union is gratefully acknowledged. Moreover, all contributions to this book were presented at the workshop 'International Sources of Policy Convergence' held at the University of Hamburg in April 2004. The workshop was generously funded by the Fritz Thyssen Foundation and the Centre for Globalization and Governance (CGG) at the University of Hamburg. My special thanks go to the colleagues who acted as anonymous referees and to Jeremy Richardson, the editor of the *JEPP.*

Christoph Knill

Introduction: Cross-national policy convergence: concepts, approaches and explanatory factors

Christoph Knill

The comparative analysis of public policies across countries is a well-developed research area with a long tradition in political science. One of the major debates in this research field centres on the question as to whether and why different countries develop similar policies over time. In the literature, there are two different answers to this question.

There are numerous studies that emphasize a striking degree of policy convergence; i.e. the development of similar or even identical policies across countries over time. For years, political scientists have been attracted by this phenomenon and its underlying causal factors (for an overview of the policy convergence literature, see Bennett 1991; Drezner 2001; Heichel *et al.* 2005). At the same time, however, there are many studies (typically in the tradition of the new institutionalism) that modify or even challenge the general expectation of cross-national policy convergence. Emphasizing important differences in national institutions and opportunity structures for domestic actors, these studies find diverging rather than converging policy developments across countries.

This debate of convergence versus divergence of national policies is closely related to the booming research industry on globalization and Europeanization. Does the strong growth of economic and institutional interlinkages between nation states lead to increasingly similar policies across countries? Or is the search for convergence emerging from the domestic impact of globalization and European integration 'an impossible quest' (Dimitrova and Steunenberg 2000: 201), as domestic responses to global or European challenges are strongly influenced by existing domestic structures and institutions (see, for example, Caporaso *et al.* 2001; Héritier *et al.* 2001; Knill 2001)?

This brief discussion clearly shows that we still have a rather limited understanding of the phenomenon of policy convergence. What explains the adoption of similar policies across countries over time? Under which conditions can we expect that domestic policies converge or rather develop further apart? Why do countries converge on some policies, but not on others? What is the direction of policy convergence? Do national policies converge at the regulatory top or bottom, and why?

Although a number of factors have been suggested in order to account for the mixed empirical evidence of both convergence and divergence, including the role of international organizations, regulatory competition between nation states, or capacities for national policy adjustment, we still have limited knowledge about the causes and conditions of cross-national policy convergence. This deficit can be not only traced back to a lack of empirical findings, but is also the result of the heterogeneous and partially inconsistent theoretical literature on policy convergence. Although policy convergence constitutes a central concept in comparative public policy, it is not always consistently used and mixed up with related but not equivalent concepts. It is therefore hardly surprising that the mechanisms and conditions affecting the degree of cross-national policy convergence are not yet well understood (cf. Seeliger 1996).

It is the objective of the following contributions to improve our understanding of policy convergence and its causes. This presupposes a clear definition of the concept of convergence. In the following sections, I will thus first clarify the analytical relationship between policy convergence and related concepts used in the literature. Moreover, different approaches for the assessment and measurement of policy convergence will be presented. I conclude with a brief discussion of the causes of policy convergence to which the following articles are related. Unless explicitly acknowledged, the contributions follow the definitions and assessment criteria as defined in the following sections.

POLICY CONVERGENCE AND RELATED CONCEPTS

While there is a broad consensus on the definition of convergence as 'the tendency of societies to grow more alike, to develop similarities in structures, processes, and performances' (Kerr 1983: 3), the empirical and theoretical assessment of policy convergence is generally hampered by the use of different, partially overlapping concepts (Tews 2002). Policy convergence is equated with related notions, such as isomorphism, policy transfer or policy diffusion. This terminological variety often coincides with analytical confusion.

This becomes most apparent when focusing on the concept of *policy transfer* (Dolowitz and Marsh 1996, 2000; Radaelli 2000; Rose 1991). Dolowitz and Marsh (2000: 5) define policy transfer as 'processes by which knowledge about policies, administrative arrangements, institutions and ideas in one political system (past or present) is used in the development of policies, administrative arrangements, institutions and ideas in another political system'. Policy transfer is therefore concerned with processes rather than results. Moreover, it prescribes a development that might, but need not, lead to cross-national policy convergence. Policy transfer is not restricted to merely imitating policies of other countries, but can include profound changes in the content of the exchanged policies (Kern *et al.* 2000; Rose 1991).

Similar to transfer, *policy diffusion* typically refers to processes (rather than outcomes) that might result in increasing policy similarities across countries, hence leading to policy convergence (Elkins and Simmons 2005: 36). Diffusion is generally defined as the socially mediated spread of policies across and within political systems, including communication and influence processes which operate both on and within populations of adopters (Rogers 1995: 13). Most of the diffusion literature is characterized by this approach. Diffusion studies typically start out from the description of adoption patterns for certain policy innovations over time. In a subsequent step, they analyse the factors that account for the empirically observed spreading process. According to this concept of diffusion, no distinction in different forms of 'spread mediation' or 'influence processes' is made. Hence, from this perspective, policy diffusion is not restricted to the operation of specific mediation mechanisms, but includes all conceivable channels of influence between countries, reaching from the voluntary adoption of policy models that have been communicated in the international system, diffusion processes triggered by legally binding harmonization requirements defined in international agreements or supranational regulations, to the imposition of policies on other countries through external actors.

In contrast to this definition, however, some authors suggest a narrower focus of the concept, explicitly restricting diffusion to processes of voluntary policy transfer (Kern 2000; Busch and Jörgens 2005). Consequently, diffusion is conceived as a distinctive causal factor that drives international policy convergence rather than a general process that is caused by the operation of varying (both voluntary and coercive) influence channels. Following this approach, Busch and Jörgens distinguish three mechanisms of policy convergence: international harmonization (legal obligation from international or supranational agreements deliberately agreed by the involved countries in multilateral negotiations), imposition of policies, and policy diffusion (where national policy-makers voluntarily adopt policy models that are communicated internationally).

We are thus confronted with two different conceptions of policy diffusion. On the one hand, the concept describes the process of spreading policies across countries with the possible result of cross-national policy convergence, regardless of the causal factors that are driving this development (e.g. regulatory competition, international harmonization, imposition). On the other hand, diffusion is conceived as a distinctive causal factor leading to policy convergence by voluntary (in contrast to obliged or imposed) transfer of policy models.

Both conceptions of diffusion are analytically well grounded and applied in the literature; it is therefore more important to point out their differences rather than arguing in favour of one or the other approach. Nevertheless, the following considerations as well as the contributions to this volume (except the article by Busch and Jörgens) follow the first definition, conceiving of diffusion as a process that can be triggered by a broad range of causal factors.

Policy diffusion and policy transfer share the assumption that governments do not learn about policy practices randomly, but rather through common affiliations, negotiations and institutional membership (Simmons and Elkins 2004). Both transfer and diffusion processes hence require that actors are informed about the policy choices of others (Strang and Meyer 1993: 488). Given these conceptual overlaps, diffusion is often equated with policy transfer (Kern 2000; Tews 2002). Notwithstanding these conceptual overlaps, however, analytical differences between diffusion and transfer should not be overlooked. Diffusion studies typically start out from a rather general perspective. While analyses of policy transfer investigate the underlying causes and contents of singular processes of bilateral policy exchange, the dependent variable in diffusion research refers to general patterns characterizing the spread of innovations within or across political systems. The diffusion literature focuses more on the spatial, structural and socioeconomic reasons for particular adoption patterns rather than on the reasons for individual adoptions as such (Bennett 1991: 221; Jordana and Levi-Faur 2005). Diffusion studies often reveal a rather robust adoption pattern, with the cumulative adoption of a policy innovation over time following an S-shaped curve (Gray 1973). Relatively few countries adopt an innovation during early stages. Over time, the rate of adoption increases, until the process gets closer to saturation, and the rate slows down again.

From these considerations it follows that policy transfer and policy diffusion differ from policy convergence in important ways. First, differences exist with respect to the underlying analytical focus. While diffusion and transfer are concerned with process patterns, convergence studies place particular emphasis on effects. Transfer and diffusion thus reflect processes which under certain circumstances might result in policy convergence. This does not imply, however, that the empirical observation of converging policies must necessarily be the result of transfer or diffusion (Drezner 2001). It is well conceivable that policy convergence is the result of similar but relatively isolated domestic events. Second, the concepts differ in their dependent variable. Convergence studies typically seek to explain changes in policy similarity over time. By contrast, transfer studies investigate the content and process of policy transfer as the dependent variable, while the focus of diffusion research is on the explanation of adoption patterns over time (Elkins and Simmons 2005; Jordana and Levi-Faur 2005; Levi-Faur 2005; Gilardi 2005).

The particular focus underlying the analysis of policy convergence places it in close proximity to the concept of *isomorphism* which has been developed in organization sociology. Isomorphism is defined as a process of homogenization that 'forces one unit in a population to resemble other units that face the same set of environmental conditions' (DiMaggio and Powell 1991: 66). The central question underlying studies on isomorphism refers to the mechanisms through which organizations become more similar over time. There is thus a broad overlap between studies on policy convergence and isomorphism, with the major difference between the two concepts being on their empirical focus. The literature on isomorphism concentrates on increasing similarity of organizational and institutional structures and cultures. Studies on policy convergence, transfer or diffusion, by contrast, focus on changes in national policy characteristics.

Following the above considerations, policy convergence can be defined as any increase in the similarity between one or more characteristics of a certain policy (e.g. policy objectives, policy instruments, policy settings) across a given set of political jurisdictions (supranational institutions, states, regions, local authorities) over a given period of time. Policy convergence thus describes the end result of a process of policy change over time towards some common point, regardless of the causal processes.

TYPES OF POLICY CONVERGENCE

Having discussed the relationship between policy convergence and other analytical concepts that are often used synonymously in the literature, we still have to address the question of how convergence can be measured and evaluated empirically. The most basic way of assessing policy convergence is to analyse the extent to which the policies of countries have become more similar to each other over time. However, depending on the underlying criteria for the assessment of similarity change over time, different types of policy convergence are applied in the literature.

Table 1 Policy convergence and related concepts

	Policy convergence	*Isomorphism*	*Policy transfer*	*Policy diffusion*
Analytical focus	Effects	Effects	Process	Process
Empirical focus	Policy characteristics	Organizational structures	Policy characteristics	Policy characteristics
Dependent variable	Similarity change	Similarity change	Transfer content transfer process	Adoption pattern

The most common convergence type in this context refers to σ-convergence. Following this approach, convergence occurs if there is a decrease in variation of policies among the countries under consideration. It has to be emphasized, however, that this is only one, albeit very common, form of assessing policy convergence. Other options that are discussed in the article of Heichel *et al.* (2005) shall only be briefly mentioned here. First, β-convergence occurs when laggard countries catch up with leader countries over time, implying, for instance, that the former strengthen their regulatory standards more quickly and fundamentally than the latter. Second, γ-convergence is measured by changes of country rankings with respect to a certain policy. Finally, we speak of δ-convergence when similarity change is operationalized by comparing countries' distance changes to an exemplary model.

Depending on the type of convergence investigated, empirical results might be interpreted very differently. Evidence of σ-convergence, for instance, does not necessarily mean that there is also γ-convergence or δ-convergence. Moreover, evidence of β-convergence does not imply that there must also be σ-convergence: the fact that laggard countries change more fundamentally than leader countries is not a sufficient condition for a decrease in variance across all countries. Especially when comparing empirical results from different studies, it is therefore crucial to be clear about the specific type of convergence that has been investigated. The following articles all concentrate on the first and most commonly used type of σ-convergence; other convergence types are not explicitly investigated. Moreover, two contributions (Holzinger and Knill; Lenschow *et al.*) not only concentrate on the degree of σ-convergence, but also analyse convergence directions; i.e. the extent to which a decrease in variation of national policies is accompanied by upward or downward shifts of the regulatory mean (e.g. setting levels of environmental standards).

CAUSES OF POLICY CONVERGENCE

The literature on convergence and its related concepts offers a broad range of causal factors in order to explain changes in the similarity of policies across countries. At a very general level, these factors can be grouped into two categories: (1) causal mechanisms triggering the convergent policy changes across countries; and (2) facilitating factors which affect the effectiveness of these mechanisms. They are discussed and analysed in detail in the following articles. The basic objective of this overview is therefore to show how these articles relate to the different factors of cross-national policy convergence.

With respect to causal mechanisms, five central factors can be found in the highly diverse literature (see, for example, Bennett 1991; DiMaggio and Powell 1991; Dolowitz and Marsh 2000; Drezner 2001; Hoberg 2001; Holzinger and Knill 2005). First, cross-national policy convergence might be simply the result of similar but independent responses of different countries to parallel problem pressure (e.g. ageing of societies, environmental pollution or economic decline); i.e. policy convergence is caused by similar policy problems to which countries are reacting (Bennett 1991: 231). Second, several studies emphasize convergence effects stemming from the imposition of policies. Imposition refers to constellations where countries or international organizations force other countries to adopt certain policies by exploiting asymmetries in political or economic power. Third, emphasis is placed on the harmonization of national policies through international or supranational law. Countries are obliged to comply with international rules on which they have deliberately agreed in multilateral negotiations. Fourth, regulatory competition emerging from the increasing economic integration of European and global markets has been identified as an important factor that drives the mutual adjustment of policies across countries. Finally, cross-national policy convergence can simply be caused by transnational communication. Under this heading, several mechanisms are summarized which all have in common that they rest purely on communication and information exchange among countries (see Holzinger and Knill 2005). They include lesson-drawing (where countries deliberately seek to learn from successful problem-solving activities in other countries), joint problem-solving activities within transnational élite networks or epistemic communities, the promotion of policy models by international organizations with the objective of accelerating and facilitating cross-national policy transfer as well as the emulation of policy models.[1] One could certainly argue that communication is also of relevance with regard to the other mechanisms of imposition, international harmonization or regulatory competition. In these cases, however, communication and information exchange are basically a background condition for the operation of the mechanisms rather than the central factor actually triggering convergence.

What are potential facilitating factors that affect the degree of cross-national policy convergence? The first group of factors in that respect refers to characteristics or, more precisely, the similarity of the countries under investigation. It is argued that converging policy developments are more likely for countries that are characterized by high institutional similarity. Policies are transferred and properly implemented only insofar as they fit with existing institutional arrangements (see, for instance, Knill and Lenschow 1998). Moreover, cultural similarity plays an important role in facilitating cross-national policy transfer. In their search for relevant policy models, decision-makers are expected to look to the experiences of those countries with which they share an especially close set of cultural ties (Strang and Meyer 1993). Finally, similarity in socioeconomic structures and development has been identified as a factor that facilitates the transfer of policies across countries (see, for instance, on environmental policy, Jänicke 1988).

The second group of facilitating factors that can be analytically distinguished is composed of characteristics of the underlying policies. In this context, the type of policy has been identified as a factor that influences the likelihood of convergence. The expectation is that policies involving high distributional conflicts between domestic actor coalitions will diffuse and hence converge to a lesser extent than regulatory policies with comparatively small redistributional consequences (Tews 2002). A second argument about the impact of policy characteristics on convergence concentrates on different policy dimensions. Hall (1993), for instance, distinguishes between policy paradigms, policy instruments and settings,[2] arguing that change (and consequently convergence) is most difficult on ideas, given their deep embeddedness in dominant beliefs of domestic actors. Instruments and, even more, settings, by contrast, can be adjusted without necessarily demanding ideational change; hence convergence on the latter dimensions is more likely than on paradigms. This view, however, is not uncontested in the convergence literature (see, for instance, the contributions of Radaelli 2005 and Lenschow *et al.* 2005).

With the exception of potential effects of different policy types, the above-mentioned causes of cross-national policy convergence are investigated in closer detail in the following articles. Two theoretical contributions concentrate especially on the development of hypotheses on the conditions under which the different factors will actually lead to convergence. While Holzinger and Knill place particular emphasis on the role of causal mechanisms, Lenschow *et al.*, using the environmental field as a reference point, analyse facilitating factors of policy convergence. Some of the theoretical expectations developed in these papers are taken up again in the more empirical articles. While Heichel *et al.* present a general overview of empirical findings and analytical deficits of research on policy convergence, the remaining articles are concerned with the

Table 2 Causal factors of policy convergence analysed in the following contributions

Causal mechanisms	Independent problem-solving	Holzinger/Knill, Marcussen
	Imposition	Busch/Jörgens; Holzinger/Knill; Marcussen
	International harmonization	Busch/Jörgens; Drezner; Holzinger/Knill, Marcussen
	Regulatory competition	Drezner; Holzinger/Knill
	Transnational communication	Albrecht/Arts; Busch/Jörgens; Holzinger/Knill; Marcussen
Facilitating factors	Cultural similarity	Lenschow/Liefferink/Veenman
Country-group related	Institutional similarity	Lenschow/Liefferink/Veenman; Radaelli
	Socioeconomic similarity	Lenschow/Liefferink/Veenman
	Policy type	
Policy-related	Policy dimension	Holzinger/Knill; Lenschow/Liefferink/Veenman; Radaelli

assessment and explanation of convergence in individual policy sectors. Drezner focuses on two empirical cases (the regulation of genetically modified organisms and money laundering) and compares the influence of international harmonization and regulatory competition on policy convergence. Busch and Jörgens compare the convergence effect of three international factors (imposition, harmonization and transnational communication [in their terminology: diffusion]) in the environmental field. Albrecht and Arts also look at environmental policy, investigating the impact of reporting requirements and non-binding guidelines of the United Nations Framework Convention on Climate Change and the Kyoto protocol on the cross-national convergence of environmental policy instruments. Marcussen, by contrast, investigates the international factors (imposition, transnational communication) that contributed to the global spread of central banks and their independence. Finally, Radaelli, in his analysis of the use of regulatory quality assessments in Europe, studies the inter-play between international (transnational communication) and domestic causes (institutional factors) of policy convergence.

While each of the mentioned contributions is characterized by the analysis of one or more specific areas of convergence research, Jordan's commentary article offers a general assessment of the findings compiled in this volume and assesses the extent to which the individual contributions succeed in fashioning the broad issue of policy convergence into a cumulative and enduring body of work within EU scholarship.

Address for correspondence: Christoph Knill, Department of Politics and Management, University of Konstanz, Box D 81, D-78457 Konstanz, Germany. Tel: 49 7531 883553. Fax: 49 7531 882381. email: christoph.knill@uni-konstanz.de

ACKNOWLEDGEMENTS

This article is based on the research project 'Environmental governance in Europe: the impact of international institutions and trade on policy convergence (ENVIPOLCON)'. The support of the EU is gratefully acknowledged. For very helpful comments on earlier versions of this paper I am grateful to Bas Arts, Katharina Holzinger, Andy Jordan, David Levi-Faur, Duncan Liefferink and Jeremy Richardson.

NOTES

1 In the terminology used by Busch and Jörgens (2005), the mechanisms summarized under transnational communication would be referred to as policy diffusion.
2 For alternative but basically compatible classifications see, for instance, Bennett (1991) or Dolowitz and Marsh (2000).

REFERENCES

Bennett, C. (1991) 'What is policy convergence and what causes it?', *British Journal of Political Science* 21: 215–33.

Busch, P.-O. and Jörgens, H. (2005) 'The international sources of policy convergence: explaining the spread of environmental policy innovations', *Journal of European Public Policy* 12(5): 860–84.

Caporaso, J., Cowles, M. and Risse, T. (eds) (2001) *Transforming Europe. Europeanization and Domestic Change*, Ithaca, NY: Cornell University Press.

DiMaggio, P.J. and Powell, W.W. (1991) 'The iron cage revisited. Institutionalized isomorphism and collective rationality in organizational fields', in W.W. Powell and P.J. DiMaggio (eds), *The New Institutionalism in Organizational Analysis*, Chicago: Chicago University Press, pp. 63–82.

Dimitrova, A. and Steunenberg, B. (2000) 'The search for convergence of national policies in the European Union. An impossible quest?', *European Union Politics* 1(2): 201–26.

Dolowitz, D.P. and Marsh, D. (1996) 'Who learns what from whom. A review of the policy transfer literature', *Political Studies* 44: 343–57.

Dolowitz, D.P. and Marsh, D. (2000) 'Learning from abroad: the role of policy transfer in contemporary policy making', *Governance* 13: 5–24.

Drezner, D.W. (2001) 'Globalization and policy convergence', *The International Studies Review* 3: 53–78.

Elkins, Z. and Simmons, B. (2005) 'On waves, clusters and diffusions: a conceptual framework', *The Annals of the American Academy of Political and Social Science* (Special Issue: The Rise of Regulatory Capitalism: The Global Diffusion of a New Order, Guest Editors: D. Levi-Faur and J. Jordana) 598: 33–51.

Gilardi, F. (2005) 'The institutional foundations of regulatory capitalism: the diffusion of independent regulatory agencies in western Europe', *The Annals of the American Academy of Political and Social Science* 598: 84–101.

Gray, V. (1973) 'Innovation in the states: a diffusion study', *American Political Science Review* 67: 1174–85.

Hall, P.A. (1993) 'Policy paradigms, social learning and the state. The case of economic policymaking in Britain', *Comparative Politics* 25: 275–96.

Heichel, S. Pape, J. and Sommerer, T. (2005) 'Is there convergence in convergence research? An overview of empirical studies on policy convergence', *Journal of European Public Policy* 12(5): 817–40.

Héritier, A., Kerwer, D., Knill, C., Lehmkuhl, D. and Teutsch, M. (2001) *Differential Europe. New Opportunities and Constraints for National Policy-Making*, Lanham: Rowman & Littlefield.

Hoberg, G. (2001) 'Globalization and policy convergence: symposium overview', *Journal of Comparative Policy Analysis: Research and Practice* 3: 127–32.

Holzinger, K. and Knill, C. (2005) 'Causes and conditions of cross-national policy convergence', *Journal of European Public Policy* 12(5): 775–96.

Jänicke, M. (1988) 'Structural change and environmental impact: empirical evidence on thirty-one countries in East and West', *Environmental Monitoring and Assessment* 12: 99–114.

Jordana, J. and Levi-Faur, D. (2005) 'The diffusion of regulatory capitalism in Latin America: sectoral and national channels in the making of a new order', *The Annals of the American Academy of Political and Social Science* (Special Issue: The Rise of Regulatory Capitalism: The Global Diffusion of a New Order, Guest Editors: D. Levi-Faur and J. Jordana) 598: 102–24.

Kern, K. (2000) *Die Diffusion von Politikinnovationen. Umweltpolitische Innovationen im Mehrebenensystem der USA*, Opladen: Leske + Budrich.

Kern, K., Jörgens, H. and Jänicke, M. (2000) 'Die Diffusion umweltpolitischer Innovationen. Ein Beitrag zur Globalisierung von Umweltpolitik', *Zeitschrift für Umweltpolitik* 23: 507–46.

Kerr, C. (1983) *The Future of Industrial Societies: Convergence or Continuing Diversity?*, Cambridge, MA: Harvard University Press.

Knill, C. (2001) *The Europeanisation of National Administrations*, Cambridge: Cambridge University Press.

Knill, C. and Lenschow A. (1998) 'Coping with Europe: the impact of British and German administrations on the implementation of EU environmental policy', *Journal of European Public Policy* 5(4): 595–614.

Lenschow, A. Liefferink, D. and Veenman, S. (2005) 'When the birds sing. A framework for analysing domestic factors behind policy convergence', *Journal of European Public Policy* 12(5): 797–816.

Levi-Faur, D. (2005) 'The global diffusion of regulatory capitalism', *The Annals of the American Academy of Political and Social Science* (Special Issue: The Rise of Regulatory Capitalism: The Global Diffusion of a New Order, Guest Editors: D. Levi-Faur and J. Jordana) 598: 12–32.

Radaelli, C. (2000) 'Policy transfer in the European Union: institutional isomorphism as a source of legitimacy', *Governance* 13: 25–43.

Rogers, E.M. (1995) *Diffusion of Innovations*, New York: Free Press.

Rose, R. (1991) 'What is lesson-drawing?', *Journal of Public Policy* 11: 3–30.

Seeliger, R. (1996) 'Conceptualizing and researching policy convergence', *Policy Studies Journal* 4: 287–306.

Simmons, B.A. and Elkins, Z. (2004) 'The globalization of liberalization: policy diffusion in the international political economy', *American Political Science Review* 98: 171–89.

Strang, D. and Meyer, J. (1993) 'Institutional conditions for diffusion', *Theory and Society* 22: 487–511.

Tews, K. (2002) 'Der Diffusionsansatz für die vergleichende Politikanalyse. Wurzeln und Potenziale eines Konzepts. Eine Literaturstudie', FU-Report 2002–02, Berlin: Environmental Policy Research Centre.

Causes and conditions of cross-national policy convergence

Katharina Holzinger and Christoph Knill

1. INTRODUCTION

The study of cross-national policy convergence is a highly popular research area in political science. While first studies date back to the early 1960s, the academic popularity of the topic significantly increased during the 1990s. This development is closely related to an increasing research interest in the domestic impact of European integration and globalization. As a consequence, there is an ever-growing body of studies that investigate the occurrence and the underlying driving forces of cross-national policy convergence. Notwithstanding these enormous research efforts, it is generally acknowledged that we still have a limited understanding of the causes and conditions of policy convergence.

This deficit can be traced to two problems. First, as Seeliger (1996) argues, much more emphasis has been placed on the presentation of empirical results than on systematic theory-building. Second, policy convergence is a rather heterogeneous research field, with scholars coming from different academic backgrounds and disciplines (including, for instance, comparative politics, policy analysis and international relations). Hence, policy convergence is typically analysed from rather diverse theoretical perspectives employed in related research areas, such as policy transfer, policy diffusion or isomorphism. It is therefore hardly surprising that we find a broad number of different factors that are mentioned as potential causes of policy convergence. At the same time, theoretical and conceptual heterogeneity poses important restrictions on the comparability of the empirical findings gained in different convergence studies.

It is the objective of this article to review the existing literature and to address theoretical deficits in the study of policy convergence. We proceed in the following steps. First, we briefly present the central indicators we apply for the assessment of policy convergence. In a second step, we identify and compare different causal mechanisms of cross-national policy convergence. Having elaborated on the major causes of policy convergence, however, we still know little about the conditions under which these factors actually lead to convergence. This is the central objective of the third part of our analysis, in which we develop theoretical expectations on different indicators of cross-national policy convergence.

2. HOW TO CONCEPTUALIZE POLICY CONVERGENCE?

The definition of policy convergence as the growing similarity of policies over time still leaves a broad range of options as to how to empirically assess and evaluate similarity changes (Heichel *et al.* 2005). In so doing, we suggest various indicators, including not only the degree but also the scope and direction of convergence.

With respect to the *degree of convergence*, we first of all have to clarify the criteria on the basis of which we judge whether policies across countries are similar or not. In this context, a general distinction can be drawn between the similarity of policy outputs (the policies adopted by a government) and policy outcomes (the actual effects of a policy in terms of goal achievement). While studies on both dimensions can be found in the literature, we concentrate in the following analysis on policy outputs only. The governments are the agents reacting to problem pressure, experience gained elsewhere, pressure of powerful external actors, economic pressure, and legal obligation. Thus, governmental programmes are what count. Policy outcomes, by contrast, are only indirectly related to the causal mechanisms of convergence, because they are usually affected by many intervening variables. The adoption of a programme is a poor predictor of its implementation.

For the measurement of similarity change, we rely on the concept of σ-convergence. According to this concept, the degree of convergence increases with the extent to which the policies of different countries have become more similar to each other over time. Thus, convergence degree is the decrease of standard deviation from time t_1 to t_2.

The *direction of convergence*, by contrast, indicates the extent to which convergence coincides with an upward or downward shift of the mean from time t_1 to t_2. Convergence at the top or bottom presupposes therefore both a decrease of standard deviation and a shift of the mean (Botcheva and Martin 2001: 4). As shown in Table 1, the comparison between the policies in time t_1 and t_2 for a number of countries can therefore yield highly different results.

The direction of convergence is usually related to the extent of state intervention or to the strictness of a regulation. Lax standards or laissez-faire policies are identified with the 'bottom', strict standards or interventionist policies with the 'top' (Drezner 2001: 59–64). The direction of convergence can only be measured whenever the policies under consideration come in degrees, which can be associated with a normative judgement on the quality of an intervention. Typical examples are the levels of environmental and consumer protection or labour standards. However, it is not always easy to identify what the top and the bottom are in a policy, because there may be different value judgements. For example, in media regulation there are competing goals of restricting harmful content, on the one hand, and freedom of information, on the other hand. Moreover, when policy instruments are compared it does not make much sense to speak of directions of convergence. Only in rare cases can a certain instrument be assumed to provide stricter (or less strict) regulation than another one. In many cases, it is therefore impossible to formulate hypotheses on the direction of convergence.

Although we are aware of the fact that countries might be exposed to several mechanisms of convergence (e.g. imposition or international harmonization) and that these mechanisms might interact (cf. Holzinger and Knill 2005), the following considerations are based on the analysis of the isolated effects of different mechanisms. Our primary interest is to theoretically investigate the effects and operation of single convergence mechanisms.

For the development of hypotheses on the degree and direction of convergence, only those subgroups of countries and policies that are of theoretical

Table 1 Potential configurations of convergence indicators

Standard deviation	*Regulatory mean*	*Interpretation*
No change	No change	Persistence of diversity and level of regulation
	Upward or downward shift	No convergence or divergence, but common movement in the same direction
Decrease	No change	Convergence, but persistence of level of regulation
	Upward or downward shift	Convergence at the top or bottom
Increase	No change	Divergence, but persistence of level of regulation
	Upward or downward shift	Divergence, but common movement in the same direction

interest can be expected to be actually affected by a certain mechanism of convergence. For example, if we talk about international harmonization, we would not expect any convergence effects on countries which are not members of the international institutions in which harmonization efforts take place. Hence, our statements about convergence degrees or directions are not related to all countries and policies under investigation, but only to the affected subgroups. It is important to emphasize that convergence within subgroups affected by a certain mechanism can, but need not, result in convergence for the whole sample of countries and policies under investigation.

To grasp potential effects of certain mechanisms on *all* countries and policies under investigation, we rely on a further indicator, namely the *scope of convergence*. The scope of convergence increases with the number of countries and policies that are actually affected by a certain convergence mechanism, with the reference point being the total number of countries and policies under study. There is no straightforward relationship between degree and scope of convergence. Although it might often be the case that an increase in the number of converging countries actually reduces the variation among all countries, there are conceivable constellations in which even the opposite might be the case. For example, a subgroup of countries might converge towards a point far away from the other countries.

3. WHAT CAUSES POLICY CONVERGENCE?

As policy convergence is a theoretically rather heterogeneous field of research, it is hardly surprising that the literature offers many factors that might lead to

Table 2 Indicators of policy convergence

Indicator	*Research question*	*Reference point*	*Operationalization*
Degree of convergence	How much similarity increase over time?	Subgroup of countries and policies affected by a certain mechanism	Decrease in standard deviation over time
Convergence direction	In what direction (upward or downward shift of the regulatory mean)?	Subgroup of countries and policies affected by a certain mechanism	Mean change
Convergence scope	How many and which countries and policies are converging?	All countries and policies under investigation	Number of countries and policies

cross-national convergence. Moreover, suggestions on causal factors can not only be found in studies explicitly concerned with policy convergence, but also in the literature on policy transfer, diffusion and isomorphism which is closely related to the study of convergence. Transfer and diffusion are processes that might result in convergence. Thus, the factors triggering these processes can be interpreted as potential causes of convergence. The same holds true for the mechanisms driving isomorphism – a concept that differs from convergence only with respect to its empirical focus on organizational structures (Knill 2005).

Although there is considerable overlap, the causal factors enumerated vary. Some authors provide lists of mechanisms, while others provide classifications. For example, Hoberg (2001) lists parallel domestic problem pressures, emulation, international legal constraints, and international economic integration as potential factors driving convergence. Bennett (1991) mentions convergence through emulation, élite networking, harmonization, and penetration. Simmons and Elkins (2004) distinguish three diffusion mechanisms: direct economic competition, informational networks, and social emulation. In DiMaggio and Powell's (1991) theory, institutional isomorphism can result from coercion, mimetic processes, and normative pressures.

Dolowitz and Marsh (1996, 2000) provide a classification along a continuum between coercive and voluntary policy transfer, ranging from perfectly rational lesson-drawing of government A learning from government B to the direct imposition of a policy on country A by country B. However, it is difficult to draw the distinction between coercive and voluntary transfer. Transfer as a result of regulatory competition, for example, is classified as direct coercion (1996: 348), while 'the desire for international acceptance' is classified as 'voluntarily but driven by perceived necessity' (2000: 13). In both cases, national governments may respond to external pressures; however, they are not 'forced' to do so. On the other side of the continuum, can there ever be perfect 'voluntariness', in the sense that there is no pressure or no incentive to react to some challenge? Even lesson-drawing implies that a government feels the need to learn. It is unclear where voluntariness ends and where coercion begins.

In the following we present a list of the potential causes of policy convergence discussed in the literature. This list is based on the analytical distinction of five causal mechanisms of policy convergence: imposition, international harmonization, regulatory competition, transnational communication and independent problem-solving. The hypotheses about policy convergence we will formulate in section 4 are based on the distinction of these mechanisms. As summarized in Table 3 below, each mechanism combines a stimulus and a corresponding response, i.e. the behaviour actually leading to convergence. The causal mechanism leads to convergence, if the response actually occurs.

Imposition

The mechanism of imposition is described in the literature under many names. For DiMaggio and Powell, 'coercive isomorphism results from both formal and

Table 3 Mechanisms of policy convergence

Mechanism	*Stimulus*	*Response*
Imposition	Political demand or pressure	Submission
International harmonization	Legal obligation through international law	Compliance
Regulatory competition	Competitive pressure	Mutual adjustment
Transnational communication		
Lesson-drawing	Problem pressure	Transfer of model found elsewhere
Transnational problem-solving	Parallel problem pressure	Adoption of commonly developed model
Emulation	Desire for conformity	Copying of widely used model
International policy promotion	Legitimacy pressure	Adoption of recommended model
Independent problem-solving	Parallel problem pressure	Independent similar response

informal pressures exerted on organizations by other organizations upon which they are dependent' (1991: 67). Dependent organizations are likely to adopt patterns of behaviour sanctioned by organizations that control critical resources (Guler *et al.* 2002: 212). Resources are used as an incentive or penalty. Similar to DiMaggio and Powell (1991), Guler *et al.* refer to organizations within the state rather than to states. Nevertheless, their definition of coercive isomorphism as 'homogeneity pressures stemming from political influence' (2002: 212) is closely related to our understanding of convergence through imposition.

Resource dependence also plays a role in the definition of imposition of policies by Meseguer Yebra (2003). She deals with the stabilization policies and adjustments of economies which many governments have introduced under the pressure of international financial institutions. In this field, the mechanism of imposition is epitomized by conditionality. The latter implies exchanging policies for loans. A quantitative empirical analysis leads Meseguer Yebra to the conclusion that governments, pressed by international financial institutions, in fact switched to liberal trade regimes.

Dolowitz and Marsh (1996: 347) treat convergence through imposition under the heading of 'direct coercive transfer'. They differentiate between two mechanisms, which they call 'direct imposition', and 'conditionality' (Dolowitz and Marsh 2000: 9). They speak of direct imposition when 'one government forces another to adopt a policy'. While direct imposition of policies on one country by another is rare, supranational institutions often play an important role in coercive policy transfer. They use the example of the spread of Western monetary policies to Third World countries. This spread was driven by conditionalities that accompanied loans given by the World Bank or the International Monetary Fund.

According to Bennett 'convergence by penetration' arises when states are forced to conform to actions taken elsewhere by external actors (1991: 227). His main examples are multinational businesses that exert pressure on governments to harmonize policies concerning products (1991: 228). However, as multinational firms can surely not *force* governments and as they have no *political* power, we subsume this kind of pressure for international co-operation under convergence through regulatory competition. Another example are voluntary international agreements, for instance at the level of the Organization for Economic Co-operation and Development (OECD) and the Council of Europe (Bennett 1991: 228). In our view, this falls under the mechanism of transnational communication (promotion of policy models) rather than reflecting convergence through imposition.

Tews identifies two conditions for 'forced policy transfer' (2002: 1181f.): first, the relations of the political units involved are characterized by structural asymmetry of power. Second, the new policy has been pushed through against the will of the legitimized politicians in the political unit forced to adopt the policy. The second condition seems to be overly restrictive. A policy imposed on a country by an international institution may not be at the top of the preference list of the national government, but it may nevertheless not be against its will; sometimes the 'imposition' may even help a democratic government to introduce a policy not favoured by its citizens.

In our definition, convergence through imposition occurs whenever an external political actor forces a government to adopt a certain policy. This presupposes asymmetry of power. Often, there is an exchange of economic resources for the adoption of the policy. There are two typical cases: the unilateral imposition of a policy on a country by another country, and the conditionality by an international institution. The first case might, for example, occur after a war. It will be rare and does not lead to far-reaching convergence, as it will hardly involve many countries. The second case is more prevalent and usually involves a greater number of countries. Moreover, the policies which form the content of the conditionality – typically economic policies or human rights – are usually already applied in wider parts of the international community.

International harmonization

The mechanism of international harmonization leads to cross-national convergence if the involved countries comply with uniform legal obligations defined in international or supranational law. Harmonization refers to a specific outcome of international co-operation, namely to constellations in which national governments are legally required to adopt similar policies and programmes as part of their obligations as members of international institutions.

International harmonization and more generally international co-operation presuppose the existence of interdependencies or externalities which push governments to resolve common problems through co-operation within international institutions, hence sacrificing some independence for the good of the community (Drezner 2001: 60; Hoberg 2001: 127). Once established, institutional arrangements will constrain and shape the domestic policy choices, even as they are constantly challenged and reformed by their member states. This way, international institutions are not only the object of state choice, but at the same time consequential for subsequent governmental activities (Martin and Simmons 1998: 743). However, as member states voluntarily engage in international co-operation and actively influence corresponding decisions and arrangements, the impact of international harmonization on national policies constitutes no hierarchical process; it can rather be interpreted as 'negotiated transfer' (Dolowitz and Marsh 2000: 15).

Regulatory competition

While the mechanism of international harmonization is based on domestic compliance with legal obligations, regulatory competition is expected to lead to cross-national convergence, as countries facing competitive pressure mutually adjust their policies. Regulatory competition presupposes economic integration among countries. Especially with the increasing integration of European and global markets and the abolition of national trade barriers, the international mobility of goods, workers and capital puts competitive pressure on the nation states to redesign domestic market regulations in order to avoid regulatory burdens restricting the competitiveness of domestic industries. The pressure arises from (potential) threats of economic actors to shift their activities elsewhere, inducing governments to lower their regulatory standards. This way, regulatory competition among governments may lead to a race to the bottom in policies, implying policy convergence (Hoberg 2001: 127; Simmons and Elkins 2004; Drezner 2001: 57–9). Theoretical work, however, suggests that there are a number of conditions that may drive policy in both directions (Vogel 1995; Scharpf 1997; Kern *et al.* 2000; Holzinger 2002, 2003), including, for example, the type of policy concerned (product or process standards), or the presence of interests other than business in national politics.

Transnational communication

Under the term of transnational communication we summarize a number of different but related mechanisms, including lesson-drawing, transnational problem-solving, emulation and the transnational promotion of policy models. In contrast to the other mechanisms discussed so far, they have in common that their operation is *purely* based on communication among countries. The other mechanisms presuppose either political pressure (imposition), legal obligation (harmonization), competitive pressure (regulatory competition) or parallel problem pressure (independent problem-solving). Communication might also play a role in these cases; however, it is not the main factor accounting for convergence effects. So far, in the literature no established heading for these different, but closely related mechanisms exists. One could certainly argue that each of the mechanisms summarized under transnational communication can be considered as a mechanism in its own right. However, they share an important characteristic that crucially distinguishes them from all other causal mechanisms, namely, they presuppose nothing but information exchange and communication with other countries. Moreover, the theoretical expectations with regard to their convergence effects are rather similar.

Lesson-drawing

The mechanism of lesson-drawing refers to constellations of policy transfer in which governments rationally utilize available experience elsewhere in order to solve domestic problems. According to Rose, who introduced the concept, lesson-drawing is based on a voluntaristic process whereby government A learns from government B's solution to a common problem what to do ('positive lessons') or what not to do ('negative lessons'). The government is modelled as a rational actor who poses the question: 'Under what circumstances and to what extent would a programme now in effect elsewhere also work here?' (Rose 1991: 4). The creation of new programmes, however, need not be based on the mere copying of other policies, but can take many different forms, reaching from hybrids of transferred and domestically developed components to completely new models. Rose also emphasizes that drawing a lesson does not require policy change: a programme elsewhere may be evaluated negatively or there may be no way to transfer it (1991: 22). Therefore, lesson-drawing is not the same as policy convergence.

A closely related concept is presented by Meseguer Yebra (2003) who applies the concept of Bayesian learning to policy learning. Bayesian learning is a mode of rational, experience-based learning. Governments are modelled as perfectly rational learners. They update their beliefs on the consequences of policies with all available information about policy outcomes in the past and elsewhere. They choose the policy that is expected to yield the best results. Bayesian learning is a formal mechanism, but the notion of learning in this concept is very similar to Rose's concept of lesson-drawing. However, in Meseguer Yebra's approach, governments will converge in their policy choices if they are exposed to the same information. This implies that there is a 'best solution' – given a certain state of information. Only if governments are not perfectly rational and do not collect all available information may divergence occur.

Transnational problem-solving

Similar to lesson-drawing, transnational problem-solving assumes processes of rational learning. In the latter case, however, convergence is not the result of bilateral transfer. Rather, it is driven by the joint development of common problem perceptions and solutions to similar domestic problems and their subsequent adoption at the domestic level. Transnational problem-solving typically occurs within transnational élite networks or epistemic communities, defined as networks of policy experts who share common principled beliefs over ends, causal beliefs over means and common standards of accruing and testing new knowledge (Haas 1992: 3). Common educational and normative backgrounds typically facilitate joint development of common policy models in such constellations (DiMaggio and Powell 1991: 73).

It is well conceivable that transnational problem-solving in élite networks can prepare the ground for subsequent activities of international harmonization. This holds true especially for problems characterized by strong interdependencies. At the same time, however, it is emphasized that international institutions play an important role in forging and promulgating transnational epistemic communities (Simmons and Elkins 2004). In other words, regular negotiations and discussions on problems subject to harmonization provide the ground for joint problem-solving in related areas that do not necessarily require a joint solution through international law. This argument is supported by the findings of Kern (2000: 144) who shows that international institutions play an important role in accelerating and facilitating cross-national policy transfer. They constitute important channels for multilateral communication and policy diffusion. Kern shows that – compared to policy exchange resting on bilateral and horizontal communication between countries – policy models spread much broader and faster if these countries are members of the same international institution.

Emulation of policies

Policy convergence through emulation is driven by the mere desire for conformity with other countries rather than the search for effective solutions to given problems. Consequently, emulation usually implies the simple copying of policies adopted elsewhere. Which factors account for this search for conformity? In the literature, various aspects are mentioned.

First, it is argued that emulation is a function of the number of countries that have already adopted a certain policy. As argued in herding theories, it can be optimal for a country to follow the behaviour of others even without using further information than the sheer number of followers. The fact that many others apply a certain policy serves as information that this might be the best thing to do (Levi-Faur 2002). In theories of population ecology, a different rationale is emphasized: emulation is the result of the socially embedded behaviour of actors (Meyer and Rowan 1977; Baum and Oliver 1992). The most widespread solution to a problem becomes the obvious way of dealing with it whereas other possible solutions are no longer considered.

Second, emulation can be driven by the striving of organizations to increase their social legitimacy by embracing forms and practices that are valued within the broader social and institutional environment (DiMaggio and Powell 1991: 70).

States might sometimes copy mimetically the policies of other states simply to legitimate conclusions already reached (Bennett 1991: 223).

Third, a psychologically based rationale for emulation is the desire of actors 'not to be left behind', a mechanism that has been transferred to the behaviour of state actors within the international system (Meyer *et al.* 1997; Finnemore 1996; Tews 2002). In the theory of DiMaggio and Powell 'mimetic isomorphism' occurs especially when an innovation is poorly understood and when its consequences are still unclear (1991: 69). The fear of not being left behind might be a result of uncertainty, but might also be a motive in itself.

Fourth, there are rational motivations. Bennett observes that emulation might be a consequence of time pressures: 'the more urgency that is perceived, the more likely will be the imitation of solutions without lengthy analysis and investigation' (1991: 223). Finally, compared with more demanding forms of learning, the costs of information are probably much lower for simple imitation (Tews 2002: 180).

International policy promotion

Countries might not only be inspired to adopt a certain policy because of rational learning or their desire for conformity. They can also be motivated to do so because of legitimacy pressures emerging from the promotion of policy models by international institutions. In contrast to the mechanism of transnational problem-solving, policy convergence is not the result of joint problem-solving efforts of countries represented in transnational networks, but is driven by the active role of international institutions that are promoting the spread of distinctive policy approaches they consider particularly promising.

Cross-national policy transfer is stimulated by non-binding international agreements or propositions on broad goals and standards that national policies should aim to achieve, institutionalized peer review and identification of best practice (benchmarking) as well as the construction of league tables ranking national policies in terms of performance to previously agreed criteria (Humphreys 2002: 54; Tews 2002: 174). International institutions, such as the European Union (EU), the OECD or the World Bank, but also non-governmental organizations (NGOs) and transnational interest organizations (Keck and Sikkink 1998), play a highly active role in this process. In constantly searching for new policy ideas, disseminating best practice and evaluating domestic policy performance, they function as mediators of cross-national policy transfer, urging national governments to adopt successful policy models (Kern *et al.* 2000: 10). Countries that deviate from recommended policy models or rank low in international league tables face pressure to legitimate their policy approaches in light of 'international scrutiny'.

In many instances, promotion activities by international institutions originate from the activities of individual states seeking to convince other countries to copy their policy models. Countries which have developed innovative policy concepts generally have a strong interest in establishing their approach as an international solution in order to minimize the costs of institutional and economic adjustment to potentially diverging internationally promoted policy models. This pattern of leaders using international institutions as leverage when trying to drag along the laggards has not only been observed in the EU (Héritier *et al.* 1996; Andersen and Liefferink 1997), but also at the level of the OECD and other international institutions (Jänicke 1998: 334; Wallace 1995: 267).

Independent problem-solving

Many authors observe that convergence of policies between several countries can arise as a result of similar but independent responses of political actors to parallel problem pressures. Just as individuals open their umbrellas simultaneously during a rainstorm, governments may decide to change their policies in the presence of tax evasion, environmental pressures, such as air pollution, or an ageing population. This causal mechanism has been discussed under the names of functional, technocratic or technological determinism (Rose 1991: 9; Bennett 1988: 417), clustering (Simmons and Elkins 2004), spurious diffusion (Gilardi 2005; Gilardi and Braun 2005), or parallel domestic pressures (Hoberg 2001: 127).

Similar responses to parallel problem pressure are not the same as policy transfer or diffusion, since under this mechanism actors do not behave in response to each other's actions (Gilardi 2005). Rather, independent problem-solving presupposes that there is no communication between countries; i.e. they are not informed about the other countries' policy choices. As Bennett notes, the analyst of policy convergence 'must avoid the pitfall of inferring from transnational similarity of public policy that a transnational explanation must be at work' (1991: 231).

4. WHEN DOES POLICY CONVERGENCE OCCUR?

Having identified the causal mechanisms of policy convergence, it is the objective of this section to develop theoretical expectations about the conditions of their operation. We aim at further specifying the mechanisms in order to develop testable hypotheses with respect to degree, direction, and scope of cross-national policy convergence for each mechanism. To answer these questions, a point of reference is needed. As a reference point, we assume a situation where no mechanism is at work and where the policies of the countries under consideration are characterized by diversity.

Imposition

As a matter of fact, imposition implies that the country forced to adopt a certain model has not much choice in modifying the policy. As a consequence, imposition can generally be expected to lead to complete similarity of the policies of the submitting country and the policies of the imposing country or institution.

While imposition hence results in a high degree of convergence, the scope of convergence is affected by the number of countries required to change their policies.

In this context, we have to distinguish between imposition by individual countries and imposition by international institutions. In the first case of unilateral imposition, usually only a few states might be affected; i.e. convergence occurs only among a small number of countries. The scope of convergence is much higher, by contrast, if imposition takes place through international institutions. Convergence will occur not only among all countries that similarly depend on the international institutions enacting the conditionality, but also among the dependent countries and the member states of the international institutions enacting the conditionality, if those members wish to export a policy which they also apply at home.

With respect to the impact of imposition on the direction of convergence, the extent to which imposition coincides with a shift of the regulatory mean depends on the level of regulation or intervention that is prescribed by the imposing country or institution. There is empirical evidence that imposition through international institutions has led to convergence at the top. This holds true especially in cases where conditionality requires compliance with certain standards in fields such as human rights, environmental protection, data protection, accounting or financial risks. In trade liberalization or privatization, by contrast, imposition implies a lower level of intervention – which is in these fields valued higher by the international community than interventionist policies. Hence, in this case, we can only identify shifts in the regulatory mean, while any judgement about whether this shift can be interpreted as upward or downward does not make much sense.

International harmonization

The scope of cross-national convergence triggered by international harmonization is affected by two factors. First, as convergence effects are restricted to those countries that are actually committed to international agreements or supranational regulations, the scope of convergence through harmonization increases with the number of countries that are members of the international institution or regime with the power to enact legally binding rules. Second, the number of policies affected through harmonization increases with the number of areas covered by the legislation of the international organization in question.

With regard to the extent to which international harmonization triggers cross-national convergence, two factors can be identified. First, the degree of convergence varies with the legal specification of international law. Specification is particularly high if international law requires the total or minimum harmonization of national standards. Convergence effects are less pronounced, by contrast, if legal rules are defined in a less rigid way, leaving member states broad leeway for selecting appropriate instruments to comply with international policy objectives. In this respect, varying discretion levels are conceivable, reaching from differentiated regulatory requirements, the prescription of broad objectives rather than detailed substantive or procedural regulations to mutual recognition and opting-out clauses.

Second, the degree of similarity will increase with the extent to which compliance with legal obligation can actually be enforced. International institutions reveal important differences in terms of their enforcement powers. The EU can be characterized as an institution in which such powers are comparatively well developed, given the direct effect and the supremacy of European law, the influential role of the European Court of Justice in the enforcement of Community law, the – albeit restricted – monitoring activities of the European Commission as well as the opportunity to financially sanction non-compliant member states. Against this background, the converging effects of European legislation can be expected to be higher than those of intergovernmental organizations or international regimes, where enforcement powers are less developed.

To what extent does convergence through international harmonization coincide with upward or downward shifts of the regulatory mean? The answer to this question basically depends on factors such as decision rules, interest constellations and the distribution of power between the involved actors (typically national governments and international organizations) which shape the negotiations at the level of international institutions. As the constellation of these factors might vary from case to case, in principle, every result within the span of regulations preferred by the involved national governments is possible. Notwithstanding this openness, the theoretical modelling generally predicts an outcome which reflects a compromise, hence lying somewhere in the middle between countries favouring extreme positions of either rather strict or weak regulations, with a strong tilt towards the preferences of the more powerful states (Drezner 2001: 61; for the EU: Holzinger 1994: 465–8; Tsebelis 2002: ch. 11).

However, even if we assume that the final agreement reflects a compromise between high-regulating and low-regulating countries, we still need to know whether and in which direction the mean of national regulatory levels will change as a result of this compromise. For this purpose, it is useful to distinguish between total and minimum harmonization.[1]

In the case of total harmonization, the expected result is that convergence coincides with no or only minimal mean changes of regulatory levels. Assuming that the international agreement on average lies in the middle between the levels of high-regulating and low-regulating countries, it can be expected that the required upward and downward moves of national standards will neutralize each other, hence implying no significant departure from the status quo.

The constellation looks different, however, if international rules are directed at minimum rather than total harmonization of national regulations. In this case, it is still possible for countries with a preference for higher regulatory levels to enact standards beyond the minimum level specified in international agreements. While deviations to the top are therefore still possible, countries with lower standards are obliged to raise their standards levels at least to the international minimum level. We thus predict that minimum harmonization is more likely to result in shifting the regulatory mean upward, as is the case with total harmonization. This expectation rests on two assumptions. First, the international minimum standard reflects a compromise between high-regulating and low-regulating countries. Second, not all high-regulating countries will lower their standards towards the minimum level.

Regulatory competition

A number of conditions can be derived from theories of regulatory competition (Vogel 1995; Scharpf 1997; Holzinger 2003) which affect our convergence indicators. To begin with, these theories point to various factors that restrict the scope of potentially converging countries and policies. On the one hand, potential convergence effects of regulatory competition presuppose economic integration between market economies. Even in constellations of high economic integration, no competitive pressures will emerge in and between non-market economies. This scenario applies in particular to the communist countries before 1990. On the other hand, a qualification applies to the policies for which convergence effects are predicted. Adjustments will be most pronounced for trade-related policies, such as product or process standards. No convergence is expected for policies, which are subject to low competitive pressures from international markets. This holds true for all policies that are not directly related to products or to production processes, such as nature or bird protection policies. It also holds true where trade-related policies are concerned, but the effects of the regulation on production costs are low. In this case they do not affect competition between industries in different countries.

In general, theories of regulatory competition predict that countries adjust policy instruments and regulatory standards in order to cope with competitive pressures emerging from international economic integration. The more exposed a country is to competitive pressures following on from high economic integration (emerging from its dependence on the trade of goods, capital and services with other countries), the more likely it is that its policies will converge with other states with international exposure. In other words, the degree of convergence depends on the level of competitive pressures to which countries are exposed.

There is an ongoing debate in the literature on the direction of convergence caused by regulatory competition. Often a distinction is made between product and production process standards (Scharpf 1997; Holzinger 2003). In the case of process standards, we find a widely shared expectation that policy convergence will occur at the lowest common denominator; states will gravitate towards the policies of the most laissez-faire country (Drezner 2001). If the regulation of production processes implies an increase in the costs of production, potentially endangering the international competitiveness of an industry, regulatory competition will generally exert downward pressures on economic regulations (Scharpf 1997: 524). It is assumed that governments are ready to lower environmental standards in the face of lobbying and exit threats exerted by the respective industry.

Expectations are less homogeneous for product standards. While industries in both low-regulating and high-regulating countries have a common interest in harmonization of product standards to avoid market segmentation, the level of harmonization can hardly be predicted without the examination of additional factors. Most important in this context is the extent to which high-regulating countries are able to factually enforce stricter standards. If it is possible to erect exceptional trade barriers, as, for example, for health or environmental reasons under EU and World Trade Organization (WTO) rules, convergence at a high level of regulation is to be expected (Scharpf 1997; Vogel 1995). If such exceptional trade barriers cannot be justified, by contrast, competitive pressure will induce governments to lower their standards (Holzinger 2003: 196).

Transnational communication

With respect to the number of countries and policies potentially affected by transnational communication, only a few restrictions apply, given the rather undemanding precondition of information about policy choices of other countries. It is therefore impossible to identify factors that restrict the scope of convergence through transnational communication for certain policies or countries.

The fact that transnational communication might potentially affect all countries and policies under investigation does not imply, however, that this mechanism produces cross-national policy convergence in each constellation. Rather, its operation varies with several factors. First, research on emulation emphasizes that the probability of adoption increases with the number of countries that have already switched to a certain policy model. In other words, the degree of existing policy similarity across countries crucially affects the likelihood of future similarity changes through emulation.

Second, as argued in the literature on lesson-drawing, the degree of convergence varies with the extent to which policy transfer occurs between countries with strong cultural linkages. In their search for relevant policy models, decision-makers are expected to look at the experiences of those countries with which they share an especially close set of cultural ties (Strang and Meyer 1993). Especially in constellations characterized by high uncertainty about the consequences of policy choices, decision-makers are likely to imitate the practices of nations with which they share linguistic, religious, historical or other cultural linkages (Friedkin 1993; Simmons and Elkins 2004).

Third, the adoption of similar policies across countries varies with the compatibility of transnational concepts and domestic policy legacies. The degree of expected convergence will decrease with the cost of adaptation implied by the adoption of the policy concept in question (Kern *et al.* 2000; Knill 2001). If, for instance, the adoption of a certain model requires far-reaching changes in existing institutional arrangements (regulatory frameworks, administrative structures), there is a high probability for only partial or even refused transfer. The same scenario applies to constellations in which the model adoption entails high economic costs or is likely to face strong political opposition (e.g. in the case of strong redistributive effects among national actor coalitions). As a consequence of these considerations, we can expect the degree of convergence to vary with two conditions: first, convergence depends on the specification of the model to be adopted. The broader its definition, the lower are potential costs of adjustment, given the high discretion for domestic application. Second, convergence will be higher among states that share similar policy legacies (e.g. welfare state traditions) and therefore face lower costs of adjustment when borrowing policy models from each other. This means that transnational communication will have stronger convergence effects among states that are already relatively similar in terms of existing institutional structures than among states that are characterized by highly different arrangements.

Fourth, as information and knowledge exchange between states is the essential requirement for most transnational communication mechanisms becoming effective (Simmons and Elkins 2004), the degree of convergence will be particularly high among those countries that are strongly interlinked in varying transnational networks. Of particular importance in this respect is common membership in international institutions that play an important role in increasing the interaction density between their members, hence intensifying transnational information exchange (Kern 2000: 267).

To what extent does convergence through transnational communication lead to shifts in the level of domestic regulations? General statements to answer this question are hardly possible. This holds true in particular for the mechanisms of lesson-drawing, transnational problem-solving and emulation. The fact that states adopt a certain innovation or copy policy concepts successfully applied in other countries does not automatically imply that this results in an increase in regulatory levels. It might well be the case that states adopt less demanding regulations, following corresponding patterns in other countries (e.g. replacing of interventionist regulation by self-regulation).

The only mechanism that allows for more precise predictions refers to the promotion of policy models. This holds true in particular where promotion is based on the dissemination and evaluation of best practice. This competition of ideas can generally be expected to result in an overall strengthening of regulatory concepts. Since international organizations will in general promote the most progressive national approach, benchmarks will be set at the level of the highest-regulating country. Hence, an upward shift of the mean will be the likely result.

Independent problem-solving

Bennett identifies two conditions for parallel problem pressure to lead to the same solution (1988: 419): first, there must be certain intrinsic characteristics of a problem that would inevitably lead to its similar treatment. Second, these characteristics must be universally recognized. The problem with this argument is, however, that the extent to which convergence might be observed is strongly dependent on the definition of 'similar treatment'.

If similarity is defined in a very demanding way, including, for instance, the choice of instruments and regulatory settings, there will rarely be only one solution to a problem (Rose 1991: 9; Hoberg 1991). This is already valid for a relatively simple problem, such as the rainstorm mentioned above. Although many people may open their umbrellas, others may put on a hat or seek shelter. This is a problem where we already have something like 'one best solution', namely the umbrella.

If we apply a less demanding definition of similarity, by contrast, there is a higher probability that we observe convergence as a result of parallel problem pressure. For example, if the problem is that it starts raining, and the 'similar solution' is that people react to it, we will probably find convergence, as most people will in fact react somehow. Or, if the problem is the ageing of society, and the solution is that the pension schemes are changed, we might also find convergence, as most governments will change pension schemes. This still implies, however, a comparatively low degree of convergence, as the new pension schemes may be very different.

As the bandwidth of possible solutions or reactions to a problem is usually very broad, in the case of parallel problem pressure convergence can be expected only in very general terms (in the sense of mere reaction). A higher degree of convergence can be expected only if some additional conditions are fulfilled; for example, if the cultural, institutional or socio-economic similarity of the affected countries is high. In other words, countries that share a broad number of characteristics are more inclined to react independently to a problem in a similar way.

While structural similarity may thus affect the degree of convergence among countries reacting to parallel problem pressures, it is impossible to develop statements about potential convergence directions. We cannot predict whether parallel problem pressure leads to convergence at a high or low level of regulation or intervention.

5. CONCLUSION

In this article, we analysed various causes and factors regarding the scope, degree and direction of cross-national policy convergence. Starting from a review of the theoretical literature on convergence and related concepts, we developed theoretical expectations on the main causal mechanisms suggested by these theories. From these considerations several general conclusions can be drawn.

First, our analysis shows that one should not expect a general increase in cross-national policy convergence – not even in the era of globalization. This is valid not only for the overall picture of the causes of policy convergence, but also for the individual causal mechanisms. Even if the mechanisms have an effect on policy convergence, it is – as a result of their differences in the

Table 4 Theoretical expectations on scope, degree and direction of convergence

Mechanism	*Factors affecting convergence scope*	*Factors affecting convergence degree*	*Expected convergence direction*
Imposition	Reach of the imposing actor (individual country vs. international institution)	(by definition full convergence to imposed model)	No prediction possible
International harmonization	Number of member countries	Degree of legal specification Capacity to enforce compliance	Upward shift for minimum harmonization Persistence for total harmonization
Regulatory competition	Market economy Trade-related policies	Trade dependence	Upward or downward shift for product standards Downward shift for process standards
Transnational communication	Apart from information about policy choices of other countries no particular restrictions apply	Degree of existing similarity (number of adopters) Cultural linkages Degree of model specification Similarity of policy legacies Degree of inter-linkage into transnational networks	Upward shift in case of policy promotion For other mechanisms no prediction possible
Independent problem-solving	Number of countries that recognize similar problem	Degree of existing similarity across countries	No prediction possible

scope of convergence – by no means justified to expect global convergence over all countries, policy areas and policy dimensions. As summarized in Table 4, the conditions and effects of convergence vary strongly across the different convergence mechanisms.

Second, and also apparent from Table 4, there is no clear picture at which level of regulation we can expect policy convergence. While some of the mechanisms might lead to an upward or downward shift of the average policy, for others no prediction is possible. In view of these findings, it is therefore hardly surprising that empirical findings on policy convergence and on races to the top or bottom are rather ambiguous.

Finally, this differentiated pattern of expectations about policy convergence was developed on the basis of the isolated analysis of each potential mechanism of convergence. Empirically, however, the mechanisms interact. It is thus an important area of future research to develop hypotheses and to undertake empirical research on the interaction effects of all potential causal mechanisms.

Addresses for correspondence: Katharina Holzinger, Institute of Political Science, University of Hamburg, Allendeplatz 1, D-20146 Hamburg, Germany. Tel: 49 40 42838 4693. Fax: 49 40 42838 3534. email: holzinger@sozialwiss.uni-hamburg.de/Christoph Knill, Department of Politics and Management, University of Konstanz, Box D 81, D-78457 Konstanz, Germany. Tel: 49 7531 883553. Fax: 49 7531 882381. email: christoph.knill@uni-konstanz.de

ACKNOWLEDGEMENTS

This article is based on the research project 'Environmental governance in Europe: the impact of international institutions and trade on policy convergence (ENVIPOLCON)'. We would like to thank the EU for providing funding for this project. For constructive criticism and helpful comments on earlier versions of this paper we are particularly grateful to Bas Arts, Fabrizio Gilardi, Helge Jörgens and Andrea Lenschow as well as the participants of the Hamburg Workshop on 'International Sources of Policy Convergence', held in April 2004.

NOTE

1 As convergence can primarily be expected if legal obligation requires the harmonization of national regulations, we will not consider regulatory options that offer more leeway for member states (e.g. mutual recognition), hence potentially leading to diverging rather than converging outputs in the member states.

REFERENCES

Andersen, M.S. and Liefferink, D. (1997) *European Environmental Policy. The Pioneers*, Manchester: Manchester University Press.

Baum, J.A.C. and Oliver, C. (1992) 'Institutional embeddedness and the dynamics of organizational populations', *American Sociological Review* 7: 540–59.

Bennett, C. (1988) 'Different processes, one result. The convergence of data protection policy in Europe and the United States', *Governance* 1: 162–83.

Bennett, C. (1991) 'What is policy convergence and what causes it?', *British Journal of Political Science* 21: 215–33.

Botcheva, L. and Martin, L.L. (2001) 'Institutional effects on state behaviour. Convergence and divergence', *International Studies Quarterly* 45: 1–26.

DiMaggio, P.J. and Powell, W.W. (1991) 'The iron cage revisited. Institutionalized isomorphism and collective rationality in organizational fields', in W.W. Powell and P.J. DiMaggio (eds), *The New Institutionalism in Organizational Analysis*, Chicago: Chicago University Press, pp. 63–82.

Dolowitz, D.P. and Marsh, D. (1996) 'Who learns what from whom? A review of the policy transfer literature', *Political Studies* 44: 343–57.

Dolowitz, D.P. and Marsh, D. (2000) 'Learning from abroad: the role of policy transfer in contemporary policy making', *Governance* 13: 5–24.

Drezner, D.W. (2001) 'Globalization and policy convergence', *The International Studies Review* 3: 53–78.

Finnemore, M. (1996) *National Interests in International Society*, Ithaca, NY: Cornell University Press.

Friedkin, N.E. (1993) 'Structural bases of interpersonal influence in groups. A longitudinal case study', *American Sociological Review* 58: 61–872.

Gilardi, F. (2005) 'The international foundations of regulatory capitalism: the diffusion of independent regulatory agencies in Western Europe', *The Annals of the American Academy of Political and Social Science* 598: 84–101.

Gilardi, F. and Braun, D. (2005) 'Taking "Galton's problem" seriously: towards a theory of policy diffusion'. Paper presented at the Convention of the International Studies Association, March 2005, Honolulu.

Guler, I., Guillén, M. and Macpherson, J. (2002) 'Global competition, institutions and the diffusion of organizational practices. The international spread of ISO 9000 quality certificates', *Administrative Science Quarterly* 47: 207–33.

Haas, P.M. (1992) 'Introduction: Epistemic communities and international policy coordination', *International Organization* 46: 1–36.

Heichel, S., Pape, J. and Sommerer, T. (2005) 'Is there convergence in convergence research? An overview of empirical studies on policy convergence', *Journal of European Public Policy* 12(5): 817–40.

Héritier, A., Knill, C. and Mingers, S. (1996) *Ringing the Changes in Europe. Regulatory Competition and the Transformation of the State*, Berlin: de Gruyter.

Hoberg, G. (2001) 'Globalization and policy convergence: symposium overview', *Journal of Comparative Policy Analysis: Research and Practice* 3: 127–32.

Holzinger, K. (1994) *Politik des kleinsten gemeinsamen Nenners. Umweltpolitische Entscheidungsprozesse in der EG am Beispiel des Katalysatorautos*, Berlin: Edition Sigma.

Holzinger, K. (2002) 'The provision of transnational common goods: regulatory competition for environmental standards', in A. Héritier (ed.), *Common Goods: Reinventing European and International Governance*, Lanham: Rowman & Littlefield, pp. 59–82.

Holzinger, K. (2003) 'Common goods, matrix games, and institutional solutions', *European Journal of International Relations* 9: 173–212.

Holzinger, K. and Knill, C. (2005) 'Competition, cooperation and communication. A theoretical analysis of different sources of environmental policy convergence and their interaction', Working Paper, Political Science Series 102, Vienna: Institute for Advanced Studies.

Humphreys, P. (2002) 'Europeanisation, globalisation and telecommunications governance: a neo-Gramscian analysis', *Convergence: The Journal of Research into New Media Technologies* 8: 52–79.

Jänicke, M. (1998) 'Umweltpolitik. Global am Ende oder am Ende global?', in U. Beck (ed.), *Perspektiven der Weltgesellschaft*, Frankfurt a. Main: Suhrkamp, pp. 332–44.

Keck, M.E. and Sikkink, K. (1998) *Articles beyond Borders. Networks in International Politics*, Ithaca, NY: Cornell University Press.

Kern, K. (2000) *Die Diffusion von Politikinnovationen. Umweltpolitische Innovationen im Mehrebenensystem der USA*, Opladen: Leske + Budrich.

Kern, K., Jörgens, H. and Jänicke, M. (2000) 'Die Diffusion umweltpolitischer Innovationen. Ein Beitrag zur Globalisierung von Umweltpolitik', *Zeitschrift für Umweltpolitik* 23: 507–46.

Knill, C. (2001) *The Europeanisation of National Administrations*, Cambridge: Cambridge University Press.

Knill, C. (2005) 'Introduction: Cross-national policy convergence: concepts, approaches and explanatory factors', *Journal of European Public Policy* 12(5): 764–74.

Levi-Faur, D. (2002) 'Herding towards a new convention. On herds, shepherds and lost sheep in the liberalization of the telecommunications and electricity industries'. Paper presented at the workshop 'Theories of Regulation', Nuffield College, University of Oxford.

Martin, L. and Simmons, B. (1998) 'Theories and empirical studies of international institutions', *International Organization* 52: 729–57.

Meseguer Yebra, C. (2003) 'Learning and economic policy choices: a Bayesian approach', EUI Working Paper RSC No. 2003/5, San Domenico: European University Institute.

Meyer, J.W. and Rowan, B. (1977) 'Institutionalized organizations. Formal structure as myth and ceremony', *American Journal of Sociology* 83: 340–63.

Meyer, J.W., Frank, D.J., Hironaka, A., Schofer, E. and Brandon-Tuma, N. (1997) 'The structuring of a world environmental regime, 1870–1990', *International Organization* 51: 623–51.

Rose, R. (1991) 'What is lesson-drawing?', *Journal of Public Policy* 11: 3–30.

Scharpf, F.W. (1997) 'Introduction: the problem-solving capacity of multi-level governance', *Journal of European Public Policy* 4: 520–38.

Seeliger, R. (1996) 'Conceptualizing and researching policy convergence', *Policy Studies Journal* 4: 287–306.

Simmons, B.A. and Elkins, Z. (2004) 'The globalization of liberalization: policy diffusion in the international political economy', *American Political Science Review* 98: 171–89.

Strang, D. and Meyer, J. (1993) 'Institutional conditions for diffusion', *Theory and Society* 22: 487–511.

Tews, K. (2002) 'Politiktransfer: Phänomen zwischen Policy-Lernen und Oktroi. Überlegungen zu unfreiwilligen Umweltpolitikimporten am Beispiel der EU-Osterweiterung', *Zeitschrift für Umweltpolitik und Umweltrecht* 2: 173–201.

Tsebelis, G. (2002) *Veto Players. How Political Institutions Work*, Princeton, NJ: Princeton University Press.

Vogel, D. (1995) *Trading Up. Consumer and Environmental Regulation in the Global Economy*, Cambridge, MA: Harvard University Press.

Wallace, D. (1995) *Environmental Policy and Industrial Innovation. Strategies in Europe, the US and Japan*, London: Earthscan.

When the birds sing. A framework for analysing domestic factors behind policy convergence

Andrea Lenschow, Duncan Liefferink
and Sietske Veenman

1. INTRODUCTION

Birds sometimes sing and sometimes they don't. In a similar vein, national policies sometimes converge and sometimes they don't. Speaking very generally and somewhat cynically, this is the key insight to be derived from several decades of studies on the convergence of national policies.

Both convergence and non-convergence have their own logic. On the one hand, all countries in the world largely face the same types of problems, ranging from the organization of the fire brigade to environmental deterioration. These countries, moreover, maintain increasingly intensive relations, for instance through trade, tourism, media, or international co-operation. This would make it plausible that policy-makers learn from each other and, on the longer term, reach some kind of implicit or even explicit agreement on which policies are considered 'optimal' and ought to be followed. On the other hand, no country is similar to another. Levels of economic development diverge enormously. Each state has its distinct way of organizing government. And cultural traditions show an endless variation, even within countries. These deeply embedded differences would make it only logical that policies will always retain strongly national traits. As with the birds, what happens in practice depends on the circumstances.

Over the years, various views have been put forward as to which forces might induce or impede change in domestic policies and under which circumstances such change might take similar directions across countries. As will be discussed in more detail below, some have concentrated on *how* policy innovations spread around the globe. Others have focused on *what* spreads and (possibly) converges, arguing, for instance, that certain types of policy innovations converge more easily than others. Yet others have stressed the importance of the '*destination*' of the spreading process, that is, the domestic setting in which innovations 'land'. Several papers in this special issue address the first aspect, i.e. the international forces behind spread and convergence. The present contribution develops the second and third aspect combined, i.e. the domestic factors that determine to what extent countries are likely to take up different types of new policies.

To this end, the next section assesses the treatment of domestic factors in the policy convergence literature and related discussions on policy diffusion and cross-national policy learning. We find there is a need to reflect more systematically and develop clear hypotheses on the impact of domestic factors on the nature and scope of cross-national policy convergence. Section 3 therefore distinguishes three central structural factors – culture, institutions and economic development. It is argued that these factors are important to different degrees, dependent on whether change involves the basic goals and ideas of a policy, the instruments applied, or the setting or 'calibration' of these instruments. Here, we focus on the environmental field, but the approach as such should be equally valid for other policy areas. Section 4 goes on to propose indicators by which the cultural, institutional and economic affinity of countries can be assessed. This leads to the basic hypothesis that countries that are culturally, institutionally or economically close may be expected to adopt similar ideas, instruments or settings in environmental policy, respectively, and thus are likely to converge on these points. This hypothesis is planned to be tested empirically at a later stage. Thus, section 5 concludes by summing up the main features of the proposed framework for analysis.

2. INTERNATIONAL POLICY CONVERGENCE: THE ROLE OF DOMESTIC STRUCTURAL FACTORS

The discussion of international policy convergence has spun off 'second image reversed' analyses (Gourevitch 1978) which trace domestic policy change to international examples and dynamics. Other contributions to this collection aim at identifying and analysing the various international mechanisms that may result in convergence while at the same time bringing some order in the terminological variety that has emerged (see Holzinger and Knill 2005; Busch and Jörgens 2005). The present contribution, in turn, returns to the original second image, that is, domestic factors shaping the process of policy change and influencing patterns of convergence. This focus is rooted in the assumption that there is always an international and a domestic side to the international spread of policy innovation and convergence. In particular, convergence patterns – defined as increasing similarity between countries – are likely to be affected not only by the voluntary or involuntary interactions of state actors on the international scene but also by the domestic predisposition to react to one impulse but not to another.

Screening the literature on policy convergence and the various processes that are frequently associated with this effect – especially policy diffusion, regulatory competition and policy learning[1] – we find little systematic discussion of domestic factors, however. Of those concepts, *policy diffusion* has the longest history, occupying several disciplines. This literature emerged from a general interest in policy innovation which was traced either to political, social or economic characteristics internal to the state or alternatively to intergovernmental diffusion processes (cf. Berry and Berry 1999: 170). In 1975 Collier and Messick argued for bringing the domestic 'prerequisite' factors and intergovernmental diffusion explanation together in one analytical framework. But instead the literature began to focus on elaborating the nature of the linkage structures facilitating diffusion between states. Only lately is this literature being complemented by an interest in domestic structural conditions affecting the rate and form of diffusion. Some authors emphasize cultural similarity (Strang and Meyer 1993; Strang and Soule 1998), others point to administrative traditions and capacities (Kern *et al.* 1999) as significant domestic framework conditions. While primarily sociologists argue that foreign models – both policies and organizational arrangements – need to be (made) socially meaningful, political scientists focus more on institutions and resources that make domestic adoption feasible. So far, there has been no attempt to think more systematically about the range of domestic structures – cultural, institutional and economic – that might affect the process of 'import' and about their relative importance with respect to the nature of the diffusing 'object' in question.[2]

The literature on *policy convergence* shares the conclusions of those sociological diffusion studies emphasizing the importance of resonance between the exported 'object' and the cultural and institutional setting of the potential importer. Van Waarden (1995), for instance, points out that policy diffusion does not automatically lead to convergence as foreign models are likely to be changed to fit national institutional structures and policy styles. In contrast to Strang and Meyer (1993), however, who speak of the need to 'theorize' foreign ideas in order to make them meaningful domestically, the convergence literature perceives national institutions and institutionalized practices generally as more 'sticky' and resistant against eradication or fundamental change. Typically this literature focuses on one structural dimension, such as the structure of the welfare state (Scharpf and Schmidt 2002) or national regulatory styles (Van Waarden 1995; Vogel 1986), and investigates to what extent patterns of convergence correspond to similarities between countries along these specific structural characteristics or whether convergence patterns cross these country groupings. Despite such explicit emphasis on the impact of domestic structures, little attempt is made to differentiate between structural categories and link those to policy characteristics that may or may not converge.

The role of socio-economic factors has been strangely neglected in the discussions cited above. However, both the cost of public policy in an international competitive context and the cost of changing these existing rules and regulations and potentially disrupting domestic social and institutional relations are relevant factors shaping the modification of public policy. Domestic policy-makers will aim at identifying 'affordable' responses to increasingly globalized economic relations and dependencies; their 'calculations' are necessarily made in light of domestic socio-economic structures. Theories of *regulatory competition*, for instance, assume differential effects on highly or poorly endowed as well as on more or less industrialized economies. While the validity of far-reaching claims within this literature about convergence on the lowest regulatory level (race to the bottom) is highly disputable (cf. Drezner 2001), the impact of the domestic economic context as such on policy choices remains generally plausible.

Besides cost calculations on the basis of economic constraints and competitive pressures, *policy learning* is a possible mechanism that might lead to domestic change. Applied to intergovernmental diffusion processes, this concept focuses on dynamics taking place in the 'importer' country. Although it is not our aim to analyse the relevance of this or other change mechanisms, the literature on policy learning also points to significant domestic framework factors for convergence. Similar to the literature on policy convergence, analysts of policy learning perceive the process of change as a culturally and institutionally pre-structured process. Actors' choices with respect to following, adapting or ignoring foreign examples are influenced by dominant ideas (policy paradigms or even more general views of the world) and institutional structures at home. Peter Hall (1989, 1993) is a pioneer of this perspective, basing his analysis on an historical institutionalist approach.

In contrast to the policy convergence literature that, when looking at domestic factors, tends to assume institutional path-dependencies, Hall adopts a more differentiated perspective, looking more closely at the policy object in question. Moving between the orders of policy change – rising from policy settings, instruments to general ideas and principles – policy-makers (typically bureaucrats) become more and more embedded in institutional and cultural structures, and hence more constrained with respect to fundamental change. As Hall is mostly concerned with analysing the balance between structure and agency in explaining different 'orders' of learning, he does not investigate the precise nature of domestic structures that impact on actors, however.[3] This is the aim of the present article. It starts from the seminal work of Hall in distinguishing between his three 'orders of policy change', but then attempts to relate these to three structural factors that, in various compositions and intensities, permit or constrain the domestic adoption of 'importable' policies. We depart from past debates that focus on international versus domestic factors or the role of structure versus agency and examine a neglected issue in both debates, namely the diverse facets of domestic structure and their potentially distinct impacts.

3. DOMESTIC FACTORS AND TYPES OF POLICY INNOVATION: A FRAMEWORK FOR ANALYSIS

3.1 Three categories of domestic factors

Given an international impulse towards policy innovation, which factors determine if a country will actually follow this stimulus? As indicated, this is not a contribution to further elaborate on the international factors and the nature of the mechanism leading toward policy convergence; our focus rather is the soil in which the seed of change is sown, i.e. those factors that make up the basic domestic opportunity structure for change. Although most of the theories just reviewed do in fact address, in one way or another, the domestic factors determining the 'likelihood of change', it is our aim to add a more systematic perspective. For this purpose, we will start working from three fundamental sets of 'framework conditions' for domestic policy change: the cultural setting, the institutional setting and the socio-economic setting.[4]

One category of factors determining the domestic opportunity structure for change is culture. Policy-specific political discourses – the ideas and narratives behind policies and policy change – are set within the broader culture of a country. Thus, culture offers an important key to understanding how policy-specific discourses are developed, interpreted and eventually integrated into the domestic policy-making context. As Hall (1993: 289) points out, 'politicians, officials, the spokesmen for society interests, and political experts all operate within the terms of political discourse that are current in the nation at a given time' and that lend 'legitimacy to some social interests more than others'. An example is provided by Hajer (1995), who describes how the UK and the Netherlands translated the discourse of ecological modernization into their national policies in quite different ways, dependent first and foremost on their national culture and relation to nature. While the concept of ecological modernization has indeed spread widely in the world, the concrete meaning given to this concept varies between countries and follows cultural predisposition.

Second, institutionalist theories emphasize the importance of institutional structures as both opportunities for and impediments to change. Steinmo and Thelen (1992), for instance, stress that institutions provide the context in which policy changes are defined. In this tradition, Knill and Lenschow (2000), for example, argue that effective implementation of European Union (EU) policies by the member states basically depends on the degree of institutional 'fit' between existing institutional arrangements and the institutional implications of the 'incoming' policy.

There are limits to institutional explanations, of course. Institutions may indeed accommodate, 'constrain or refract policies but they can never be the sole "cause"' of policy change (Steinmo and Thelen 1992: 3). Institutional analysis argues that institutions are the main independent variable to explain political outcomes in periods of stability. Under highly dynamic circumstances, such as political or economic crises, however, institutions may break down. In that case, they become the dependent variable themselves (Knill 2001). The sociological branch of institutionalism adopts a very wide notion of institutions – including norms and mutual understandings – and thus develops a cultural understanding of their influence on behaviour. Since we want to analytically distinguish between institutional and cultural factors, we follow a thinner definition of institutions, limiting it to organizational structures, formal and informal rules, and policy-making procedures.

Institutions and culture are inextricably linked to a third set of factors, i.e. socio-economic structure and development. As Inglehart (1977) has argued, highly developed industrialized nations tend to pay more attention to 'post-materialist' (e.g. environmental) values. Jänicke (1988) investigated the de-linking of economic performance and environmental pollution and found that structural economic change in the broad sense of the word, such as the growth of the service sector in highly developed economies, can have an environment-friendly result. These examples stress the importance of socio-economic structure as a third determinant for the likelihood of domestic policy change.

To sum up, this paper distinguishes three basic sets of 'framework conditions' for domestic policy change: institutional, cultural and socio-economic factors. These are, as was already hinted at, interlinked and the extent to which a policy innovation is accommodated and adopted by a given country can never be explained with reference to one single factor. Nevertheless, it will be argued below that one factor may be more important than others, depending on the specific type of policy change at stake.

3.2 Three dimensions of change

The innovation of policy may come in different forms. It may involve the development of a new set of ideas, such as ecological modernization in the example above, or the introduction of a new policy principle. But it may also be a new type of policy instrument, for instance emissions trading, or a tendency towards stricter standards for a certain pollutant, owing for instance to new scientific insight. Following Hall (1993), moreover, it seems likely that these different types of policy change will have different implications domestically. Consequently, institutional, cultural and economic factors may be differently relevant as 'framework conditions' for their uptake at the domestic level.

For the purpose of this paper, we adopt Hall's three basic dimensions of policy content. First, we consider the overarching goals that guide policy in a particular field. These goals operate within a policy paradigm or a 'framework of ideas', specifying the very nature of the problems to be addressed by the policy. Examples are the precautionary principle or the idea of human 'stewardship' over nature. Second, there are the instruments or techniques by which policy goals are attained, e.g. direct regulation, fiscal instruments or voluntary agreements. Countries with different traditions may adopt different instruments to regulate the same policy issue. Third, it is important to look at the precise setting, or 'calibration', of these instruments, e.g. the level of emission standards or taxes, the chemicals included in 'grey' and 'black' lists, etc.

3.3 Combining domestic factors and dimensions of change: a systematic approach

Our search for structural predispositions to change, adaptation and diffusion will be rather well known to readers tuned into the institutionalist literature. Institutional factors are cited to (a) affect a country's general likelihood to depart from existing structures and practices (e.g. presence of veto points in the political systems) as well as (b) group countries into 'families' that share important features and, by implication, sensitivities during reform processes on the level of policy sectors (e.g. models of welfare states or degree of liberalization of the national economy).

Taking a closer look at this literature one sometimes gets the feeling that everything is institutional. Institutional factors range from organizational structures, to normative traditions or belief systems, even to traditional characteristics of the national economy. Using longevity and embeddedness as the main criteria for institutionalization, such wide understanding of the term institution is certainly defensible. To the extent that one aims to develop a differentiated understanding of domestic structural predispositions to change, the distinction into institutions (focusing on organizational, legal and procedural structures), culture (or normative traditions) and the socio-economic framework carries clear advantages, however. Each factor can be further operationalized with respect to the specific question (or policy) in mind and testable hypotheses can be derived.

We begin by suggesting a matrix (Figure 1) indicating the primary domestic factor influencing convergence on the three policy dimensions in general terms, before turning to the operationalization and development of hypotheses with respect to convergence in section 4. In illustrating our arguments we use environmental policy references, but we like to emphasize that this framework presumes more general applicability.

Ideas and principles

Ideas and principles on the policy level establish basic notions on the nature of the problem and legitimate means for handling it. In the environment policy field, for instance, the perception of pollution as a problem depends on an 'idea' of nature as something fragile and worthy of protection (be it for

	Culture	Institutions	Socio-economic structure
Ideas/Principles	■		
Instruments		■	
Settings			■

Figure 1 Hypothesized primary structural factors (dark shades) for the three orders of policy change

instrumental or 'genuine' reasons). The principles translating this idea into guidance for human behaviour, in turn, may establish concrete notions of responsibility (towards local or global society, future generations as well as nature). In Thompson's words (1983: 233): 'When we look at our environment we do not see it with the naked eye. We see it as it is filtered through a cultural screen – our idea of nature.' In this formulation, culture appears policy-specific; but we argue that there is a strong link between general cultural characteristics of a given society and ideas related to a particular policy. In Hofstede's (1992) classification of national cultures the more or less anthropogenic interpretation of environmental protection and notion of responsibility are tapped by the general cultural dimensions of 'masculinity versus femininity' and 'uncertainty avoidance'. The former measures a nation's general inclination to value collective goals as opposed to egoistic objectives; the latter contrasts a pragmatic handling of uncertainty with an emphasis on notions of truth as basis for action. Hofstede shows some links of both dimensions to the dominant religion of a country, i.e. an even more general cultural dimension. Catholicism and orthodox religion is being associated with uncertainty avoidance and a more masculine culture; Protestantism is linked to worldly and pragmatic ways to cope with uncertainty and a more feminine culture. The link between religion and environmental policy has been pursued by Vogel (2002) and Inglehart and Carballo (1997). The significant role of religious factors has also been shown for economic (Simmons and Elkins 2004) and welfare (Castles 1994; Manow 2004) policy, for instance.

Strang and Meyer (1993) relate cultural factors to diffusion processes – and by implication to convergence.[5] They 'argue that diffusion is importantly shaped and accelerated by culturally analyzed similarities among actors' (p. 487). The impact of culture on diffusion is considered especially large once cultural categories are situated in a general 'formulation of patterned relationships such as chains of cause and effect' (p. 492) which facilitate the meaningful communication between countries, and hence diffusion. Culture transformed into such 'meaningful formulation' moves down a level of abstraction and close to a policy-specific framework of ideas and principles. In other words, policy ideas and principles are specific, reasoned embodiments of culture. This leads us to hypothesize that the general cultural framework will be the dominant factor structuring domestic adaptation to foreign input at the level of ideas and principles.

Institutional and socio-economic structures are thought of as potentially significant but secondary domestic factors shaping patterns of convergence. Institutional 'fit' (Cowles *et al.* 2000; Knill and Lenschow 1998) is the shorthand for policy-specific institutional structures that require no fundamental reorientation for the implementation of new ideas. Especially as long as new (fashionable) ideas are merely adopted for symbolic rather than problem-oriented reasons, moreover, their institutional implications may be ignored by the political decision-makers.

As the economic implications of ideas are (or appear) often 'harmless' and are hidden behind abstract formulations, we assume that the stage of economic development forms only a moderate constraint (or opportunity) for change. This is true under the assumption that the level of economic development does not form a threshold for adopting environmental ideas in the first place; hence it is plausible especially for analyses focusing on so-called developed countries. From a more long-term perspective, changes in the economic structure and development may contribute to the emergence of new value systems and cultural change which, in turn, is likely to impact on the reception of new ideas. Specific to environmental policy, Ronald Inglehart and associates (1977, 1997) have traced the emergence of so-called post-material values to increasing economic security and modernization (both within and across societies). This research points to the linkage of the three structural categories under investigation.[6] For our purposes it is relevant, however, that the cultural soil, regardless of its deeper historical foundations, provides the immediate ground for implanting foreign ideas and principles.

Policy instruments

Policy instruments define how, who and within which organizational structures to do things in order to attain the defined goals and objectives. The choice of policy instruments is typically taken rather autonomously by actors within the state apparatus (cf. Hall 1993: 281–4) who may respond to internal dissatisfaction with past experiences and/or copy or imitate new techniques perceived successful in other settings. The literature on bureaucratic and organizational behaviour suggests, however, that these actors tend to orient their choices on the already existing repertoire of institutional procedures, technologies and organizational forms. New institutional patterns that break with established forms and procedures or appear costly, as considerable time, personnel and financial resources may be required to run a new set of policy instruments (see Pierson (1996) on the notion of 'sunk costs'), are considered rather unlikely.

The crucial role of institutional path-dependencies for the adaptation of new policy instruments has been shown in several policy areas in the EU. For examples in the environmental field, see Knill and Lenschow (1998), Jordan *et al.* (2003), Jordan and Liefferink (2004); similarly, Duina (1997) points to the relevance of institutional 'fit' in social policy; Buller (2002) shows that the reformed European agricultural policy meets distinct national reactions linked to the respective organizational structure of that sector. Typically, policy instruments follow more general governance patterns in a country such as the type of state–society relations, the level of state intervention or the importance attached to the law.

But policy instruments are also embedded in a more general political culture of governing and it is not easy to establish priority. Hofstede's categorization is again instructive. His power distance index sets apart the 'Latin' countries from the rest of Europe when measuring attitudes toward human equality versus authority. These are likely to be reflected in the country's preference of legally enforceable rules versus more participatory approaches. His individualism versus collectivism index, which distinguishes all Anglo-Saxon countries and the Netherlands on the individualistic side from the rest of the investigated countries, will impact on market versus state dominance in governing the society with an equally close link to the choice of policy instruments. Arguably, institutional categories focusing on the role of the state and the law in governing society can be viewed as institutionalized forms of the political culture dimensions just described. Previewing the operationalization chosen below, pluralism builds on equality-based and individualistic cultural characteristics; neo-corporatism represents a middle category on both cultural dimensions; while statism is linked to more authoritarian and collectivist cultural patterns. The question whether the proposed institutionalist short-cut, by-passing more complex cultural categories, is justifiable needs to be tested empirically. Generally, the empirical test (not included in this paper) needs to control for the risk of multicollinearity that runs through this analysis.

Notwithstanding that the choice of a policy instrument implies economic costs and benefits, an analytical linkage between the socio-economic structure of a country and its pattern in adopting new policy instruments appears remote. Modernization theory, pointing to an interdependent relationship between economic and democratic development, suggests more participatory patterns in economically advanced countries; similarly, the use and diffusion of market instruments may be associated with the level of economic (and hence market) activity. Given the somewhat speculative link between these factors in the literature we consider economic structure as a merely secondary factor.

Settings

The choice of policy settings, by contrast, is primarily influenced by the question 'can we afford this?' Meeting certain standards or norms, the introduction of taxes, fees or subsidies as well as procedural settings such as the duration of review processes, for instance, affect the resource base of a country and of social or economic groups within a country.

Especially in cases where the competitiveness of the country is affected by regulatory settings, the level of economic development and the structure of the workforce will be major determinants in choosing a setting. The choice-theoretical literature on races to the top or bottom in setting regulatory standards (cf. Holzinger 2003; Scharpf 1996) is based on this notion. While generally the economic rationale will call for a setting of low standards, hence keeping production costs low and internationally competitive, we may witness an international trend towards the top if high regulating states make a credible threat of closing their markets to products of lower standard. The setting of policy instruments is therefore a consequence of comparing the costs of (new) settings with the benefits of market access.

Such economic rationale becomes problematic when the policy settings do not refer to tradable goods but production processes. In order to explain that we may witness a race to the top here as well, reference to economic structure and development may not suffice. While it may be true that a country will orient the setting of policy instruments on budgetary constraints and the relative strength of the economy (or the sector affected), it will also be guided by social and cultural understandings of appropriateness and the answer to the question 'Do we want high standards or tight controls?' Besides economic features such as the level of industrialization, the intensity of agricultural production, the degree of urbanization, etc. which are closely tied to levels of environmental destruction in a country, the culturally determined problem perception and the search for 'appropriate' responses impact on the settings of a policy instrument. In a risk-averse culture the regulatory constraints on economic activity are likely to be set at a more severe level than in a culture of risk-takers. A country with a predominant Protestant culture may not only show particular sensitivity to human-induced threats to the eco-system but will also be willing to adopt such policies earlier and with higher standards than other countries. Similarly, a country with an authoritarian culture will not only be hesitant in the very adoption of communication-based instruments, but also more restrictive in setting such instruments once they may have entered the national repertoire of policy tools. Institutional structures by contrast can be generally assumed to play only a secondary role in the setting of policies, as usually they are not themselves challenged but merely operate as filters.

4. SIMILAR POLICIES IN SIMILAR COUNTRIES? THREE HYPOTHESES

In the preceding section, we proposed an ordering of domestic factors in relation to their anticipated impact on the adoption of different types of policy innovations. On this basis we will now formulate three testable hypotheses and, to this end, we will operationalize our three domestic factors – culture, institutions and socio-economic structure – with the help of indicators, one for each factor.

In selecting these indicators, we chose rather basic indicators frequently used to characterize the policy-making of countries in cultural, institutional and economic terms. We focus on environmental policy in our illustrations and our indicators were chosen to resonate with environmental policy debates. Nevertheless, none of the indicators is specific to environmental policy as the cited literature confirms. Our indicators allow us to cluster countries that share certain domestic factors. In this section, by way of thought experiment, we will do so for a sample of almost all – Western and Eastern – European countries plus the US, Mexico and Japan. This sample coincides with the focus of an ongoing research project[7] which investigates the degree and causes of convergence of policies around twenty-seven environmental issues in twenty-three countries over a period of three decades. On the basis of expert surveys, it brings together detailed information on the development of policy ideas, instruments and settings over time. These data will enable us to test our hypotheses empirically at a later stage. It should be emphasized that this rather tentative exercise is not meant to 'label' countries as a goal in itself. Its only purpose is to make our hypotheses more concrete and testable. Furthermore, this exercise is not designed to explain single cases, but rather to suggest probable convergence trends in larger N samples. While section 4.1 deals with the cultural 'opportunity structure', sections 4.2 and 4.3 discuss the institutional and socio-economic structures, respectively.

4.1 Culture

General hypothesis: Convergence of ideas, principles and goals of environmental policy can be accounted for by cultural rather than institutional or socio-economic similarity between countries.

According to this hypothesis, clusters of countries that are culturally close may be expected to adopt more or less similar ideas, in this case about environmental policy, around the same time. Culture, moreover, is expected to account better for such convergence than institutional and socio-economic factors.

In an illuminating article, Vogel (2002) reviews a number of possible explanations for differences in environmental ethics among twenty-four rich countries. For this purpose, he distinguishes between 'light green' environmentalism, focusing on domestic health and safety concerns, and 'dark green' environmentalism, with a much broader, less anthropocentric scope. Among factors such as relative wealth, the pathway towards industrialization, and civic culture, religion is found to be the only one fully correlating with the 'shades of green' observed in his sample. Vogel elaborates on this by claiming that 'dark green' environmentalism is more likely to be found in countries that are (or historically have been) dominated by Protestantism, given their pervasive sense of morals, an emphasis on individual responsibility, a pessimistic or even apocalyptic world view, and a tendency towards self-discipline (Vogel 2002: 317). According to Vogel, this is an important reason why Protestant countries have generally facilitated earlier and more eco-centric environmental policies than others. The usefulness of religion as a shorthand for cultural attributes that may have an impact on the spread of ideas is supported by a recent study by Simmons and Elkins (2004). They convincingly show that having a similar religious tradition corresponds well – and much better than other cultural factors – with the uptake of certain ideas about the liberalization of the national economy.

Following this logic, one would expect predominantly Protestant countries to base their environmental policies on roughly similar ideas and principles, which can be distinguished from those adopted by Roman Catholic or other countries. Protestant countries, with their tradition of moral responsibility, for instance, may be more inclined to adopt the precautionary principle than Roman Catholic ones (Vogel 2002: 317–18). Basically drawing upon Vogel's paper, we use the categories of countries set out in Table 1 (Vogel 2002; see also http://www.nationmaster.com).[8] Note that for the present purposes, only the distinction between Protestant and 'other' (i.e. Roman Catholic, Orthodox, Buddhist, etc.) countries is relevant.

4.2 Institutions

General hypothesis: Convergence of environmental policy instruments can be accounted for by institutional rather than cultural or socio-economic similarity between countries.

This hypothesis claims that similar types of instruments are most likely to be adopted in countries with a roughly comparable institutional structure. It also presupposes that institutional factors are more important in this respect than cultural or socio-economic ones.

The governance discussion captures this institutional dimension of national policy-making rather well. Governance signifies 'das Gesamt aller nebeneinander bestehenden Formen der kollektiven Regelung gesellschaftlicher Sachverhalte: von der institutionalisierten zivilgesellschaftlichen Selbstregelung über verschiedene Formen des Zusammenwirkens staatlicher und privater Akteure bis hin zu hoheitlichem Handeln staatlicher Akteure' (Mayntz 2003: 72).[9] These basic principles of political rule-making correspond to the conventional categories of (liberal) pluralism, neo-corporatism and statism, respectively (e.g. Van Waarden 1995; Schmidt 1999).[10]

Apart from legal prohibitions or obligations, which generally are the dominant tools in regulatory policy, alternative instruments may also be applied to influence the behaviour of industry or societal actors. We suggest that the likelihood of using economic or society-based instruments varies across governance systems. National systems generally characterized as statist may be expected to exhibit the strongest preference for 'state-centred' legal instruments and direct regulation ranging from prohibitions and bans to obligatory product and production standards. Liberal-pluralist countries, in contrast, will be relatively more inclined to try 'hands-off' approaches and choose market-based instruments such as taxes, levies or emissions trading. The key to neo-corporatism, finally, is *negotiated* rule-making and the exchange of influence (on the content of policies) against co-operation (in the implementation of these policies) (Schmitter 1974). Neo-corporatist systems would therefore be most inclined to apply instruments based upon negotiation, consensus and trust, such as voluntary agreements. Table 1 presents our clustering of countries as regards the basic orientation of public/private relations, based upon Williamson (1989) and Van Waarden (1995).

4.3 Socio-economic structure

General hypothesis: Convergence of environmental policy settings can be accounted for by socio-economic rather than cultural or institutional similarity between countries.

The claim here is that, as far as domestic factors are concerned, the precise level at which environmental policies are calibrated (standards, norms, levies, etc.) primarily depends on socio-economic parameters.

Intuitively, economic development and environmental quality in a country are negatively correlated. Increasing production and consumption typically leads to more pollution. Since the 1960s, however, environmental policies have been introduced to bring about a 'de-linkage' of economic growth and environmental deterioration within the group of developed countries (Jänicke 1988). Particularly in the most highly developed countries, moreover, a shift is taking place away from traditional industrial activities to 'high-tech' production and a more service-based economy, allegedly leading to a further 'de-linkage', an increase of post-materialist values (Inglehart 1977), and better opportunities for advanced environmental policies (Huber 1982).[11]

Richer countries, in sum, have both more reason and more means to control pollution. We thus expect that more developed economies will tend to have stricter standards in environmental policy than less developed ones (Vogel 1997). In Table 1 we have grouped our countries according to the basic indicator of gross domestic product (GDP) per capita (UNDP 2003).

5. CONCLUSIONS AND OUTLOOK

In this paper, we have tried to systematically link a number of very basic properties of countries to the likelihood of them taking up different types of policy innovations from abroad. More particularly, we have argued that new *ideas, principles and goals* impinge first and foremost on national *culture.* Therefore, countries that share important aspects of their cultural foundations might be expected to more quickly adopt similar ideas, principles and goals than countries that are culturally less close to each other. As a proxy for the aspects of cultural affinity between countries relevant for environmental policy, we proposed religion. Likewise, it was claimed that new policy *instruments* primarily have organizational consequences, rendering *institutional* factors crucial for their adoption. Thus, countries with a similar governance orientation were hypothesized to share preferences for the same types of instruments. The precise *setting* of the instruments, finally, was considered to be a matter primarily of *socio-economic* patterns. Countries with comparable levels of economic development were therefore expected to adopt roughly similar levels of environmental protection.

Table 1 Clustering of countries on the basis of cultural, institutional and economic indicators*

	Countries[12]	*BG*	*BE*	*DK*	*DE*	*EL*	*ES*	*FR*	*IE*	*IT*	*HU*	*NL*	*AT*	*PL*	*PT*	*RO*	*SK*	*FI*	*SE*	*UK*	*CH*	*JP*	*MX*	*NO*	*US*
Culture	Protestant			+	+							+						+	+	+	+			+	+
(indicator: religion)	Other	+	+			+	+	+	+	+	+		+	+	+	+	+					+	+		
Institutions	Neo-corporatist		+	+	+							+	+					+	+		+	+		+	
(indicator: public/	Liberal								+											+					+
private relations)[13]	Statist	+				+	+	+		+	+?			+	+	+	+						+		
Economy	Above			+					+			+	+								+			+	+
(indicator: GDP	Moderate		+		+		+	+		+					+			+	+	+		+			
per capita	Below	+				+					+			+		+	+						+		
(PPP US $))[14]																									

**Explanation and sources: see text.*

This analysis is a simplification of reality in at least two ways. First, the adoption of, for instance, new ideas can of course in practice never be *only* dependent upon cultural factors. As pointed out, all three basic factors must be supposed to play an interrelated role in the uptake of all types of policy innovations. Nevertheless, we do think to have made plausible that for the adoption of each type of policy innovation (idea, instrument or setting), one basic domestic factor (culture, institutions or economy) is generally more important than the other two. Second, policy innovations in practice hardly ever consist of new ideas, new instruments or new standards exclusively. Most often, to be sure, one implies the other. In a new instrument, for instance, some new way of thinking about the problem at stake is almost inevitably implicit. As soon as the instrument is adopted, moreover, it usually requires some sort of calibration, e.g. a concrete emission standard or a tax level. We argue, however, that this should not necessarily prevent us from identifying, for analytical reasons, the essence of any given policy innovation: either idea or instrument or setting.

The principal advantage of this two-fold simplification is that it allows for a systematic study of the impact of domestic factors on convergence. So far, most studies of convergence, and particularly those paying due attention to the domestic setting of 'importer' countries, have been based on in-depth process tracing. Although good case study work can be extremely valuable – we will be the last to deny that! – its results usually remain difficult to generalize. The three hypotheses derived from our ranking of cultural, institutional and socio-economic factors according to their expected impact upon the adoption of different types of policy innovations, in contrast, can be tested empirically across a large number of cases. As mentioned earlier, we intend to do so, on the basis of data being collected at present.

An empirical study of this kind will not tell us *why* the birds sing. It will not help us to understand the process of policy spreading across countries. But it will provide better insight into *where* and *when*, i.e. under which circumstances, they sing. Our basic argument, in fact, is that birds of a feather are more likely to burst into song. By using data over a large number of cases and a large number of countries, it can now be tested if different structural domestic characteristics in the 'importer' countries are indeed significant variables for explaining patterns of convergence.

Addresses for correspondence: Andrea Lenschow, University of Osnabrück, Faculty of Social Sciences, Seminarstraße 33, D-49069 Osnabrück, Germany. Tel: +49 541 969 4632. Fax: +49 541 969 4600. email: Andrea.Lenschow@uos.de/Duncan Liefferink, Radboud University Nijmegen, Department of Environmental Policy Sciences, PO Box 9108, NL-6500 HK Nijmegen, The Netherlands. Tel: +31 24 3611925. Fax: +31 24 3611841. email: D.Liefferink@fm.ru.nl/Sietske Veenman, Radboud University Nijmegen, Department of Environmental Policy Sciences, PO Box 9108, NL-6500 HK Nijmegen, The Netherlands. Tel: +31 24 3611925. Fax: +31 24 3611841. email: S.Veenman@fm.ru.nl

ACKNOWLEDGEMENTS

This paper was written in the context of the project 'Environmental governance in Europe: the impact of international institutions and trade on policy convergence'. We would like to thank the EU for providing funding for this project (contract no. HPSE-CT-2002-00103). Apart from that, we thank Daniel Drezner, Christoph Knill, the other participants in the Hamburg workshop of 24–25 April 2004 as well as one anonymous reviewer for their very helpful comments on earlier drafts of this paper.

NOTES

1 There are other mechanisms, including coercion, multilateral co-operation or policy transfer. In this review section we focus on those where the literature has at least touched on domestic structural factors. Implicit in our treatment of the literature is the assumption that we can investigate domestic factors as a discrete explanatory category, independent of the nature of international factors. Hence, we do not reflect on the weight of single domestic factors depending on the nature of the international impulse – e.g. coercive or co-operative. Rather we will focus on the weight of single domestic factors in relation to the policy 'object' that may or may not spread between states.

2 It must be noted at this point that we are focusing on relatively stable domestic structures rather than on the full range of domestic factors that might affect policy change – such as technological or scientific innovations, problem pressure, changes in government or public opinion. While some of these factors may be conceived of as specific facets of the structural factors mentioned – technological development as well as problem pressure have links to the socio-economic structure of a country, cultural as well as socio-economic factors may influence a country's scientific potential (though not specific innovations) – in this general paper we will not trace the relations between structural and policy specific domestic factors. Importantly, we also abstract from political factors. While, for example, the views of the electorate and the composition of the government undoubtedly play a role in adopting new policy approaches (potentially converging to international examples), these do not result in stable convergence patterns across time and policy areas, in which we are interested in this paper.

3 Implicit in his analysis is a mixed picture of cultural (ideational) and institutional factors, without placing them in any order. Economic *structure* receives no special attention, in contrast to the impact of economic *crisis* which may induce public pressure challenging even deeply embedded policy patterns.

4 We are not, in this paper, interested in the behaviour of individual actors, but in the domestic structural opportunities and constraints they face in converging with practices in other countries. This focus allows us to develop hypotheses for a large N country comparison.

5 See also Kern (1999) for an analysis specific to environmental policy.

6 The causal direction is far from clear, however. Max Weber in his 'Protestant Ethic', for instance, suggests the opposite causal chain in tracing capitalist development to cultural (religious) conditions.

7 The project 'Environmental governance in Europe: the impact of international institutions and trade on policy convergence' (2003–2005), for short 'ENVIPOLCON', is financed by the EU and carried out by the Universities of Konstanz, Nijmegen, Hamburg, Berlin (FU) and Salzburg.

8 The classification of Germany as Protestant is problematic although it corresponds to a general practice in the literature. The empirical analysis may watch for 'irregular' German patterns.

9 In our translation: 'the total of all existing forms for collectively handling society's affairs: from the institutionalized, private self-regulation to various forms of co-operation between state and private actors and to the exclusive and hierarchical rule of state actors'.

10 An even more parsimonious alternative could be the 'varieties of capitalism' approach, which distinguishes between co-ordinated and liberal market economies (Hall and Soskice 2001). As this approach focuses on relations *within* the market sector it has difficulties accommodating more state-dominated systems like France and Italy which, however, form a distinct class in regulatory policy-making.

11 Economists refer to the environmental Kuznets curve, which has the shape of an inverted 'U', to reflect the turn from a negative to a positive relationship between income and environmental quality of a country.

12 For the EU and candidate countries we have used the country code and country order as applied by the EU (http://publications.eu.int/code/en/en-370101.htm). The remaining countries we have put at the end of the table in alphabetic order by their English names.

13 The institutional classification of East European states raises certain problems. In an initial step, Bulgaria, Hungary, Poland, Slovakia and Romania have been classified as statist countries in view of their history as statist and the relatively brief period, only since 1989, in which changes have taken place in those countries. Recent work on the nature of labour relations in East European states (cf. Kohl and Platzer 2004), i.e. a policy field with particularly pronounced patterns of state–society relations, confirms that the level of state intervention in these countries remains very high (p. 280). A partial exception is Hungary which is approaching corporatist structures of Germany and Austria. Kohl and Platzer also refer, however, to certain specific features of these transformation countries as well as to the existence of different speeds of institutional change. Hence, it will be necessary to investigate the convergence behaviour of East European states carefully.

14 Three groups are distinguished, based upon the average of the GDP (Purchasing Power Parity (PPP) US $) over all countries plus respectively minus half of the standard deviation.

REFERENCES

Berry, F.S. and Berry, W.D. (1999) 'Innovation and diffusion models in policy research', in P. Sabatier (ed.), *Theories of the Policy Process*, Boulder, CO: Westview Press, pp. 169–200.

Buller, H. (2002) 'Integrating EU environmental and agricultural policy', in A. Lenschow (ed.), *Environmental Policy Integration. Greening Sectoral Policies in Europe*, London: Earthscan, pp. 103–26.

Busch, P.-O. and Jörgens, H. (2005) 'The international sources of policy convergence: explaining the spread of environmental policy innovations', *Journal of European Public Policy* 12(5): 860–84.

Castles, F. (1994) 'On religion and public policy: does Catholicism make a difference?', *European Journal of Political Research* 25: 19–40.

Collier, D. and Messick, R.E. (1975) 'Prerequisites versus diffusion: testing alternative explanations of social security adoption', *American Political Science Review* 69: 1299–355.

Cowles, M.G., Caporaso, J. and Risse, T. (eds) (2000) *Transforming Europe*, Ithaca: Cornell University Press.

Drezner, D.W. (2001) 'Globalization and policy convergence', *The International Studies Review* 3(1): 53–78.

Duina, F.G. (1997) 'Explaining legal implementation in the European Union', *International Journal of the Sociology of Law* 25: 155–79.

Gourevitch, P. (1978) 'The second image reversed: the international sources of domestic politics', *International Organization* 32(4): 881–912.

Hajer, M. (1995) *The Politics of Environmental Discourse: Ecological Modernization and the Policy Process*, Oxford: Clarendon Press.

Hall, P.A. (ed.) (1989) *The Political Power of Economic Ideas: Keynesianism Across Nations*, Princeton: Princeton University Press.

Hall, P.A. (1993) 'Policy paradigms, social learning, and the state. The case of economic policymaking in Britain', *Comparative Politics* 25(3): 275–96.

Hall, P.A. and Soskice, D. (eds) (2001) *Varieties of Capitalism. The Institutional Foundations of Comparative Advantage*, Oxford: Oxford University Press.

Hofstede, G. (1992) *Culture's Consequences. Comparing Values, Behaviors, Institutions, and Organizations Across Nations*, 2nd edn, Thousand Oaks and London: Sage.

Holzinger, K. (2003) 'Common goods, matrix games, and institutional solutions', *European Journal of International Relations* 9: 173–212.

Holzinger, K. and Knill, C. (2005) 'Causes and conditions of cross-national policy convergence', *Journal of European Public Policy* 12(5): 775–96.

Huber, J. (1982) *Die verlorene Unschuld der Ökologie. Neue Technologien und superindustrielle Entwicklung*, Frankfurt: Fischer Verlag.

Inglehart, R. (1977) *The Silent Revolution: Changing Values and Political Styles among Western Publics*, Princeton: Princeton University Press.

Inglehart, R. and Carballo, M. (1997) 'Does Latin America exist? (and is there a Confucian culture?): a global analysis of cross cultural differences', *Political Science and Politics* 30: 34–46.

Jänicke, M. (1988) 'Structural change and environmental impact: empirical evidence on thirty-one countries in East and West', *Environmental Monitoring and Assessment* 12: 99–114.

Jordan, A. and Liefferink, D. (eds) (2004) *Environmental Policy in Europe. The Europeanization of National Environmental Policy*, London: Routledge.

Jordan, A., Wurzel, R. and Zito, A. (eds) (2003) *New Instruments of Environmental Governance: National Experiences and Prospects*, Special issue of *Environmental Politics* 12(1): 1–224.

Kern, K. (1999) *Politische Kultur und Umweltpolitik. Die amerikanischen Einzelstaaten im Vergleich*, Berlin: Freie Universität, Forschungsstelle für Umweltpolitik, FFU Report 99–8.

Kern, K., Jörgens, H. and Jänicke, M. (1999) *Die Diffusion umweltpolitischer Innovationen. Ein Beitrag zur Globalisierung von Umweltpolitik*, Berlin: Freie Universität, Forschungsstelle für Umweltpolitik, FFU Report 99–11.

Knill, C. (2001) *The Europeanisation of National Administrations. Patterns of Institutional Change and Persistence*, Cambridge: Cambridge University Press.

Knill, C. and Lenschow, A. (1998) 'Coping with Europe: the impact of British and German administrations on the implementation of EU environmental policy', *Journal of European Public Policy* 5(4): 595–614.

Knill, C. and Lenschow, A. (2000) *Implementing EU Environmental Policy, New Directions and Old Problems*, Manchester and New York: Manchester University Press.

Kohl, H. and Platzer, H.-W. (2004) *Arbeitsbeziehungen in Mittelosteuropa. Transformation und Integration. Die acht neuen EU-Mitgliedsländer im Vergleich*, 2nd edn, Baden-Baden: Nomos.

Manow, P. (2004) *'The Good, the Bad, and the Ugly' – Esping-Andersen's Regime Typology and the Religious Roots of the Western Welfare State*, Köln: MPIfG Working Paper 04/3.

Mayntz, R. (2003) 'Governance im modernen Staat', in A. Benz *et al.* (eds), *Governance. Eine Einführung*, Dreifachkurseinheit der FernUniversität Hagen, pp. 71–83.

Pierson, P. (1996) 'The path to European integration. A historical institutionalist analysis', *Comparative Political Studies* 29(2): 123–63.

Scharpf, F.W. (1996) 'Politische Optionen im Vollendeten Binnenmarkt', in M. Jachtenfuchs and B. Kohler-Koch (eds), *Europäische Integration*, Baden-Baden: Nomos Verlag, pp. 109–40.

Scharpf, F.W. and Schmidt, V.A. (eds) (2002) *Welfare and Work in the Open Economy. From Vulnerability to Competitiveness*, Oxford: Oxford University Press.

Schmidt, V.A. (1999) 'National patterns of governance under siege. The impact of European integration', in B. Kohler-Koch and R. Eising (eds), *The Transformation of Governance in the European Union*, London and New York: Routledge.

Schmitter, P.C. (1974) 'Still the century of corporatism?', *The Review of Politics* 36: 85–131.

Simmons, B.A. and Elkins, Z. (2004) 'The globalization of liberalization: policy diffusion in the international political economy', *American Political Science Review* 98(1): 171–89.

Steinmo, S. and Thelen, K. (1992) 'Historical institutionalism in comparative politics', in S. Steinmo, K. Thelen and F. Longstreth (eds), *Structuring Politics. Historical Institutionalism in Comparative Analysis*, Cambridge: Cambridge University Press, pp. 1–33.

Strang, D. and Meyer, J. (1993) 'Institutional conditions for diffusion', *Theory and Society* 22(4): 487–511.

Strang, D. and Soule, S.A. (1998) 'Diffusion in organisations and social movements: from hybrid corn to poison pills', *Annual Review of Sociology* 24: 265–90.

Thompson, M. (1983) 'Postscript: a cultural basis for comparison', in H.C. Kunreuther and J. Linnerooth (eds), *Risk Analysis and Decision Processes. The Siting of Liquefied Energy Gas Facilities in Four Countries*, Berlin: Springer Verlag, pp. 232–62.

UNDP (United National Development Programme) (2003) *Human Development Report 2003*, see http://www.undp.org/hdr2003/indicator/indic_4_2_1.html

Van Waarden, F. (1995) 'Persistence of national policy styles: a study of their institutional foundations', in B. Unger and F. van Waarden (eds), *Convergence or Diversity: Internationalization and Economic Policy Response*, Aldershot: Avebury, pp. 333–72.

Vogel, D. (1986) *National Styles of Regulation. Environmental Policy in Great Britain and the United States*, Ithaca: Cornell University Press.

Vogel, D. (1997) 'Trading up and governing across: transnational governance and environmental protection', *Journal of European Public Policy* 4(4): 556–71.

Vogel, D. (2002) 'The Protestant ethic and the spirit of environmentalism: exploring the cultural roots of contemporary green politics', *Zeitschrift für Umweltpolitik und Umweltrecht* 25(3): 297–322.

Williamson, P. (1989) *Corporatism in Perspective: An Introductory Guide to Corporatist Theory*, Thousand Oaks and London: Sage.

Is there convergence in convergence research? An overview of empirical studies on policy convergence

Stephan Heichel, Jessica Pape and Thomas Sommerer

INTRODUCTION

When looking at empirical studies on policy convergence, it is striking that there are different schools of thought which employ the term 'convergence'. They come from different academic backgrounds, apply both different theoretical approaches and concepts as well as diverse explanatory variables for convergence. Given the widespread popularity of this research topic, it may seem appealing to review the literature that focuses on causal factors. However, as in comparative studies in general, ensuring the comparability of the outcomes is a major problem (Feick 1992). We argue that this is particularly the case for empirical convergence literature. Therefore, trying to detect a 'common ground' that allows for an overall judgement deserves equal attention in a review article. We attempt to pinpoint the main factors that allow or hinder comparability between various studies on policy convergence.

To this end, we illustrate empirical literature on policy convergence, while focusing on whether convergence or divergence was determined and which countries, periods and policy fields were examined. Moreover, we analyse the different definitions and conceptualizations of policy convergence and the policy dimensions employed. In addition, a closer look at the structures of the methodological approaches will enable us to assess comparability of results in a systematic manner. We limit ourselves to research that focuses explicitly on policy convergence (and related concepts).[1]

EMPIRICAL POLICY CONVERGENCE RESEARCH

The introduction by Knill (2005) presents some definitions of policy convergence and related concepts we apply here. Although they comply with these definitions, we treat the concepts of policy convergence, policy diffusion, policy transfer and policy learning as comparable for the purpose of this review. This is justified since a common feature of the empirical studies applying the concepts is their general interest in the subject of increasing policy similarity (dissimilarity respectively). While the concept of policy convergence is more directly concerned with this effect as an observable phenomenon, policy transfer, diffusion, and learning describe mechanisms that can lead to policy similarity, hence constituting pathways towards convergence.

This linkage is proposed by policy diffusion researchers (see Kern *et al.* 2000: 510, 521; Tews *et al.* 2003: 571) and policy transfer scholars (see Jones and Newburn 2002: 104; Lavenex 2002: 716, 718). However, policy convergence is not necessarily the result of policy transfer or policy diffusion, but can also result from parallel problem pressure, for example (Knill 2005). We selected empirical studies for this review that fulfil the following criteria:[2] first, a study should address at least one clearly identifiable public policy or policy field in relation to at least two countries providing information on the development over time.[3] Second, researching policy similarity or related processes should be the central theme of the analysis (in many cases, this implies that policy convergence is the dependent variable). Third, a study should include an investigation of policy similarity between the countries in terms of concept and measurement. We argue that passing this threshold 'makes the difference'. Many studies on 'globalization', for example, are disregarded because they focus on other aspects and therefore do not comply with them.

In the following, we analyse the selected empirical policy convergence studies with regard to two dimensions, the **findings in convergence research** (including the policy area, region, observation period and explanatory factors) as well as aspects of the **research design** (policy dimensions, time factor and measurement).

While analysing the **findings in convergence research**, we look at four different categories: we conceive 'policy area' as the policy field, e.g. social policy or environmental policy. 'Region' refers to the geographic area for which studies exist, e.g. the European Union (EU) or the Organization for Economic Co-operation and Development (OECD) countries. A closer examination can reveal whether some regions dominate the research or if geographic areas are equally distributed. The 'observation period' refers to the time span

Table 1 Foci of the article

Sections	*Categories*
Findings in convergence research	Policy area Region Observation period Explanatory factors
Concepts and operationalizations in research designs	Policy dimension Time factor Measurement

covered in a study. We address this in order to determine whether policy convergence is mainly studied for recent phases or whether studies have a more long-term scope of analysis. In addition, we will summarize the 'explanatory factors' typically found in convergence literature.

With regard to the **research design** of the examined studies, we focus on 'policy dimensions', which we conceive as policy sub-elements, such as policy content or policy style. The 'time factor' is an important category as it relates to the degree of precision with which studies examine policy similarity over time – a clearly defined time-frame is important but not always the rule in convergence studies. Finally, the 'measurement' of convergence deals with operationalization and shows that various methods of assessing convergence exist. Different methods can consequently lead to different results in convergence studies.

FINDINGS IN CONVERGENCE RESEARCH

In the following, we give an overview of the findings in our sample of empirical convergence literature, including seventy-four studies (see Table 2). The order of the policy fields in the table follows the number of their appearance in our sample: areas with a transnational character and a high level of externalities such as environmental policy dominate; this also holds for globalization-related areas of financial, economic or social policy. Studies analysing policy fields such as education, health, agriculture, migration or telecommunication, etc. are dealt with to a lesser degree. Some policy fields were hardly represented at all – foreign policy was the subject of only one study in our sample (Hill 1997).

Looking at the regions covered by convergence literature, it is noticeable that most studies cover exclusively EU or OECD countries. Studies that focus on developing or Latin American countries are the exception (e.g. Brune and Garrett 2000; Martin and Schneider 2004; Meseguer 2003). One explanation for this phenomenon is the lack of available data (especially for quantitative analyses). Along with that, many authors are interested in the effects of globalization and Europeanization, which can be examined more clearly in integrated

Table 2 Empirical findings in convergence literature

Policy fields	*Source*	*Regions*	*Period*	*Convergence*
Social policy	Andersen *et al.* (2000)	13 EU countries	1970–1998	limited convergence
	Armingeon (1999)	18 OECD countries	1974–1978; 1990–1994	no
	Brooks (2004)	59 countries	1980–1999	limited convergence
	Dolowitz (1997)	UK, USA	1980s	yes
	Ferrara *et al.* (2001)	EU-15	1995–1999	no
	Gibson and Means (2000)	Australia, UK	1966–1998	yes
	Gornick and Meyers (2001)	14 European countries and USA	1980–1995	limited convergence
	Greve (1996)	12 EU countries	1980–1993	yes
	Montanari (2001)	18 OECD countries	1930–1990	limited convergence
	O'Connor (1988)	17 OECD countries	1960–1980	limited convergence
	Orenstein (2003)	152 countries	1981–2000	yes
	Overbye (1994)	22 European and Anglo-American countries	1970–1991	yes
	Pierson (2003)	Australia, UK	1990–1996	limited convergence
	Saint-Arnaud and Bernard (2003)	20 OECD countries	1985–1995	no
	Tavits (2003)	Estonia, Latvia	1990s	no
Fiscal policy (spending and taxing)	Bernauer and Achini (2000)	21 OECD countries and non-OECD	1970–1994	no
	Bouget (2003)	21 OECD countries	1980–1998	limited convergence
	De Bandt and Mongelli (2000)	17 OECD countries	1970–1998	limited convergence
	Gemmell and Kneller (2002)	16 OECD countries	1970–1995	limited convergence

(*Table continued*)

Table 2 Continued

Policy fields	*Source*	*Regions*	*Period*	*Convergence*
	Kautto and Kvist (2002)	EU-15, Norway	1980–2000	limited convergence
	Olewiler (1999)	20 OECD countries	1975–1996	yes
	Sanz and Velazquez (2003)	26 OECD countries	1970–1997	yes
	Slemrod (2004)	96 countries	1975–1995	yes
	Swank (2002)	16 OECD countries	1981–1998	yes
	Tomka (2003)	11 EU countries, Norway, Switzerland	1918–1990	yes
	Wolf (2002)	EU-15	1980–1997	yes
	Wunder (1999)	14 OECD countries	1985–1997	yes
Environmental policy	Aguilar Fernández (1994)	Germany, Spain	1980s and 1990s	no
	Botcheva and Martin (2001)	21 OECD countries	1986–1994	yes
	Harrison (2002)	Canada, Sweden, USA	1982–1999	no
	Hoberg (1991)	Canada, USA	1980s	yes
	Howlett (2000)	Canada, USA	1960–2000	limited convergence
	Howlett (1994)	Canada, USA	1980–2000	no
	Kern *et al.* (2000)	OECD, CEE, Africa	1970–2000	limited convergence
	Liefferink and Jordan (2002)	10 European countries	1980s and 1990s	limited convergence
	Oberthür and Tänzler (2002)	EU-15	1992–2001	yes
	Ostergren and Hollenhorst (1999)	Russia–USA	1930–1996	yes
	Seeliger (2001)	Canada, Germany, USA	1970–1996	limited convergence
	Tews *et al.* (2003)	48 OECD and CEE countries	1948–2000	yes

Trade policy	Brune and Garrett (2000)	148 developing countries	1988–1997	limited convergence
	Martin and Schneider (2004)	90 developing countries	1978–1999	limited convergence
	Meseguer (2003)	51 developing countries	1964–1990	yes
	Nicoletti and Scarpetta (2003)	22 OECD countries	1980–2000	no
	Simmons and Elkins (2004)	182 IMF member states	1967–1996	yes
Banking regulation	Busch (2002, 2003)	Germany, Switzerland, UK, USA	1974–1999	no
	Castro and McNamara (2003)	70 countries	1970–2000	yes
	Coleman (1994)	Canada, France, Germany, UK, USA	1973–1983	limited convergence
	Lütz (2004)	Germany, UK, USA	1960s–2002	limited convergence
Telecommunication, electricity and media	Bartle (2002)	France, Germany, UK	1980s and 1990s	yes
	Harcourt (2002)	France, Germany, UK, Italy, Spain	mid-1980s and 1990s	yes
	Levy (1997)	France, Germany	1990s	no
	Padgett (2003)	EU-15	1980s and 1990s	yes
Health policy	Gibson and Means (2000)	Australia, UK	1950s–1990s	yes
	Greener (2002)	UK–USA	1980–1990	yes
	Harrison *et al.* (2002)	UK–USA	1990s	yes
	O'Neill (2000)	UK–USA	1980s	yes
Monetary policy (EMU)	Angeloni and Dedola (1999)	6 EU countries	1980–1997	yes
	Brada and Kutan (2002)	5 EU, 9 EU candidate countries	1993–2000	limited convergence
	Bredin and Fountas (1998)	7 EU countries	1979–1992	no

(*Table continued*)

Table 2 Continued

Policy fields	*Source*	*Regions*	*Period*	*Convergence*
Migration policy	Holzer and Schneider (2002)	19 OECD countries	1983–1995	limited convergence
	Lavenex (2002)	10 CEE countries	1990s–2002	limited convergence
	Meyers (2002)	9 OECD countries	1870–2000	yes
Organizational practices and infrastructure	Bissessar (2002)	4 states of the Caribbean Commonwealth	1980s and 1990s	limited convergence
	Guler *et al.* (2002)	85 countries	1993–1998	no
	Kerwer and Teutsch (2001)	France, Germany, Italy	1980s and 1990s	no
Competition policy	Eyre and Lodge (2000)	UK, Germany	1990s	no
	Waarden and Drahos (2002)	Austria, Germany, Netherlands	1950–2000	yes
Justice and data protection policy	Bennett (1988)	Germany, Sweden, UK, USA	1968–1984	limited convergence
	Jones and Newburn (2002)	UK, USA	1990s	yes
Agricultural policy	Coleman and Grant (1998)	Australia, Canada, Ireland, UK, USA	1970–1995	limited convergence
	Coleman (2001)	Australia, Canada, USA	1983–2000	yes
Education policy	Bleiklie (2001)	England, Norway, Sweden	1980s and 1990s	limited convergence
	Hackl (2001)	EU-15	1970–2001	yes
Foreign policy	Hill (1997)	EU-15	1969–1997	limited convergence

markets. Since the 1990s, studies covering Eastern European countries have emerged (Lavenex 2002; Tavits 2003). However, it is still not possible to characterize convergence research as a global phenomenon: Africa and Asia, for example, are still underrepresented regions.

The country samples analysed by the authors range from the comparison of two countries (e.g. Aguilar Fernández 1994; Gibson and Means 2000; Hoberg 1991) to samples of more than ninety countries (Martin and Schneider 2004; Orenstein 2003; Simmons and Elkins 2004).[4]

An assessment of the observation periods reveals that most studies cover ten to thirty years, mainly between 1970 and 2000. Studies covering considerably longer observation periods are the exception (but see Meyers 2002 [migration policy]; Montanari 2001 [social policy]; Ostergren and Hollenhorst 1999; Tews *et al.* 2003 [environmental policy]; Tomka 2003 [fiscal policy]). This can partly be explained by the research interest of many authors: globalization as well as Europeanization processes became more pronounced in this period. At the same time, a research design covering a longer observation period (for example, the twentieth century) poses the problem of data collection. For quantitative analyses, data sets for the first half of the century hardly exist. For (recent) qualitative analyses, a similar problem emerges from the lack of interview partners that can give information on observations periods which are longer than ten to twenty years ago.

The last column of Table 2 illustrates whether convergence was found in the respective studies. Nearly half of the sample (thirty-three studies) claimed to find convergence whereas only fifteen reported a lack of convergence or divergence. A large number of studies (twenty-six) arrived at more ambiguous results by detecting limited convergence, which means that they found convergence in some but not in all areas of their analysis. For example, some authors found convergence in subgroups of the examined country sample (e.g. Montanari 2001) or in certain periods only (Kautto and Kvist 2002; Lütz 2004; O'Connor 1988). In some cases, convergence was limited to certain policy dimensions: in the field of environmental policy, Liefferink and Jordan (2002) detected convergence in terms of policy content (limits, instruments) but less in terms of general goals and principles. In contrast, Seeliger (2001) found for the same policy field convergence with respect to policy goals only.

In the context of empirical findings in convergence literature, the level[5] at which convergence occurs is important, as it relates to races to the top or bottom (a convergence process with an upward (top) or downward (bottom) shift of the mean). Interestingly, a race to the bottom was hardly ever observed by the authors – this aspect will be elaborated in more detail below for selected policy fields.

Comparing the **explanatory factors** for policy convergence brought forward by the authors, several categorizations are possible – as already described by Holzinger and Knill (2005), causal factors for convergence can be categorized into national, international and policy-specific factors (see also Kern *et al.* 2000). Another possibility is to differentiate between economic and ideational pressure (Drezner 2001). Although these categorizations refer to different dimensions, one could argue that economic and ideational pressures mainly relate to international factors.[6]

Regarding the explanations brought forward by the authors who did find (at least limited) convergence, the differentiation between economic and ideational pressure seems useful: ideational pressure was suggested, for example, by Tews *et al.* (2003) ('efficiency improvement' and 'generating legitimacy' in environmental policy), Hackl (2001) ('national pride and competitiveness' in education policy) or Harrison *et al.* (2002) (importance of 'scientific communities' for health policy).

Economic pressure was suggested, for example, by Coleman (2001), who claimed that international competition was as an important factor for agricultural policy convergence. Competition for capital and trade is often regarded as the main reason for the liberalization of policies – in this regard, Simmons and Elkins (2004) found that policy innovations in one country can alter payoffs in other countries. Following the same line of argument, Martin and Schneider (2004) argue that convergence towards less restrictive trade policies was influenced by interactions between so-called 'leader' and 'follower' countries. Brune and Garrett (2000: 3) attribute the diffusion of pension privatization to the influence of peer nations being more influential than globalization or the domestic political and economic landscape (see also Brooks 2004).

A typical explanation often raised for the absence of convergence is the argument that 'domestic aspects act as filters', and that national differences persist (see, for example, Busch 2002; Bissessar 2002; Bleiklie 2001; Coleman and Grant 1998; De Bandt and Mongelli 2000; Eyre and Lodge 2000; K. Harrison 2002; Howlett 1994; Lütz 2004). Nation states are still the key actors, even in the face of globalization and Europeanization processes (Brune and Garrett 2000; Ferrara *et al.* 2001; Guler *et al.* 2002). Some authors emphasized that even the EU was 'no sufficient motor' to induce convergence in the face of national institutional differences (e.g. Aguilar Fernández 1994: 52; Kerwer and Teutsch 2001; Nicoletti and Scarpetta 2003).

Regarding the explanatory factors for convergence, it seems fair to say that the causes of convergence are often based on international (economic or ideational) factors, whereas the explanations for limited convergence or divergence are often rooted in national (institutional) factors. Policy-specific explanations for convergence have been brought forward to a lesser degree (e.g. Tews *et al.* 2003: 592). Regarding the different policy fields portrayed in the studies, an interesting question is therefore whether policy-specific factors can also explain part of the variation found in the findings. Are some policy areas more likely to converge than others and, if so, at which level and degree of convergence does this occur?[7] The level of convergence is often explained by the economic pressure exerted by regulatory competition. The intensity of this pressure is assumed to vary between policy fields. Besides, the strength of the political forces defending existing levels of national regulation and social protection should also differ across policy fields (Scharpf 1997: 532). The interest heterogeneity of actors should be more accentuated within redistributive policy fields such as social policy or taxation than within regulative policy fields such as environmental policy, which in turn should have implications for the probability that policy change occurs (Scharpf 1997; see also Tews *et al.* 2003).

As we cannot describe all studies of our sample in more detail, we will exemplarily portray findings in the fields of taxation, environmental and social policy as these areas represent to different degrees the policy-specific factors assumed to be relevant for policy change: costs, political salience and interest heterogeneity (Scharpf 1997).

Taxation

One line of argument regarding fiscal policy and particularly the field of taxation is the assumption that mobile entities can avoid taxes of one state by moving the tax base to another state with lower rates. This in turn should lead states to cut tax rates in order to increase their tax base (Scharpf 1997: 525). Several studies in our sample do indeed find a downwards shift of rates for taxes on *corporate* income, as well as an increase of similarity of those tax rates, which could be interpreted as a race to the bottom. Wunder (1999) observes that the average corporate income tax rates of fourteen OECD countries dropped from 46 per cent in 1985 to 35 per cent in 1997. During the same period, the standard deviation was reduced as well (pp. 343ff.), which indicates convergence. In the same vein, Swank (2002) detects a reduction of the average corporate income tax rate between 1981 and 1998 from 45 to 34 per cent in sixteen OECD countries. A similar pattern is observed by Slemrod (2004) for corporate income tax rates in ninety-six countries between 1975 and 1995.

In contrast, studies focusing on the taxation of individuals (labour) found a race to the top rather than a race to the bottom. Focusing on top marginal *personal* income tax rates in OECD countries, Olewiler (1999: 350) found upward convergence between 1978 and 1995. Most high-income earners faced higher legal burdens at a later point in time. At the same time, marginal tax rates for low-income earners have also risen since 1978. These findings correspond with the hypothesis that, in the case of taxing, convergence is likely to occur at the bottom for mobile entities. However, for relatively immobile entities (labour), a race to the bottom is not likely, as the avoidance of tax burdens by moving to another country is more difficult because of language and certification barriers.

Environmental policy

Owing to the comparatively low cost factor for an economy to comply with environmental regulations (Scharpf 1997: 524) as well as the political salience of environmental issues, a race to the bottom is not likely and has not been reported in the literature. Convergence found by authors was instead characterized by a race to the top or at least as a move towards more encompassing environmental policies in countries (see e.g. Hoberg 1991; Kern *et al.* 2000; Ostergren and Hollenhorst 1999: 309; Tews *et al.* 2003).

Interest heterogeneity seems to be less pronounced in the regulative field of environmental policy than in other (redistributive) policy fields, which facilitates international co-operation. This has been observed, for example, by Oberthür and Tänzler (2002), who argue that international institutions, in particular the international climate change regime, were decisive in the diffusion of climate policy instruments in EU member states. Similarly, Botcheva and Martin (2001) observe considerable convergence in state behaviour since the signing of the Montreal Protocol. They argue that high negative externalities (both environmental and economic) make states benefit from choosing the same course of action, which leads to convergence. This confirms the proposition stated above that explanations brought forward for convergence often relate to international economic and ideational pressures.

Kern *et al.* (2000) observe a slower diffusion of policies, which leads to a redistribution of income (in particular when organized economic interests are the losers in this process). They observed that, for these reasons, policies like CO_2/energy taxes and soil protection laws were not as easily implemented as environmental agencies, eco-labelling and national environmental plans in OECD countries between 1970 and 2000.

Some authors argue that competing domestic interests can impede the convergence of policies; despite a considerable consensus among environmental scientists Kathryn Harrison (2002) argues that regulations for dioxin effluents in Canada, Sweden and the USA did not converge; again, national (institutional) factors explain a lack of convergence.

Social policy

It has been argued that globalization and Europeanization processes trigger a race to the bottom in the field of social policy which might result in the decline of the welfare state. The redistributive character of the policy field, however, suggests pronounced interest heterogeneity, which should make policy change more difficult. When looking at the empirical findings, it is striking that even though a convergence of welfare states has been detected (Greve 1996; Tomka 2003), a race to the bottom is seldom observed. Andersen *et al.* (2000: 20) analyse EU labour markets and find that even though a wage convergence in Europe has taken place owing to a 'European wage norm' supported by the European Commission, there is still a role for domestic labour markets and for social policy at the level of the nation state.

Some authors claim that there has been a shift towards neo-liberal strategies, mostly advocated by the activities of international organizations such as the World Bank (Orenstein 2003). However, this argument is contested. Ferrara *et al.* (2001: 12) argue that no race to the 'neo-liberal bottom' can be observed, claiming that the race has been in the other direction, with the southern countries advancing to northern European levels of social expenditure. Despite differences in spending priorities or replacement rates (e.g. unemployment), all European countries spent between a quarter and a third of their gross domestic product (GDP) on social security by the late 1990s (Ferrara *et al.* 2001: 12).

It seems that although the costs of implementing social policy are high, a race to the bottom is unlikely, given the political salience and the interest heterogeneity of the topic. However, even though a race to the bottom has not been reported in the convergence literature, it may just be a matter of time until this can be observed empirically (Overbye 2003: 163).

These examples only hint at the role that policy-specific characteristics might play in the level and degree of policy convergence. Further research is required to examine the causal linkages between policy fields and convergence. However, the examples have demonstrated that such an attempt seems promising. In the following, we illustrate the research designs of the studies in more detail.

CONCEPTS AND OPERATIONALIZATIONS IN RESEARCH DESIGNS

In order to properly interpret the results of the studies and assess the comparability of their findings, we must address how the authors have conceptualized 'policy convergence' and how these concepts have guided the research process in terms of operationalization.

Policy dimensions in research designs

A problem often found in empirical policy convergence studies is an insufficient level of precision with regard to the policy dimension investigated. Bennett (1991: 218) argues that 'public policy is a complex multidimensional phenomenon' and that it is hence 'crucial to be absolutely precise as to the aspects of policy being compared to ensure cross-national equivalence'. A number of empirical analyses have followed this research stringency to distinguish between *policy goals, policy content, policy instruments, policy outcomes,* and *policy style.* They investigate the occurrence and degree of convergence of policies with regard to one or more of these policy categories. Coleman and Grant (1998) analyse convergence of policy content, instruments and outcomes separately (see also Coleman (1994) for a comparable study on banking regulation with a focus on policy styles only). Liefferink and Jordan (2002) distinguish between convergence of policy content, policy structure, policy style and policy instruments while analysing national environmental policies in EU states.

Other texts are mostly limited to two of these policy sub-categories. Gibson and Means (2000: 45) distinguish between policy goals and strategies while searching for social policy convergence in the UK and Australia. Ostergren and Hollenhorst (1999: 294) examine the convergence of policy goals and policy content in wildlife protection regulations of the USA and Russia (USSR). Howlett (1994, 2000), in contrast, is mostly concerned with the policy (implementation) styles and the procedures by which policies are developed. Van Waarden and Drahos's (2002: 918ff.) conceptualization is remarkable because they present a very fine-graded scheme of policy content elements which they investigate individually. Focusing on the regulation of the banking sector, Busch (2002: 11ff.) also offers a unique approach by investigating policy content, politics and polity convergence. Analyses focusing on policy content, however, are dominant in the convergence literature (e.g. Armingeon 1999; Harrison 2002; Hoberg 1991; Meyers 2002).

In a similar vein, several studies on policy transfer have followed the theoretical proposals by Dolowitz and Marsh (1996: 350) to look for the transfer of *policy goals, content, instruments, structure* and *policy concepts, attitudes, ideas* as well as *administrative structures* and *techniques* separately (e.g. Dolowitz 1997; Larmour 2002; Pierson 2003). With their focus on environmental policy instruments, Tews *et al.* 2003 provide a good example of policy dimension specification within diffusion research.

However, many empirical studies are less precise with regard to the question which policy elements are compared; a number of analyses do not distinguish between dimensions, but compare 'policies' in general (e.g. Harcourt 2002; Kerwer and Teutsch 2001; Overbye 1994).

The quality and comparability of results is certainly hampered by imprecision with respect to policy dimensions. What conclusion should be drawn, for example, if one study finds general convergence in a policy field, while another demonstrates the convergence of policy content and policy goals but divergence regarding policy styles and instruments? Similar problems can occur for policy transfer and diffusion studies. This problem is less severe for analyses on government spending, tax policy and monetary policy since they are based on single dimension data.

Time factor in research designs – convergence as a process

The theoretical contributions by Bennett (1991: 219, 296ff.) and Unger and van Waarden (1995: 3) have convincingly demonstrated that, by definition, convergence means the development of policy similarity over time. Convergence or divergence is a process and the decisive reference point, besides space, is thus time (Knill 2005). Hence, an appropriate convergence concept needs a precise time-frame that sets rigid standards for the interpretation of the findings.

The basic approach to operationalize the time-frame in genuine convergence studies would be to establish the initial degree of policy similarity between the observed units in t_1, and compare it to a second measurement at point t_2. Unfortunately, this procedure is not always applied, which indicates general problems in convergence research (cf. Seeliger 1996: 287). It is not enough to speak of convergence if one merely implies similarity in terms of being alike. It is also problematic if one cannot clearly recognize that convergence did occur between two points in time (Aguilar Fernández 1994; Levy 1997).

Owing to a focus on processes, the lack of a clear time-frame (set ex ante) seems to be a general but not that problematic a feature of policy transfer studies (a notable exception is Pierson 2003: 79). A time-frame is also not considered to be an important factor in demonstrating policy diffusion and hence hardly applied in diffusion studies (but see Brune and Garrett 2000: 1; True and Mintrom 2001: 32). The starting point for the policy diffusion research is usually the year when the policy of interest is first introduced to one entity (the invention). It ends when the last political unit in the sample adopts it. This implies that research periods vary if more than one policy is investigated. However, even if disregarding clear time-frames cannot be considered a shortcoming of policy transfer and diffusion studies, their inclusion seems nonetheless advisable.

Even if references to time are made, it is very common to present only rough observation periods such as 'the last fifteen years' (see, for example, Gibson and Means 2000) or nothing specific at all (Hoberg 1991). Classical case study design makes it difficult to find more than one point of comparison for policy similarities (Aguilar Fernández 1994; Busch 2002; Lavenex 2002; Ostergren and Hollenhorst 1999; Seeliger 2001). In this regard, it is helpful to give the history of events a prominent place in the structure of the study itself (Larmour 2002). A parallel description of policy changes for all countries also seems to be advantageous (Bennett 1988, 1997; Bissessar 2002; Bleiklie 2001; Padgett 2003).

Strict implementations of precise time-frames are presented by Armingeon (1999) on labour market policy convergence in OECD countries (1974–1994), by Bennett (1988) on data protection policy convergence in four countries (1968–1984), by van Waarden and Drahos (2002) on competition policy convergence in Europe (1950–2000), or by Coleman and Grant (1998) on agriculture policy convergence in OECD countries. Here, the data are categorized into few periods (mainly between two and five) and policy similarity is assessed for each of them.

A similar longitudinal design is applied in quantitative studies of fiscal or monetary policy convergence alternatively to the use of time-series (Angeloni and Dedola 1999; Bredin and Fountas 1998; Gemmell and Kneller 2002; Gornick and Meyers 2001; Nicoletti and Scarpetta 2003; Sanz and Velásquez 2003). Pure applications of time-series design are not common in convergence studies, although they are found in Bernauer and Achini (2000) and De Bandt and Mongelli (2000) and in the study of policy adoption over longer periods (Brune and Garrett 2000; Meseguer 2003).

This rare occurrence is justified by the fact that, except for government expenditure or monetary policy parameters, annual data may not be adequate. Policies are not expected to underlie yearly changes. Fewer points in time may be better to make out substantial changes, as the concept of policy convergence refers to long-term changes. This also requires setting at least a 'medium' time-frame of fifteen to thirty years and it is questionable to analyse convergence with time-frames that cover only ten years (e.g. Howlett 1994). Longer periods are rarely covered, although some exceptional studies span eighty years (Ostergren and Hollenhorst 1999) or half a century (Van Waarden and Drahos 2002).

Four basic approaches to assess convergence

The empirical literature varies not only in terms of longitudinal design, but also in terms of the interpretation of 'increasing similarity'. This basic but vague definition of convergence leaves the question as to what similarity it is referring unanswered. By portraying four different approaches to assess policy convergence, a categorization is deduced from the empirical literature that will display communalities and differences in research design and their consequences for the results. Even if this classification follows the nomenclature of quantitative measures, the basic ideas behind each type of convergence are compatible with qualitative research designs as well.

Sigma-convergence as growing together

Starting with the logic that comes closest to a common understanding of convergence, a first group of studies under review analyses the decrease in variation of domestic policies. This measurement is called sigma-convergence, named after the algebraic notation for variance (Sala-I-Martin 1996: 1326ff.). In its classic form, a decreasing coefficient of variance (also known as dispersion index) indicates convergence. If changes in the mean are added, sigma-convergence can be linked to hypotheses on so-called 'races to the bottom/top' (Gornick and Meyers 2001; Montanari 2001; Wolf 2002). This approach is found in areas where forces of economic globalization seem to play a dominant role, i.e. mainly in studies on tax revenue and governmental expenditure (Alber and Standing 2000; Bernauer and Achini 2000; Bouget 2003; Gornick and Meyers 2001; Sanz and Velázquez 2003; Wolf 2002) or on tax rates (Ganghof 2004; Slemrod 2004; Wunder 1999) as well as in trade policy (Martin and Schneider 2004). Few other areas are covered by this approach, with an exception being immigration policy (Holzer and Schneider 2002).

Extensions of the classical understanding of sigma-convergence are found where authors apply similarity measures such as Euclidian distance (Saint-Arnaud and Bernard 2003), Gini-coefficients (Gemmell and Kneller 2002), graphical illustrations such as boxplots (Nicoletti and Scarpetta 2003: 19) or analyse the diffuse approximation of national policies as well. In doing so, they are not limited to metrical data, which is a clear advantage of applications to policy analysis.

For studies measuring the similarity of policies or regulatory instruments, such as Montanari's (2001: 475) work on convergence in social insurance regimes, sigma-convergence as 'growing together' is also the basic logic. The same holds true for studies from the diffusion literature, where the spread of ideas, instruments and organizational forms is displayed in rates of adoption, indicating the degree of homogeneity (Brooks 2004; Castro and McNamara

2003; Kern *et al.* 2000; Meseguer 2003; Tews *et al.* 2003; True and Mintrom 2001).

Even if quantitative papers seem to dominate, sigma-convergence also stretches to pure qualitative designs. Many case studies generally interested in 'exploring variation and similarities between countries' (Bleiklie 2001: 10) compare the development of selected policies over time (Bennett 1988, 1997; Busch 2002, 2003; Harrison 2002; Ostergren and Hollenhorst 1999; Seeliger 2001). Their less formal way of defining similarity makes it difficult to identify patterns of convergence and compare findings to other studies. Deficits of qualitative studies in measuring combined with a biased selection of cases may lead to overrated findings of convergence. On the other hand, with their open design, they compensate for the disadvantages of quantitative approaches. The latter are vulnerable to outliers and often not attentive to convergence on a subgroup level (for an exception, see Martin and Schneider 2004). As it is inaccurate in this respect, the classical 'aggregate' approach may lead to an underestimation of policy convergence.

Beta-convergence as catching up

In the economic literature, the second approach to investigate similarities across countries is 'beta-convergence'. It occurs when poor economies grow faster than rich ones and it is named after the growth coefficient (Sala-I-Martin 1996: 1326ff.). Beta-convergence often goes along with sigma-convergence, as 'growing together' presupposes a process of catching-up indicated by beta-convergence. However, there are differences between them, for example, cases where high beta-convergence leads to weak decrease in variation only (Ganghof 2004: 21). Alternatively, catching-up may entail overtaking and thus a greater dissimilarity than before.

An example of an adequate transformation from economics to the context of analysing policy laggards and policy frontrunners in immigration policy shows the valuable contribution of this logic to policy analysis (Holzer and Schneider 2002: 64). Here beta-convergence occurs when the degree and speed of tightening asylum regulations in formerly liberal countries is higher than in formerly restrictive ones. The possibility of including aspects of 'speed' to analyse convergence makes this procedure highly interesting. However, it requires metrical and time series-like data and only a few applications can be found (Alber and Standing 2000; Sanz and Velásquez 2003). In qualitative studies, this approach plays a minor role, although attempts to assess speed exist (Coleman 1994).

Gamma-convergence as mobility

A recent variant of convergence research is 'gamma-convergence'. It was developed in response to beta-convergence, which has been criticized for not capturing sufficient aspects of cross-country dynamics (Boyle and McCarthy 1999). For the analysis of gamma-convergence, country rankings for different points in time are compared to assess the mobility of countries. If countries in the first ranks fall behind or catch up over time, convergence occurs.

Policy change is analysed by simple measures of association, like the Kendall index of rank concordance (Boyle and McCarthy 1999). A low degree of similarity between rankings indicates high mobility of countries over time.

Gamma-convergence adds an additional perspective to the study of policy convergence. If the ranking of countries is stable or if it changes over time it obviously makes a difference for the interpretation of sigma- or delta-convergence. On the other hand, gamma-convergence can occur where other approaches do not detect changes. Country rankings may, for example, change without a significant decrease of cross-country variation or without an approximation towards an exemplary policy model. This review contains only one paper applying this logic to fiscal policy (Sanz and Vélasquez 2003: 11). Although the study of gamma-convergence is not common yet, it nonetheless represents a promising tool for policy studies, as the idea of comparing ordinal classifications is also compatible with a qualitative research design.

Delta-convergence as minimizing distance to an exemplary model

The main categories of traditional economic convergence analysis have been outlined but many studies under review have yet to be classified. What they have in common is their approach to convergence based on the decreasing distance of policies towards an exemplary model, for example, a model promoted by an international organization or a frontrunner country. Based on the algebraic notation of 'distance', we refer to this category here as 'delta-convergence'.[8] Empirically, sigma- and delta-convergence often occur simultaneously. If countries reach total similarity relative to a policy model, variance between them is obviously reduced. However, if delta-convergence is not complete, policies may approach the model by parallel moves without becoming more similar. In a study of higher education policy Bleiklie (2001: 27) states that policies moved in the same direction. With different points of departure, however, this development enabled states to maintain their national peculiarities. As sigma-convergence does not have to be directed towards a certain model, though, distance minimizing constitutes a logic of convergence in its own right.

While the other approaches had a significant bias towards fiscal and welfare policy, delta-convergence was found across all policy areas. In conceptual terms, this holds for studies on Europeanization, to the extent that they analyse the convergence of member states towards the European model (Hackl 2001; Harcourt 2002). By reference to exemplary policies, studies on policy transfer can also be easily assigned to delta-convergence (Lavenex 2002; Padgett 2003). Moreover, the diffusion literature often includes aspects of 'distance'. For example, scholars have investigated how far countries converged to a private pension scheme (Brooks 2004), or to organizational practices (Guler *et al.* 2002). If the policy choice of adopting is a discrete one, delta-convergence will coincide with decreasing national varieties.

Many studies generally dealing with 'convergence' include the notion of reducing variation and distance without being explicit on the concept of convergence that is applied. This is often the case for studies on two countries only (Aguilar Fernández 1994; Eyre and Lodge 2000; Howlett 2000).

A policy model can be a helpful criterion to define similarity that allows for a better comparability of findings. In the studies listed above, this is seldom applied. An explicit measurement of distances, which goes beyond a mere description of the model and the similarity of policies to it, is rarely found – even checklists are more the exception than the norm (Bissessar 2002: 117; Padgett 2003: 32). In one study on banking policy, Coleman (1994: 287) uses a similarity index for the distance of five countries to the model of corporatism. Coleman and Grant (1998: 231) also construct an index for different types of agricultural finance regimes, assessing how far countries converged towards it over time.

In monetary policy, delta-convergence (understood as 'co-integration') occurs when national currencies have a long-term relationship or a 'common root' with a leading one, be it the Deutschmark or the Euro. Statistical tests of homogeneity (Angeloni and Dedola 1999; Brada and Kutan 2002) or cross-correlation (De Bandt and Mongelli 2000) are most frequently applied.

The domination of small-n designs in delta convergence research is not only caused by difficulties in quantifying distance to policy models. In addition, many scholars are not interested in convergence directly. They analyse the process, giving justifiable preference to in-depth case study analysis. However, when focusing on causal factors, one should not lose sight of the analysis of convergence itself, which is often taken for granted.

CONCLUSION

In the current empirical convergence literature, much attention is paid to the exploration of causal factors that are supposed to lead to growing similarities among nation states – like theories on regulatory competition, policy learning or transnational harmonization. Excellent review articles already exist on this issue (Drezner 2001). The main focus of this paper is a different one: it presents a systematic overview on findings and different research designs, in order to provide a guideline for future assessment of empirical convergence.

The analysis of findings in convergence research has revealed that empirical studies differ according to regions, observation periods and the degree of convergence detected by the authors. In addition, it was observed that a 'race to the bottom' was hardly ever confirmed empirically – many authors argued that domestic factors act as 'filters' of globalization processes. The findings in the policy fields of taxation, social and environmental policy indicate, furthermore, that policy-specific characteristics play a relevant role for policy convergence which should be elaborated in future research.

The increasing interest in convergence research over the past years has led to a diversification in research design rather than to a 'convergence in convergence studies'. The second part of the paper therefore attempts to establish a common ground with respect to different dimensions like policy goals, instruments or outcomes and to four different approaches to measure convergence. We have demonstrated that an investigation of convergence or divergence is difficult when clear criteria for comparison do not exist. A 'general' judgement on the degree of policy convergence as a global phenomenon is impossible, as there is not enough common ground with respect to research designs, concepts and operationalizations.

Both for quantitative and qualitative work, the categorization in sigma-, beta-, gamma and delta-convergence covers comprehensive views of the assessment of growing similarity over time. Facilitating the comparison of findings across different studies, this could also be seen as an inspiration to the structure of a future research agenda in convergence studies.

Address for correspondence: Stephan Heichel, University of Konstanz, Fach D 91, D-78457 Konstanz, Germany. Tel: +49(0)7531 885183. Fax: +49(0)7531 882381. email: stephan.heichel@uni-konstanz.de

ACKNOWLEDGEMENTS

The authors would like to thank Christoph Knill, Kerstin Tews and Helge Jörgens for helpful comments, insights and assistance relating to this article. However, the authors alone are responsible for the arguments made and for any errors or omissions contained herein. Michael Dobbins, Jale Oenel and Natascha Warta deserve credit for assistance in general and language editing.

NOTES

1 By related concepts of policy convergence, we mean policy diffusion, policy transfer, policy learning and isomorphism (see Knill 2005).

2 We applied an encompassing search procedure using several bibliographical databases, including the SSCI. We also checked the literature quoted in other studies (especially reviews). Thereby we ended up with about 450 studies of general interest (not only empirical research) which we scrutinized in more detail. Key words for searching were 'policy convergence', 'policy divergence', 'policy diffusion', 'policy transfer', 'policy learning', 'lesson drawing' and 'isomorphism'. Empirical studies which address policy convergence issues but cannot be found with those key words, i.e. those in comparative politics in general dealing with the topic, might have been overlooked. Research published up to the middle of 2004 was considered.

3 Hence, we selected only literature dealing with policies at the national level.

4 We are aware that this phenomenon (large versus small-n studies) differentiates qualitative and quantitative literature; however, we treat these studies as comparable while bearing in mind their respective advantages and disadvantages.

5 See Holzinger and Knill (2005) for the concept of the level of convergence.

6 See, for example, Tews *et al.* (2003: 574) who define 'regulatory' and 'ideational' competition as the two main international driving mechanisms for convergence.

7 See Holzinger and Knill (2005) for the concept of the degree of convergence.

8 The concept we introduce here was already applied by Howlett (2000: 306, 309) and named 'strong convergence'. However, Howlett refers to Unger and van Waarden (1995) as a source for this term although those authors mean

something different, namely the approximation of two countries' policies towards each other, not towards another policy (model) (Unger and van Waarden 1995: 3).

REFERENCES

Aguilar Fernández, S. (1994) 'Convergence in environmental policy? The resilience of national institutional designs in Spain and Germany', *Journal of Public Policy* 14(1): 39–56.

Alber, J. and Standing, G. (2000) 'Social dumping, catch up, or convergence? Europe in a comparative global context', *Journal of European Social Policy* 10(2): 99–119.

Andersen, T.M., Haldrup, N. and Sorensen, J.R. (2000) 'Labour market implications of EU product market integration', *Economic Policy* 15(30): 107–33.

Angeloni, I. and Dedola, L. (1999) 'From the ERM to the euro: new evidence on economic and policy convergence among EU countries', *Working Paper* No. 4, Frankfurt: European Central Bank.

Armingeon, K. (1999) 'Politische Reaktionen auf steigende Arbeitslosigkeit', in A. Busch and T. Plümper (eds), *Nationaler Staat und internationale Wirtschaft: Anmerkungen zum Thema Globalisierung*, Baden-Baden: Nomos, pp. 169–96.

Bartle, I. (2002) 'When institutions no longer matter: reform of telecommunications and electricity in Germany, France and Britain', *Journal of Public Policy* 22(1): 1–27.

Bennett, C.J. (1988) 'Different processes, one result: the convergence of data protection policy in Europe and the United States', *Governance: An International Journal of Policy and Administration* 1(4): 415–41.

Bennett, C.J. (1991) 'Review article: What is policy convergence and what causes it?', *British Journal of Political Science* 21: 215–33.

Bennett, C.J. (1997) 'Understanding ripple effects: the cross-national adoption of policy instruments for bureaucratic accountability', *Governance: An International Journal of Policy and Administration* 10(3): 213–33.

Bernauer, T. and Achini, C. (2000) 'From "real" to "virtual" states? Integration of the world economy and its effects on government activity', *European Journal of International Relations* 6(2): 223–76.

Bissessar, A.M. (2002) 'Globalization, domestic politics and the introduction of new public management in the Commonwealth Caribbean', *International Review of Administrative Sciences* 68: 113–35.

Bleiklie, I. (2001) 'Towards European convergence of higher education policy?', *Higher Education Management* 13(3): 9–29.

Botcheva, L. and Martin, L.L. (2001) 'Institutional effects on state behavior: convergence and divergence', *International Studies Quarterly* 45(1): 1–26.

Bouget, D. (2003) 'Convergence in the social welfare systems in Europe', *Social Policy and Administration* 37(6): 674–93.

Boyle, G.E. and McCarthy, T.G. (1999) 'Simple measures of convergence in per capita GDP: a note on some further international evidence', *Applied Economics Letters* 6: 343–7.

Brada, J.C. and Kutan, A.M. (2002) 'Balkan and Mediterranean candidates for European Union membership: the convergence of their monetary policy with that of the European Central Bank', *Eastern European Economics* 40(4): 31–44.

Bredin, D. and Fountas, S. (1998) 'Testing for monetary policy convergence in European countries', *Journal of Economic Studies* 25(5): 353–69.

Brooks, S.M. (2004) 'Interdependent and domestic foundations of policy change: the diffusion of pension privatization around the world'. Paper presented at Annual Conference, International Studies Association, Montreal, 19 March.

Brune, N. and Garrett, G. (2000) 'The diffusion of privatization in the developing world'. Paper prepared for presentation at Annual Meeting, APSA, Washington, DC, 30 August–3 September.

Busch, A. (2002) 'Divergence or convergence? State regulation of the banking system in Western Europe and the United States'. Paper presented at Workshop on Theories of Regulation, Nuffield College, Oxford, 25–26 May 2002.

Busch, A. (2003) *Staat und Globalisierung: Das Politikfeld der Bankenregulierung im internationalen Vergleich*, Wiesbaden: Westdeutscher Verlag.

Castro, E. and McNamara, K.R. (2003) 'The diffusion of central bank independence'. Paper prepared for presentation at 'Interdependence, Diffusion and Sovereignty' (Conference), Los Angeles, University of California, 7–8 March.

Coleman, W.D. (1994) 'Policy convergence in banking: a comparative study', *Political Studies* 42: 274–92.

Coleman, W.D. (2001) 'Agricultural policy reform and policy convergence: an actor-centered institutionalist approach', *Journal of Comparative Policy Analysis: Research and Practice* 3: 219–41.

Coleman, W.D. and Grant, W.P. (1998) 'Policy convergence and policy feedback: agricultural finance policies in a globalizing era', *European Journal of Political Research* 34: 225–47.

De Bandt, O. and Mongelli, F.P. (2000) 'Convergence of fiscal policies in the euro area', *Working Paper* 2000/20, Frankfurt: European Central Bank.

Dolowitz, D.P. (1997) 'British employment policy in the 1980s: learning from the American experience', *Governance: An International Journal of Policy and Administration* 10(1): 22–42.

Dolowitz, D.P. and Marsh, D. (1996) 'Who learns from whom? A review of the policy transfer literature', *Political Studies* 44: 343–57.

Drezner, D.W. (2001) 'Globalization and policy convergence', *International Studies Review* 3: 53–78.

Eyre, S. and Lodge, M. (2000) 'National tunes and a European melody? Competition law reform in the UK and Germany', *Journal of European Public Policy* 7(1): 63–79.

Feick, J. (1992) 'Comparing comparative policy studies: a path towards integration', *Journal of Public Policy* 12(3): 257–85.

Ferrara, M., Hemerijck, A. and Rhodes, M. (2001) 'The future of the European "social model" in the global economy', *Journal of Comparative Policy Analysis: Research and Practice* 3: 163–90.

Ganghof, S. (2004) 'Konditionale Konvergenz, Standortwettbewerb, Policy-Lernen und politische Institutionen in der Steuerpolitik von EU- und OECD-Ländern'. Paper presented at Sources of Cross-national Policy Convergence, DVPW, Hamburg, 23–25 April.

Gemmell, N. and Kneller, R. (2002) 'Fiscal policy, growth and convergence in Europe', European Economic Group, *Working Paper* No. 14/2002.

Gibson, D. and Means, R. (2000) 'Policy convergence: restructuring long-term care in Australia and the UK', *Policy & Politics* 29(1): 43–58.

Gornick, J.C. and Meyers, M.K. (2001) 'Lesson-drawing in familiy policy: media reports and empirical evidence about European developments', *Journal of Comparative Policy Analysis: Research and Practice* 3: 31–57.

Greener, I. (2002) 'Understanding NHS reform: the policy-transfer, social learning, and path-dependency', *Governance: An International Journal of Policy and Administration* 15(2): 161–83.

Greve, B. (1996) 'Indications of social policy convergence in Europe', *Social Policy and Administration* 30(4): 348–67.

Guler, I., Guillén, M. and MacPherson, J. (2002) 'Global competition, institutions and the diffusion of organizational practices: the international spread of ISO 9000 quality certificates', *Administrative Science Quarterly* 47: 207–33.

Hackl, E. (2001) 'Towards a European area of higher education: change and convergence in European higher education', *Working Paper RSC* No. 2001/09, San Domenico, Italy: EUI.

Harcourt, A. (2002) 'Engineering Europeanization: the role of the European institutions in shaping national media regulation', *Journal of European Public Policy* 9(5): 736–55.

Harrison, K. (2002) 'Ideas and environmental standard-setting: a comparative study of regulation of the pulp and paper industry', *Governance: An International Journal of Policy and Administration* 15(1): 65–96.

Harrison, S., Moran, M. and Wood, B. (2002) 'Policy emergence and policy convergence: the case of "scientific-bureaucratic medicine" in the United States and United Kingdom', *British Journal of Politics and International Relations* 4(1): 1–24.

Hill, C.J. (1997) 'Convergence, divergence and dialectics: national foreign policies and the CFSP: paradoxes of European foreign policy', *Working Paper RSC* No. 97/66, San Domenico, Italy: EUI.

Hoberg, G. (1991) 'Sleeping with an elephant: the American influence on Canadian environmental regulation', *Journal of Public Policy* 11: 107–32.

Holzer, T. and Schneider, G. (2002) *Asylpolitik auf Abwegen: Nationalstaatliche und europäische Reaktionen auf die Globalisierung der Flüchtlingsströme*, Opladen: Leske + Budrich.

Holzinger, K. and Knill, C. (2005) 'Causes and conditions of cross-national policy convergence', *Journal of European Public Policy* 12(5): 775–96.

Howlett, M. (1994) 'The judicialization of Canadian environmental policy, 1980–1990: a test of the Canada–United States convergence thesis', *Canadian Journal of Political Science* 27(1): 99–127.

Howlett, M. (2000) 'Beyond legalism? Policy ideas, implementation styles and emulation-based convergence in Canadian and US environmental policy', *Journal of Public Policy* 20(3): 305–29.

Jones, T. and Newburn, T. (2002) 'Learning from Uncle Sam? Exploring US influences on British crime control policy', *Governance: An International Journal of Policy and Administration* 15(1): 97–119.

Kautto, M. and Kvist, J. (2002) 'Parallel trends, persistent diversity: Nordic welfare states in the European context', *Global Social Policy* 2(2): 189–208.

Kern, K., Jörgens, H. and Jänicke, M. (2000) 'Die Diffusion umweltpolitischer Innovationen: Ein Beitrag zur Globalisierung von Umweltpolitik', *Zeitschrift für Umweltpolitik und Umweltrecht* 23(4): 507–46.

Kerwer, D. and Teutsch, M. (2001) 'Elusive Europeanization: liberalizing road haulage in the European Union', *Journal of European Public Policy* 8(1): 124–43.

Knill, C. (2005) 'Introduction: Cross-national policy convergence: concepts, approaches and explanatory factors', *Journal of European Public Policy* 12(5): 764–74.

Larmour, P. (2002) 'Policy transfer and reversal: customary land registration from Africa to Melanesia', *Public Administration and Development* 22(2): 151–61.

Lavenex, S. (2002) 'EU enlargement and the challenge of policy transfer: the case of refugee policy', *Journal of Ethnic and Migration Studies* 28(4): 701–21.

Levy, D.L. (1997) 'Regulating digital broadcasting in Europe: the limits of policy convergence', *West European Politics* 20(4): 24–42.

Liefferink, D. and Jordan, A. (2002) 'The Europeanisation of national environmental policy: a comparative analysis', *Working Paper* 2002/14, Nijmegen, Netherlands: NSM.

Lütz, S. (2004) 'Convergence within national diversity: the regulatory state in finance', *Journal of Public Policy* 24(2): 169–97.

Martin, C. and Schneider, G. (2004) 'Foreign economic liberalization, regulatory competition and policy convergence: global trends, regional differences'. Paper presented at Sources of Cross-national Policy Convergence, DVPW, Hamburg, 23–25 April.

Meseguer, C. (2003) 'Learning and economic policy choice: a Bayesian approach', *Working Paper RSC* No. 2003/5, San Domenico, Italy: EUI.

Meyers, E. (2002) 'The causes of convergence in western immigration control', *Review of International Studies* 28: 123–41.

Montanari, I.J. (2001) 'Modernization, globalization and the welfare state: a comparative analysis of old and new convergence of social insurance since 1930', *British Journal of Sociology* 52(3): 469–94.

Nicoletti, G. and Scarpetta, S. (2003) 'Regulation, productivity and growth: OECD evidence', *Economic Policy* 18: 9–72.

Oberthür, S. and Tänzler, D. (2002) 'International regimes as a trigger of policy diffusion: the development of climate policies in the European Union', in F. Biermann, R. Brohm and K. Dingwerth (eds), *Proceedings of the 2001 Berlin Conference on the Human Dimensions of Global Climate Change 'Global Environmental Change and the Nation State'*, Potsdam: Potsdam Institute for Climate Change Impact Research, pp. 317–28.

O'Connor, J. (1988) 'Convergence or divergence? Change in welfare spending in OECD countries 1960–1980', *European Journal of Political Research* 16: 277–99.

Olewiler, N. (1999) 'National tax policy for an international economy: divergence in a converging world?', in T.J. Courchene (ed.), *Room to Manoeuvre? Globalization and Policy Convergence*, Montreal: McGill-Queen's University Press, pp. 345–82.

O'Neill, F. (2000) 'Health: the "internal market" and the reform of the National Health Service', in D.P. Dolowitz, R. Hulme, M. Nellis and F. O'Neill (eds), *Policy Transfer and British Social Policy: Learning from the USA?*, Buckingham: Open University Press, pp. 59–76.

Orenstein, M.A. (2003) 'Mapping the diffusion of pension innovation', in R. Holzmann, M.A. Orenstein and M. Rutkowski (eds), *Pension Reform in Europe: Process and Progress*, Washington, DC: World Bank, pp. 171–92.

Ostergren, D.M. and Hollenhorst, S.J. (1999) 'Convergence in protected area policy: a comparison of Russian Zapovednik and American wilderness systems', *Society & Natural Resources* 12: 293–313.

Overbye, E. (1994) 'Convergence in policy outcome: social security systems in perspective', *Journal of Public Policy* 14: 147–74.

Overbye, E. (2003) 'Globalisation and the design of the welfare state', in D. Pieters (ed.), *European Social Security and Global Politics*, London: Kluwer Academic Press, pp. 145–65.

Padgett, S. (2003) 'Between synthesis and emulation: EU policy transfer in the power sector', *Journal of European Public Policy* 10(2): 227–45.

Pierson, C. (2003) 'Learning from labour? Welfare policy transfer between Australia and Britain', *Commonwealth & Comparative Politics* 41(1): 77–100.

Saint-Arnaud, S. and Bernard, P. (2003) 'Convergence or resilience? A hierarchical cluster analysis of the welfare regimes in advanced countries', *Current Sociology* 51(5): 499–527.

Sala-I-Martin, X.X. (1996) 'Regional cohesion: evidence and theories of regional growth and convergence', *European Economic Review* 40: 1325–52.

Sanz, I. and Velázquez, F.J. (2003) 'Has the European integration approximated the composition of government expenditures?', Leverhulme Centre for Research on

Globalisation and Economic Policy, *Working Paper* 2003/09, Nottingham: University of Nottingham.
Scharpf, F.W. (1997) 'Introduction: The problem-solving capacity of multi-level governance', *Journal of European Public Policy* 4(4): 520–38.
Seeliger, R. (1996) 'Conceptualizing and researching policy convergence', *Policy Studies Journal* 24(2): 287–306.
Seeliger, R. (2001) *Konvergenz oder Divergenz? Sonderabfallpolitik in Deutschland, Kanada und den USA 1970 bis 1996*, Tübingen: Unpublished Ph.D. dissertation.
Simmons, B.A. and Elkins, Z. (2004) 'The globalization of liberalization: policy diffusion in the international political economy', *American Political Science Review* 98(1): 171–89.
Slemrod, J. (2004) 'Are corporate tax rates, or countries, converging?', *Journal of Public Economics* 88: 1169–86.
Swank, D. (2002) 'The transformation of tax policy in an era of internationalization: an assessment of a conditional diffusion model'. Paper prepared for presentation at Annual Meeting, APSA, Boston, MA, 29 August–1 September.
Tavits, M. (2003) 'Policy learning and uncertainty: the case of pension reform in Estonia and Latvia', *Policy Studies Journal* 31(4): 643–60.
Tews, K., Busch, P.-O. and Jörgens, H. (2003) 'The diffusion of new environmental policy instruments', *European Journal of Political Research* 42(3): 569–600.
Tomka, B. (2003) 'Western European welfare states in the 20th century: convergences and divergences in a long-run perspective', *International Journal of Social Welfare* 12: 249–60.
True, J. and Mintrom, M. (2001) 'Transnational networks and policy diffusion: the case of gender mainstreaming', *International Studies Quarterly* 45(1): 27–57.
Unger, B. and Waarden, F. van (1995) 'Introduction: An interdisciplinary approach to convergence', in B. Unger and F. van Waarden (eds), *Convergence or Diversity? Internationalization and Economic Policy Response*, Aldershot: Avebury, pp. 1–35.
Waarden, F. van and Drahos, M. (2002) 'Courts and (epistemic) communities in the convergence of competition policies', *Journal of European Public Policy* 9(6): 913–34.
Wolf, H. (2002) 'Globalization and the convergence of social expenditure in the European Union', *Occasional Paper Series*, Washington, DC: The GW Center for the Study of Globalization.
Wunder, H.F. (1999) 'International tax reform: its effect on repatriation decisions of multinational corporations', *Journal of International Accounting, Auditing & Taxation* 8(2): 337–53.

Globalization, harmonization, and competition: the different pathways to policy convergence

Daniel W. Drezner

INTRODUCTION

Economic globalization – defined here as the cluster of technological, economic, and political innovations that reduce the barriers to economic, political, and cultural exchange – is frequently cited as a source for policy convergence. However, the precise causal links between these two variables often go unexplored.[1] Multiple narratives are available, including the influence of global civil society (Wapner 1995; Keck and Sikkink 1998), the role of international governmental organizations (Meyer *et al.* 1997; Finnemore 1996), the prominence of epistemic communities (Haas 1992; Braithwaite and Drahos 1999), and the dominance of capital markets (Goodman and Pauly 1993). However, the trouble with most of these theoretical approaches is the lack of variation in the independent variable. According to these theories, globalization increases the number and power of factors and actors that inexorably promote policy convergence. Structural theories lack the capacity to explain variation in convergence outcomes (Drezner 2001).

The common thread missing from existing arguments is the role that state agency continues to play in the regulation of the global political economy. This paper builds on a simple game-theoretic model of policy coordination to argue that the great powers – defined as governments that possess large internal markets – remain the most important actors in determining the extent of policy convergence. When great powers act in concert, there will be effective policy harmonization through the exercise of both market power and coercive power.[2] When the great powers fail to agree, policy convergence *of a sort* will take place. The increasing returns to scale of regulatory harmonization will lead powerful actors to compete for as many allies as possible, leading strong policy convergence, but at multiple nodes. To use the terminology provided by Knill (2005), when great powers cannot achieve a concert, policy convergence will take place through competition rather than harmonization.

These arguments are tested by examining the variation in outcomes of two different issue areas: money laundering and genetically modified organisms (GMOs). In both of the relevant sectors – finance and agriculture – markets that were heavily protected against international influences have been dramatically liberalized in the last twenty years. In the case of finance, the true liberalization of capital markets beyond the United States started only in the mid-1980s (Cohen 1996). The globalization of capital markets generated benefits to participating countries, but also facilitated the laundering of illicit assets. Agriculture is perceived as a more heavily protected market. However, by empirical measures such as tariff levels, subsidies as a percentage of output, or the decline of commodity cartels, the agricultural sector underwent considerable liberalization between 1975 and 1995 (Davis 2003: ch. 1).

Over the past five years, there has been significant convergence in the development of anti-money laundering rules and regulations. There has been no great power convergence on the treatment of genetically modified foods – however, there has been a great deal of convergence by other states to either the US or the European Union (EU) position. In the money laundering case, a convergence of interests among the United States and key EU actors led to rapid policy harmonization. In the latter case, divergent US and EU preferences on this issue – and the competition by the economic superpowers to win the standard-setting game – have led to policy convergence at two different nodes.

This paper is organized into seven sections. The following section discusses why great powers retain their importance in determining the pattern of policy convergence. The third section develops and analyzes a simple game-theoretic model of regulatory coordination. The fourth section discusses the disparate pathways to policy convergence. The fifth section examines the case of anti-money laundering standards, and the sixth section looks at the GMO case. The final section summarizes and concludes.

WHY GOVERNMENTS MATTER

The assumption that states are the primary actors in setting regulatory standards is hardly novel to this project. There is a burgeoning literature that discusses how states determine the pattern of transnational regulation (Vogel 1995; Simmons 2001; Mattli 2001; Koremenos *et al.* 2001). Like other scholars in this tradition, I will assume that governments are the primary actors in global economic governance. This does not mean that states are insensitive to market forces and market pressures. In a globalized market economy, one would expect states to act in a manner that maximizes capital inflows and labor productivity. However, while many authors recognize the state's structural dependence on capital, capital's structural dependence on the state must also be acknowledged. Firms rely on governments to establish and enforce the rules of the game for economic interactions. Business traits that range from corporate governance to innovation strategies to procurement policies are often contingent on pre-existing state structures (Hall and Soskice 2001). States act as the primary negotiating agents in international fora, and retain the final say in crafting the domestic rules that govern economic activity.

Governments are differentiated by their relative power. Power is defined as the relative size and diversity of an actor's internal market. Markets have a gravitational effect on producers – the larger the economy, the stronger the pull for producers to secure and exploit market access.[3] As demand increases, firms will have greater incentives to mirror that market's preferences. Similarly, the diversity of a state's economy determines how vulnerable it is to becoming asymmetrically interdependent on other actors. The more diverse the variety of goods produced and consumed in the national market, the less vulnerable the state to external pressure, be it private or public. A great power has an economy of sufficient size and diversity such that it acts as a natural attractor for profit-seeking actors while being able to rebuff potential coercers. Great powers are price-makers, not price-takers – they have 'go-it-alone' power (Gruber 2000).

Empirically, the economic great powers for the current era of globalization are the United States and the EU. These are the only two entities that combine relatively large markets with low vulnerability, as Table 1 indicates. As measured by aggregate market size, the US and EU both had economies over $10 trillion at the end of 2003. The American and European shares of global merchandise trade are more than twice that of any other 'candidate' great power. Using market exchange rates, both the US and EU are twice as large as Japan, the next biggest economy. When their market size is combined, the United States and the EU are responsible for roughly 40 percent of global output, 41 percent of world imports, 59 percent of inward foreign direct investment, 78 percent of outward foreign direct investment, and 88 percent of global mergers and acquisitions (Quinlan 2003). No other economic entity comes close to great power status.[4]

Describing the United States as an economic great power is straightforward – both its market size and economic diversity are unquestioned (Wohlforth

Table 1 Basic economic statistics of great power candidates

Measure of economic power	*United States*	*European Union*	*Japan*	*Russia*	*China*	*India*
Population (in millions)	290	379	127	145	1,286	1,050
GDP (market exchange rates, in 2001 billions)	10,020	10,400	4,176	310	1,159	483
GDP (purchasing power parity, in 2002 billions)	10,450	9,571	3,651	1,409	5,989	2,664
Share of global merchandise trade	18.6	18.5	7.5	1.7	6.2	1.1
Merchandise trade as a % of GDP (market exchange rates)	18.5	16.6	16.2	53.2	54.3	20.4
Capital market size (in billions)	54,488	51,546	21,628	>800	>5,000	>5,000

Sources: CIA World Factbook; OECD; Eurostat; United Nations Statistical Division; WTO.

1999). The EU presents a trickier problem for international relations theory. It would be problematic to describe the EU as a unitary actor in matters of foreign and security policy. For economic regulation, however, a strong case can be made for treating the EU as a single actor (Bretherton and Vogler 1999; Pollack 2004). Post-Maastricht, the member governments have delegated significant regulatory and bargaining powers to the European Commission. As Pollack (2004: 41–2) observes, 'the EU is at or near the end of the continuum in terms of delegation to executive, judicial, and legislative agents. Indeed, no other international executive enjoys both the regulatory and agenda-setting powers of the European Commission.' Systematic comparative research confirms this assessment (Haftel 2003). This does not mean that member governments cannot influence the direction of EU policy – just as regional or sectoral interests constrain the government of the United States. Treating the EU as a single actor in the coordination of global economic regulations is a significant assumption, but it is no longer a heroic one.

A SIMPLE COORDINATION GAME

Figure 1 shows the simplified form of the general coordination game that states face. The intuition behind the game is as follows: I assume that global regulatory coordination generates positive benefits for all participating actors – but that

		State B	
		Switch to country A's standards (a)	Retain national standards (b)
State A	Retain national standards (a)	*Coordinate at A* (π, $\pi - d$)	*No coordination* (0, 0)
	Switch to country B's standards (b)	*No coordination* (−d, −d)	*Coordinate at B* ($\pi - d$, π)

Figure 1 The coordination game
π = benefits from regulatory coordination
d = adjustment costs of switching standards

these benefits come with adjustment costs for those states that need to make changes in the status quo.[5] Economic globalization reduces the barriers to exchange across borders, acting to increase the benefits derived from coordination. The lower the transaction costs of economic exchange – whether through technological innovation or political accommodation – the greater the rewards that are conferred through policy coordination. Regulatory convergence permits companies to maintain single production processes, rather than multiple processes to accommodate for multiple standards regimes (Lazer 2001). A coordinated regulatory regime also clarifies the political process by which regulatory standards can be changed. Coordination helps to generate clear decision-making rules for any future changes in regulation. Globalization lowers the barriers to entry for all market participants and thereby increases the number of economic actors that stand to benefit from regulatory coordination. Concomitantly, globalization increases the economic benefits to governments for coordination.

While governments may receive benefits from the development of a single global standard, this does not mean that states will prefer *any* global standard. For governments, any agreement to coordinate standards at a point that diverges from the domestic status quo comes with economic and political costs. Firms incur economic costs when they retool their operations to the new standard. Local producers are by definition more comfortable with local rules than any international standard that diverges from those rules. Governments incur costs from the retraining of regulators, and from the restructuring or creation of new regulatory infrastructures. They also incur the political costs of getting new standards ratified by other branches of the state, or from dissatisfaction with the new standards among voters, interest groups, or members of the selectorate.

For now, I assume coordination is a two-player game with no coercive option. Two states, A and B, have the choice of coordinating their market regulation or not. There exists a unidimensional measure of regulatory stringency, with a higher value implying more stringent regulation. It will be assumed that state A's regulatory standards (a) are always more stringent than state B's (b) – in other words, $a > b$. States can choose to stick to their own regulatory framework or agree to switch to the other country's framework. The payoffs for the status quo – each state retaining their own regulatory standards – are normalized to zero. π_i represents the public good benefits country i derives from the enhanced economic efficiency achieved through regulatory coordination. π is a function of the intrinsic nature of the regulatory issue in question, the national attributes of country i, and the value of coordinating with country j. To start, however, I will assume that for all i, $\pi_i = \pi$.

The term d_i equals the economic and political costs of making the necessary adjustments to new regulatory standards for country i. Like π, d is a function of the intrinsic nature of the regulatory issue in question, the national attributes of country i, and the value of coordinating with country j. As with π, to start I will assume that for all i, $d_i = d$, and that $d = f(a - b)$. This makes the adjustment costs a function of the gap in the preexisting standards between countries A and B. It is logical to assume that the adjustment costs increase as the gap in initial standards between A and B increases.

Actors must choose whether to adhere to their national standard or be willing to switch to the other player's prior standard. Regulatory coordination increases the size of the public good but can also impose costs on actors that must adjust from the previous status quo. For all states, the most preferred option is coordination at their set of national standard. Because of adjustment costs, a state's worst outcome is to agree to another country's standards but fail to successfully coordinate. This model is consistent with but not identical to other international relations models of coordination (Krasner 1991; Gruber 2000).

Solving the most simple version of this game reveals two important facts. First, if the costs of adjustment outweigh the perceived benefits of harmonizing regulatory standards, an actor's dominant strategy is to retain its national standards.[6] This leads to an equilibrium outcome of no coordination. If $d > \pi$, then the *only* equilibrium outcome that exists is no coordination.

This simple result is worth emphasizing because the implicit bias in much of the international relations literature is that cooperation is a socially efficient outcome relative to the status quo. More formally, international relations theorists assume that international interactions are variations on simple 'games of cooperation,' in that cooperation generates a unique and socially efficient outcome that Pareto-dominates non-cooperative outcomes.[7] This is true even of models that allow for distributional conflicts among participating actors. Rather than assume *ex ante* that cooperation is the socially efficient outcome, the model described above allows for the possibility that mutual cooperation does not Pareto-dominate mutual defection.

The second insight from this game presumes that $\pi > d$; i.e. the public benefits from coordination outweigh the economic and political costs of adjustment. This makes coordination a possible equilibrium outcome. As the public good from cooperation increases and the costs from adjusting to new standards decrease, a coordinated outcome becomes more likely. In other words, regulatory coordination is an increasing function of π but a decreasing function of d. Again, this is a straightforward result that is nevertheless worthy of note. Most game-theoretic approaches are concerned with what happens within a bargaining core. This emphasis elides over the fact that coordination is more likely when the size of the bargaining core increases.

So far, the model has assumed symmetrical payoffs between the negotiating countries. However, a more reasonable conjecture would be to say that the public good benefits from regulatory coordination depend upon the size of the newly opened market. For example, if the United States and Jordan coordinate their regulatory standards, Jordanian firms would reap much greater potential benefits from access to American markets than US firms reap from enhanced access to Jordan. This simple example demonstrates why the positive benefits that come from regulatory coordination should vary according to the actor. So, let Y_i equal the market size of country i. And, instead of $\pi_i = \pi$, let π_i be a function of the relative market shares of the two countries, such that a country i receives a bigger payoff from coordination as the market size of the partner country increases.[8]

How does this affect the dynamics of the coordination game? Two hypotheses clearly emerge from this alteration.[9] First, the likelihood of a coordination equilibrium at one country's standards is an increasing function of that country's market size. This probabilistic statement comes from the concept of 'stability sets' suggested by Harsanyi and Selten (1988) and developed by Medina (2004). The intuition behind this hypothesis stems from how market size affects the perceptions both actors have about the likelihood of their strategic choices. Each country's reaction function is based on the possible distribution of payoffs in the game. Increasing the market size of government A decreases that actor's reward for coordination, while simultaneously increasing B's payoff from coordination at any set of standards. This means that the cost of adjustment carries a larger weight for the more powerful actor's decision-making calculus, while the reverse is true of the smaller actor. Both governments process this information into their reaction functions. The result is that there is a larger zone of beliefs – the stability set – where both players will prefer to select the great power's set of preferred standards.

The second hypothesis is that, *ceteris paribus*, once an economy amasses enough relative size, the *only* equilibrium outcome is coordination at that country's standards. Assume that country A is the great power. After a certain point, increasing A's market size *vis-à-vis* country B reduces A's benefit of coordinating at B's standards to the point that it prefers the status quo to coordination at B's regulatory standards. So, once its market reaches a certain size, country A's dominant strategy is to adhere to its preexisting standards. Given A's choice, country B will switch its standards to A's preferred position as long as the benefits from coordination outweigh the adjustment costs. Since B's benefits from coordination increase with A's market size, after a certain point A's economy is big enough to ensure that this will be the case.

The introduction of market power alone increases the likelihood that coordination will take place at the larger country's preferred set of standards. However, great powers have another mechanism through which they can influence the coordination game – the threat of active economic coercion. It is easy to point to circumstances in which great powers have threatened or employed economic sanctions over regulatory differences. There is considerable debate about the utility of economic sanctions in the pursuit of political goals (Drezner 1999). However, there is strong empirical evidence that the threat or use of sanctions can yield significant concessions in regulatory disputes (Drezner 2003).

With this tactic, a state that prefers to retain its own standards will impose economic sanctions if the other state refuses to switch its standards. Figure 2 demonstrates how the option to employ pressure tactics changes the payoffs of the coordination game. States with the capability to employ economic coercion can alter the payoff structure. They can penalize the other actor for choosing to retain their preexisting standards when the great power would prefer the target country to switch its regulations.

The introduction of economic coercion alters the dynamics of the coordination game in two ways. First, it widens the size of the bargaining core – the distribution of costs and benefits under which a coordinated outcome is an equilibrium outcome. For the targeted state, the preference to switch standards is no longer a question of whether the benefits exceed the adjustment costs. The question is whether the costs exceed the benefits such that switching is costlier than economic sanctions. Even if the targeted state is worse off from switching, it may represent the least bad alternative when faced with the possibility of sanctions (Gruber 2000). The second way in which coercion alters the dynamic of the game is to reduce the threshold market size necessary to lock in coordination at the great power's standards as

		State B	
		Switch to country A's standards	Retain national standards
State A	Retain national standards	*Coordinate at A* $(\pi_a, \pi_b - d)$	*No coordination* $(-c_a, -c_b)$
	Switch to country B's standards	*No coordination* $(-d, -d)$	*Coordinate at B* $(\pi_a - d, \pi_b)$

Figure 2 The modified coordination game

π = benefits from regulatory coordination

d_i = adjustment costs of switching standards for country i

$-c$ = costs to B of maintaining the status quo

the only possible equilibrium outcome. The shadow of potential sanctions lowers the threshold at which the targeted state would prefer switching to the great power's standards rather than accept the status quo.

Market power and coercive power shift the contours of the coordination game in a way that favors large markets. However, there is an important caveat to this conclusion: only relative power matters. When the two interacting countries are both great powers, neither actor possesses a distinct bargaining advantage, even if one of the two actors has more relative power. Given the size of both economies, the likelihood that the difference in market size is sufficient to alter the payoffs enough to generate a single equilibrium outcome is mathematically impossible.[10] As for the coercion option, it is highly unlikely that either actor would be able to satisfy the necessary conditions for making a credible threat of economic sanctions. Empirically, sanctions among great powers have generated meager results at best (Drezner 1999). Between governments with large internal markets, the effects of market power and coercive power wash out.

From this simple two-actor game-theoretic exercise, we can draw several conclusions. First, there exist some regulatory issue areas for which no coordination is the equilibrium outcome. For those issues where π is sufficiently low and d is sufficiently high, there is no incentive to coordinate regulatory standards in the absence of a colossal hegemon.

Second, power matters. Great powers are more likely to achieve regulatory coordination at their preferred level of standards. Their power affects the location of regulatory coordination in two ways. First, their market size can alter the incentives of actors such that their preferred outcome becomes the only equilibrium. Second, the threat of economic coercion can accelerate the lock-in effect of coordinating at the great power's ideal point.

THE DISPARATE PATHWAYS TO REGULATORY CONVERGENCE

In moving from a two-actor version of the game to a multi-actor version of the game, it is clear that there are two key stages of a nested game. The first stage involves only the great powers – the second stage involves other actors. If the great powers can coordinate their regulatory standards, then global regulatory convergence is a likely outcome. If no coordination is the equilibrium outcome among the great powers, then global regulatory competition will be the outcome.

When great powers can agree upon common regulatory standards, there is little that the other actors in the system can do to prevent global regulatory convergence. A great power concert can generate the necessary market size to lock in their preferred set of standards as the unique equilibrium outcome for almost all actors. The addition of these actors to the club of coordinated states would merely increase the incentives for coordination for laggard states (Schelling 1978). The only actors capable of resisting would have to possess dramatically high adjustment costs. Even those actors would be compelled to adjust under the threat of economic coercion. Therefore, when great powers can coordinate their regulatory standards, the outcome is rapid regulatory convergence.

The absence of a bargaining core among the great powers alters both the process and outcome of regulatory negotiations. As previously noted, coercive tactics are less likely to yield results than in the club standards outcome. Great powers are by definition less vulnerable to economic coercion. They can also thwart any organized multilateral attempt at pressure, and *ad hoc* pressure coalitions have a low probability of success.

However, the dynamics of the regulatory game are such that each actor has an incentive to maximize the size of the market that conforms to its preferred regulatory arrangements. The obvious strategy for a great power is to try and amass as many allies as possible to its preferred set of regulatory standards. In theory, a great power could amass the combined market power of a larger coalition of actors. Such a tactic would cross the tipping point and induce rival states to switch standards. However, *all* great powers would have an incentive to adopt this strategy.

The predicted result is one of partial convergence through competition. Great powers will use inducements, coercive tactics, persuasion, and forum-shifting in an effort to woo as many actors as possible to their preferred regulatory position. All the while, these governments will expend considerable effort to weaken the legitimacy of competing standards. Because all great powers have an incentive to engage in these tactics, the rest of the actors in the system will be asked – or forced – to choose which set of standards to endorse earlier than they otherwise would have. Through this competitive process, states will converge to a small number of possible regulatory standards – but among those standards 'blocs,' the outcome is one of repeated cycles of bargaining, contestation, and conflict.

It should be noted that the extent of convergence through competition is a function of the number of economic great powers in the system. In an economically bipolar world – as currently exists – both poles will try to create as large a regulatory bloc as possible. As the distribution of economic power shifts to a more multipolar world, the dynamic changes. The increased number of great powers implies reduced market and coercive power *vis-à-vis* the rest of the world. Therefore, as the distribution of economic power increases, so should regulatory divergence.

COERCED STANDARDS: THE CASE OF MONEY LAUNDERING

Money laundering is defined as the conversion of wealth derived from the proceeds of crime into untraceable and seemingly legal financial holdings. The size of these flows has been estimated at approximately 2–5 percent of global gross domestic product (GDP), or upwards of $2 trillion (Camdessus 1998). The bulk of international money laundering is conducted in support of transnational criminal organizations. Money laundering also has the potential to stunt the proper development of capital markets, retard economic growth, and weaken the rule of law (Quirk 1996).

The benefits to the US and EU from cracking down on money laundering were transparent – doing so helped to preserve the reputation of their financial systems and reduce incentives for corruption. In the wake of the 1989 BCCI scandal, the G-7 states along with the European Commission created the Financial Action Task Force on Money Laundering (FATF) to address the problem. FATF worked over the next year to develop a set of recommended best practices affecting financial supervision and regulation, appropriate law enforcement guidelines, and protocols for international cooperation. These practices were called the FATF Forty Recommendations.[11]

Originally, the FATF Forty Recommendations were designed to coordinate regulatory systems among the advanced industrial democracies. However, the growth of offshore financial centers (OFCs) and their role in the proliferation of private banking scandals and crony capitalism led both the United States and the EU to the decision to treat money laundering as a *global* problem in the mid-1990s (Wechsler 2001).

The moves towards regulatory coordination took place out of the public eye, and inspired neither strong support nor strong opposition within the US and EU. The financial sectors in these countries were more concerned about the costs of complying with new regulations. Banks, for example, were concerned about the added cost of implementing know-your-customer regulations (Florini 1999). Attempts were made by the larger financial firms to set up a 'private order' as a means of warding off further state regulations (Peith and Aiolfi 2003). In the United States, firms in the financial sector expressed concern to Treasury officials about the regulatory shift. However, those pressures failed to dissuade US officials from their course of action.

The mere establishment of the FATF Forty Recommendations encouraged many countries to take the necessary steps towards implementation. However, some developing countries faced significant adjustment costs at the prospect of coordinating their regulatory standards at FATF levels. Developing country governments can exploit repressed capital markets and privileged access to scarce foreign exchange to reward favored interests, political supporters, or simply enrich themselves (Lindsey 2002). For emerging markets, the tolerance of OFCs provides black market entrepreneurs – such as narcotics traffickers – with the opportunity to insert assets into the global financial marketplace. Although there are long-term risks to reputation for the emerging markets, many of these governments operate on the principle of 'any capital is good capital' and are therefore loath to displace such investments in the name of regulatory coordination (Quirk 1996).

To correct this problem, the US and EU used persuasion and inducements as well to ensure policy harmonization. FATF enlarged its membership to include most of the membership in the Organization for Economic Cooperation and Development (OECD). FATF also expanded to include key developing countries, such as Argentina, Brazil, South Africa, and the Russian Federation.[12] The great powers encouraged the creation of FATF-style regional bodies in the developing world, such as the Asia-Pacific Group on Money Laundering.[13] By 2003, there were five regional bodies with a collective membership of 108 jurisdictions.[14] The G-7 proffered technical assistance to cooperating countries to ensure adherence and recognition of the FATF Forty Recommendations on Money Laundering. By August 2001, over 140 countries and territories had publicly acknowledged the FATF Forty as the accepted international standard for anti-money laundering.

The specter of coercive economic power also played a role. In June 1999, the G-7 Heads of State and the European Commission pushed for FATF to take an even more aggressive posture towards non-members whose laws appeared to tolerate money laundering.[15] In February 2000, FATF (2000a: 8) published criteria to identify 'non-cooperative countries and territories' (NCCTs), a schedule for selecting and evaluating jurisdictions for NCCT status, and a menu of 'countermeasures' for those governments that refused to comply with FATF requests. The countermeasures ranged from the issuance of advisories to domestic financial institutions to the most serious possible sanction: 'conditioning, restricting, targeting, or even prohibiting financial transactions with non-cooperative jurisdictions.'

FATF members reviewed the first group of possible NCCTs between February and June 2000. Twenty-nine jurisdictions were assessed, and fifteen were listed as NCCTs. FATF demanded that these countries take the legislative and administrative steps to criminalize money laundering, establish centralized financial intelligence units, cooperate with other national authorities in money laundering investigations, and require banks to file suspicious activity reports to the government. With regard to the NCCTs, FATF (2000b: 12) warned, 'should those countries or territories identified as non-cooperative maintain their detrimental rules and practices despite having been encouraged to make certain reforms, FATF members would then need to consider the adoption of countermeasures.' A month later, the G-7 Finance Ministers strongly supported FATF's NCCT initiative as well as the potential sanctions that backed up the threat. The G-7 Heads of State communiqué stated: 'We are prepared to act together when required and appropriate to implement coordinated countermeasures against those NCCTs that do not take steps to reform their system appropriately, including the possibility to condition or restrict financial transactions with those jurisdictions.'[16]

Within a year, 73 percent of the targeted countries made major concessions prior to the implementation of any economic sanctions. There is clear evidence to support the contention that these jurisdictions altered their laws in direct response to the FATF threat of economic coercion. When Lebanon passed its anti-money laundering legislation, its central bank governor explicitly stated that the law was designed to meet FATF's criteria.[17] Dominica's Finance Minister urged for the passage of an anti-money laundering bill in order to escape the FATF 'blacklist.'[18] Other targets expressed similar sentiments, either in public or in negotiations with FATF officials.[19] Although media coverage of the FATF initiative prior to the September 11th attacks was scant, what reporting there was confirmed this assessment.[20]

The demonstration effect of the first round of the NCCT process, combined with the enhanced salience of money laundering in the wake of the 9/11 attacks, caused several other potential targets of coercion to preemptively adopt rigorous anti-money laundering measures. Within five years, the great powers were able to use a combination of market power and coercive power to cajole, coerce, and induce the rest of the world into harmonizing their anti-money laundering policies towards the FATF Forty Recommendations.

COMPETING STANDARDS: THE CASE OF GMOs

Genetically modified organisms (GMOs) are designed to improve the yield of agricultural goods while reducing the need for herbicides, pesticides, and other chemicals. No scientific evidence exists to demonstrate that genetically modified products are harmful to humans (Kuiper *et al.* 2001). However, there are concerns about whether transgenic crops would cross-pollinate with neighboring crops, overwhelming indigenous flora and fauna and reducing biodiversity (Conner *et al.* 2003).

GMOs trigger strong and conflicting preferences. Competitive agricultural producers and biotech firms have invested heavily in assets specific to GMO technology (Bullock and Desquilbet 2002; Newell 2003), ratcheting up their adjustment costs to more stringent GM standards. Among European consumers, however, the concerns generated by mad cow disease in the late 1980s generated deep suspicion of large-scale agricultural innovations. Since then, EU officials, the European Parliament, and member governments have acted to reduce competitive pressures on their agricultural sector and allay public concerns about 'Frankenfoods' (Prakash and Kollman 2003).

As Prakash and Kollman (2003: 626) observe, 'The two paths taken by the EU and the US in the area of biotech regulation could hardly be more different.' The US opposes most regulatory restrictions on GMOs, arguing that there is no scientific basis for such a regulatory position. Until March 2004, the EU had an unofficial moratorium in place on the sale of GMO crops. Even with the end of the moratorium, powerful member states are committed to prohibiting all GMO imports (Young 2003). Officially, EU institutions prefer to place restrictions and/or labels on GMO products. Developing countries are also split between agricultural exporters who have embraced the technology and other states that fear a loss of biodiversity from using GMOs (Millstone and van Zwanenberg 2003).

The United States has relied on the World Trade Organization's (WTO's) legal authority to delegitimize EU policies restricting trade in GMOs. The US also holds sway over the Codex Alimentarius Commission, a United Nations emanation that establishes food codes based on scientific principles. In the Sanitary and Phytosanitary (SPS) agreement established during the Uruguay round, the General Agreement on Tariffs and Trade (GATT) defers to the Codex to establish appropriate sanitary measures. Not surprisingly, WTO panel rulings consistently support the American position that attempts to restrict agricultural products without credible scientific evidence of possible harm violate international trade law (Davis 2003: ch. 9).

Having failed at altering the rules in these intergovernmental organizations (IGOs), the EU switched fora to another United Nations emanation to advance its regulatory preferences. In January 2000, the Cartagena Protocol on Biosafety, an outgrowth of the 1992 Rio Convention on Biodiversity, endorsed using the 'precautionary principle' in the treatment of large modified organisms (Falkner 2000). This principle states that potentially dangerous activities can be restricted or prohibited *before* they are scientifically proven to cause serious damage. The result is a legal stalemate, with the Biosafety Protocol's precautionary principle flatly contradicting the trade regime's norm of scientific proof of harm. It will be difficult at best to reconcile the WTO and Cartagena regimes (Millstone and van Zwanenberg 2003).

The transatlantic divergence of preferences has stymied efforts to develop common global regulations on GMOs. Furthermore, both great powers have expended considerable resources in converting other states to adopt their position. The Department of Agriculture and the US Trade Representative have lobbied governments across the globe on the virtues of GMO crops. Beginning with the Clinton administration's Initiative on Biotechnology, the US Department of Agriculture openly stated that facilitating the marketing of GM products was one of its goals. The United States Agency for International Development made a similar pledge in 2002 (Paarlberg 2003). At the 2002 World Food Summit, the US Agriculture Secretary announced a ten-year, $100 million Collaborative Agriculture Biotechnology Initiative to advance research on GM varieties better suited to developing countries.

The United States also pushed countries to accept US safety certifications for GMO products or to develop their own protocols as quickly as possible. For example, Chinese officials told US officials in fall 2001 that they would accept US safety certifications for GMO crops. After Beijing reversed course in early 2002, the US Trade Representative and Agriculture Secretary issued a joint statement characterizing the situation as 'unacceptable.' In response, the Chinese government issued temporary safety certificates permitting GMO imports until permanent regulations were drafted in February 2004.[21] One non-governmental organization (NGO) official complained in early 2004 that 'the US is trying to impose its standards on the rest of the world.'[22]

Implicit in US diplomacy over the GMO issue has been the specter of WTO arbitration rulings in their favor. Beginning with the EU beef hormone case, WTO panels have consistently sided with the American position that attempts to restrict agricultural products without credible scientific evidence of possible harm violate international trade law (Davis 2003). In 1998, the US Trade Representative used the shadow of the WTO to attack the EU's labeling requirements for foods containing transgenic material, arguing that 'such labeling is unnecessary, in the absence of an identified and documented risk to safety or health.' That language was consciously phrased to invoke the SPS agreement.

These uses of economic statecraft had a powerful effect on countries asymmetrically dependent on access to US markets. The first two countries to agree with American standards for GMO labeling were Mexico and Canada.[23] In 2002, the

Indian government approved the commercial cultivation of Bt cotton.[24] As large developing markets accept GM seeds, the competitive incentive for other countries to coordinate standards at a level that permits GM cultivation increases. One assessment (Nap *et al.* 2003: 6) concluded, 'The global adoption rate of GM crops is among the highest for any new technology in agriculture.'

Using similar tools of statecraft, European actors have pushed equally hard to promote the precautionary principle and resist the diffusion of GMO-friendly regulations. The EU has lobbied developing governments to ratify the Cartagena Protocol, and offered technical assistance to set up regulatory systems that embrace the precautionary principle (Paarlberg 2003). The European campaign against GMO proliferation, combined with the six-year EU moratorium on GMO imports, encouraged trade-dependent countries to adopt the EU position on GM crops. As the EU expanded into Central and Eastern Europe, those countries agreed to pass laws on GMOs consistent with the EU position. Most potential entrants have taken steps to conform to EU regulations with regard to GMOs (Nap *et al.* 2003).

The EU position has had its strongest impact on African countries. In August 2002, European Commission officials rebuffed a US request to reassure famine-stricken African countries about the safety of American-supplied GM food aid.[25] Zambia's President said in early 2003 that his nation would 'rather starve' than accept food aid with GM corn. The country's Agriculture Minister expressed concern that if the GM corn seed were to pollute the country's seed stock, Zambian agricultural exports would be blocked from the EU. Other African nations followed suit; governments in Zimbabwe, Mozambique, and Malawi also feared being shut out of European markets if they invest in GMO technology (Wu and Butz 2004).

The result of the combined US and EU pressure has been a single global cleavage on the GMO issue (Nap *et al.* 2003). In one camp are countries that specialize in agricultural exports, have internal markets of sufficient size to exploit the possibilities of GMOs, or are vulnerable to US coercive pressure. In the other category are countries that either rely on subsistence agriculture or are trade dependent on the EU. Efforts to develop policy regarding GMOs in IGOs like the World Bank and the Food and Agricultural Organization have foundered over the EU–US split (Paarlberg 2003). Wu and Butz (2004: 54) conclude: 'The regulations in these two parts of the world, and the battle between these two factions over the place of GM crops in global food production, are shaping the regulations in other nations worldwide.'

CONCLUSION

Even in a globalizing economy, governments possessing large internal markets are the most important actors contributing to regulatory convergence. In a bipolar economic world, two kinds of convergence mechanisms exist. When the great powers achieve a concert on the preferred regulatory standard, global policy coordination is the predicted outcome. Great powers can use their combined market and coercive power to lead other countries into accepting their preferred regulatory arrangements as quickly as possible. The case of money laundering provides an excellent example of this kind of convergence process.

When the great powers' adjustment costs are too high for coordination to be possible, the result is an intriguing paradox – great power rivalries can be a powerful source of policy convergence. Divergent preferences among large states, combined with the increasing returns to scale of regulatory harmonization, lead these actors to attract as many allies as possible. In a bipolar distribution of power, the result is a bifurcation of policies, but strong policy convergence at two different nodes. Without this great power rivalry, it is highly unlikely that any degree of policy convergence would have taken place. The case of GMOs strongly underscores this type of convergence process.

The cases provided here are merely plausibility probes – further theoretical work is clearly needed. However, the results suggest some possible modifications to the theory detailed above. For example, in both the GMO and money laundering case, great powers used incentives as well as coercive pressure to get other countries to change their regulatory positions. They also cooperated with private actors, suggesting some complementarities between great powers and global civil society. Further empirical work is also necessary to establish scope conditions for the model presented here.

Finally, if the theory presented here holds, there are reasons to believe that regulatory harmonization will be an increasingly difficult task over time. The long-term growth of India and China will shift what is currently a bipolar economic distribution of power into a more multipolar world (Wilson and Purushothaman 2003). As the number of actors increases, the likelihood of creating a concert of common preferences among them necessarily declines (Axelrod and Keohane 1985). This holds with particular force if these countries achieve great power market size while still having low per capita incomes. In addition to the current tension between the American and European varieties of capitalism, another source of preference divergence could emerge among the great powers: the tension between rich countries willing to trade off economic growth for quality of life issues, and still-developing countries that are more reluctant to sacrifice growth.

Address for correspondence: Daniel W. Drezner, Assistant Professor of Political Science, University of Chicago, 5828 South University Ave., Chicago, IL 60637, USA. Tel: (773) 702-0234. Fax: (773) 702-1689. email: ddrezner@uchicago.edu

ACKNOWLEDGEMENTS

Draft versions of this paper were presented at the 2004 International Studies Association annual meeting, Montreal, Canada, 17–20 March, and at the special *Journal of European Public Policy* forum on 'Policy Convergence in Europe' at the University of Hamburg. The University of Chicago's Social

Science Division provided vital research support during the drafting of this paper. I am grateful to Mark Aspinwall, Christoph Knill, Andy Jordan, Duncan Liefferink, Yves Tiberghien, Alasdair Young, and an anonymous referee for their comments.

NOTES

1 For an exception, see Bernstein and Cashore (2000).
2 On distinction between the two forms of power, see James and Lake (1989).
3 This is one reason why econometric methods to predict international trade flows are called 'gravity models'; the presumption is that the larger an economy – and the closer it is to other markets – the more traded goods that economy will naturally attract.
4 China and India have rapidly growing economies and sizeable populations. For the time period under study, however, these markets remain emerging and not emerged.
5 Space constraints prevent a further discussion of the factors that determine the values of both the coordination benefits and the adjustment costs of great power governments. For more, see Drezner (n.d.)
6 If state B chooses to switch standards, state A's utility from retaining its standards is greater than switching ($\pi > -d$). If state B retains its national standard, state A's utility from retaining its standards is still greater than switching standards ($0 > \pi - d$). By symmetry, this holds for state B as well.
7 For a formal definition of 'games of cooperation,' see Bendor and Swistak (1997).
8 Formally, let Y_i equal the size of country i's economy. Then for all i, $\pi_i =$ a linear transformation of: $Y_j/(Y_i + Y_j)$.
9 For formal derivations of these hypotheses, see Drezner (n.d.)
10 The asymptotic nature of ratios explains this fact. With small countries, a great power's size can appear greater due to its market size, but as the size of the smaller country increases, the ratio falls exponentially.
11 The FATF Forty Recommendations have since been revised twice – in 1996 and in 2003.
12 A complete membership list can be accessed at http://www.fatf-gafi.org/Members_en.htm#MEMBERS.
13 Other FATF-style regional bodies have been established in Eastern Europe, South America, and Eastern and Southern Africa.
14 Membership lists can be found at http://www1.oecd.org/fatf/Members_en.htm#OBSERVERS.
15 See the 18 June 1999 Communiqué by G-7 Heads of State and Government at http://www.g7.utoronto.ca/g7/summit/1999koln/g7statement_june18.htm.
16 Both communiqués can be accessed at http://www.g7.utoronto.ca/g7/summit/2000okinawa/.
17 'Lebanon Approves Money Laundering Law,' Reuters, 10 April 2001.
18 'Opposition in Dominica Blasts Anti-Money Laundering Bill,' Reuters, 16 June 2001.
19 Canute James and Michael Peel, 'Tax Havens Tighten Rules,' *Financial Times*, 17 June 2001.
20 See *Economist*, 'Fighting the Dirt,' 21 June 2001.
21 *Dow Jones Newswires*, 'China Says No GMO Permits Needed From Health Ministry for Now,' 1 July 2002; *People's Daily Online*, 'Gene-Altered Crops are Safe: Official,' 26 February 2004.
22 Sean Young, 'Countries "Polarized" on Safety of Genetically Modified Products,' Associated Press, 23 February 2004.
23 Mark Stevenson, 'Mexico becomes first importer nation to adopt US-backed standards on labeling for genetically modified grains,' Associated Press, 12 February 2004.

24 Edward Luce, 'India allows Farms to Grow Genetically Modified Cotton,' *Financial Times*, 27 March 2002.
25 US State Department, 'Biotechnology and US Food Assistance to Southern Africa,' 21 August 2002.

REFERENCES

Axelrod, R. and Keohane, R. (1985) 'Achieving cooperation under anarchy', *World Politics* 38: 226–54.
Bendor, J. and Swistak, P. (1997) 'The evolutionary stability of cooperation', *American Political Science Review* 91: 297–308.
Bernstein, S. and Cashore, B. (2000) 'Globalization, four paths of internationalization and domestic policy change', *Canadian Journal of Political Science* 33: 67–99.
Braithwaite, J. and Drahos, P. (1999) *Global Business Regulation*, New York: Cambridge University Press.
Bretherton, C. and Vogler, J. (1999) *The European Union as a Global Actor*, New York: Routledge.
Bullock, D.S. and Desquilbet, M. (2002) 'The economics of non-GMO segregation and identity preservation', *Food Policy* 27: 82–100.
Camdessus, M. (1998) 'Money laundering: the importance of international countermeasures'. Speech delivered to the Financial Action Task Force, 10 February 1998, Paris.
Cohen, B.J. (1996) 'Phoenix risen: the resurrection of global finance', *World Politics* 48: 268–96.
Conner, A. *et al.* (2003) 'The release of genetically modified crops into the environment', *The Plant Journal* 33: 19–46.
Davis, C. (2003) *Food Fights Over Free Trade*, Princeton: Princeton University Press.
Drezner, D.W. (1999) *The Sanctions Paradox*, Cambridge: Cambridge University Press.
Drezner, D.W. (2001) 'Globalization and policy convergence', *International Studies Review* 3: 53–78.
Drezner, D.W. (2003) 'The hidden hand of economic coercion', *International Organization* 57: 643–59.
Drezner, D.W. (n.d.) 'Who rules?'. Unpublished book ms, Chicago, IL.
Falkner, R. (2000) 'Regulating biotech trade', *International Affairs* 76: 300–15.
Financial Action Task Force (2000a) *Report on Non-Cooperative Countries and Territories*, Paris: OECD.
Financial Action Task Force (2000b) *Review to Identify Non-Cooperative Countries and Territories*, Paris: OECD.
Finnemore, M. (1996) *National Interests and International Society*, Ithaca: Cornell University Press.
Florini, A. (1999) 'Does the invisible hand need a transparent glove?'. Paper prepared for annual World Bank Conference on Development Economics, Washington, DC, April.
Goodman, J. and Pauly, L. (1993) 'The obsolescence of capital controls?', *World Politics* 46: 50–82.
Gruber, L. (2000) *Ruling the World*, Princeton: Princeton University Press.
Haas, P. (1992) 'Epistemic communities and international policy coordination', *International Organization* 46: 1–35.
Haftel, Y. (2003) 'Regional arrangements and institutionalization'. Paper presented at the Midwestern Political Science Association annual meeting, Chicago, IL.
Hall, P. and Soskice, D. (eds) (2001) *Varieties of Capitalism*, Oxford: Oxford University Press.
Harsanyi, J. and Selten, R. (1988) *A General Theory of Equilibrium Selection*, Cambridge: MIT Press.

James, S. and Lake, D. (1989) 'The second face of hegemony', *International Organization* 43: 1–29.
Keck, M. and Sikkink, K. (1998) *Activists Beyond Borders*, Ithaca: Cornell University Press.
Knill, C. (2005) 'Introduction: Cross-national policy convergence: concepts, approaches and explanatory factors', *Journal of European Public Policy* 12(5): 764–74.
Koremenos, B., Lipson, C. and Snidal, D. (eds) (2001) 'The rational design of international institutions', *International Organization* special issue 55: 761–1103.
Krasner, S.D. (1991) 'Global communications and national power', *World Politics* 43: 336–66.
Kuiper, H. *et al.* (2001) 'Assessment of the food safety issues related to genetically modified foods', *The Plant Journal* 27: 503–28.
Lazer, D. (2001) 'Regulatory interdependence and international governance', *Journal of European Public Policy* 8: 474–92.
Lindsey, B. (2002) *Against the Dead Hand*, New York: John Wiley.
Mattli, W. (2001) 'The politics and economics of international institutional standards setting: an introduction', *Journal of European Public Policy* special issue 8: 328–44.
Medina, L.F. (2004) 'The comparative statics of collective action', Working Paper, University of Chicago, Chicago, IL.
Meyer, J.W. *et al.* (1997) 'World society and the nation-state', *American Journal of Sociology* 103: 144–81.
Millstone, E. and van Zwanenberg, P. (2003) 'Food and agricultural biotechnology policy', *Development Policy Review* 21: 655–67.
Nap, J.-P. *et al.* (2003) 'The release of genetically modified crops into the environment', *The Plant Journal* 33: 19–46.
Newell, P. (2003) 'Globalization and the governance of biotechnology', *Global Environmental Politics* 3: 56–71.
Paarlberg, R. (2003) 'Reinvigorating genetically modified crops', *Issues in Science and Technology* 19: 86–93.
Peith, M. and Aiolfi, G. (2003) 'The private sector becomes active: the Wolfsberg process', *Journal of Financial Crime* 10: 359–65.
Pollack, M. (2004) 'The delegation of powers to the European Commission'. Paper presented at the International Studies Association, Montreal, Canada.
Prakash, A. and Kollman, K. (2003) 'Biopolitics in the EU and the US', *International Studies Quarterly* 47: 617–42.
Quinlan, J. (2003) 'Drifting apart or growing together?', Center for Transatlantic Relations, Washington, DC.
Quirk, P. (1996) 'Macroeconomic implications of money laundering', IMF Working Paper 96/66, Washington, DC.
Schelling, T. (1978) *Micromotives and Macrobehavior*, New York: W.W. Norton.
Simmons, B. (2001) 'The international politics of harmonization', *International Organization* 55: 589–620.
Vogel, D. (1995) *Trading Up*, Cambridge: Cambridge University Press.
Wapner, P. (1995) 'Politics beyond the state', *World Politics* 47: 311–40.
Wechsler, W. (2001) 'Follow the money', *Foreign Affairs* 80: 40–57.
Wilson, D. and Purushothaman, R. (2003) 'Dreaming with BRICs', Goldman Sachs Global Economics Paper No. 99.
Wohlforth, W. (1999) 'The stability of a unipolar world', *International Security* 24: 5–44.
Wu, F. and Butz, W. (2004) *The Future of Genetically Modified Crops*, Santa Monica: RAND.
Young, A. (2003) 'Political transfer and "trading up"', *World Politics* 55: 457–84.

The international sources of policy convergence: explaining the spread of environmental policy innovations

Per-Olof Busch and Helge Jörgens

INTRODUCTION

What explains the adoption of similar policy innovations, i.e. laws, policies, instruments and institutions, across different nations? An abundant and still growing body of literature mainly in comparative politics and international relations addresses this question or, more generally speaking, the puzzle of policy convergence and its sources. While this literature has generated a variety of theoretically informed hypotheses, its focus is often limited to the analysis of single mechanisms or classes of mechanisms through which policy convergence may occur and a systematic empirical illustration of how the different mechanisms of convergence actually work is still largely missing (see for state of the art Heichel *et al.* 2005; Bennett 1991b; Drezner 2001). In this article, we seek to address this gap by devising a systematic conceptualization of three analytically distinct classes of mechanisms that contribute to policy convergence and by applying this conceptualization empirically.

Starting from the assumption that international actors, processes and institutions increasingly affect domestic policy changes, our efforts are guided by the question as to through which mechanisms they reach the domestic level and contribute to policy convergence. While this approach is not new and pertains to the long-standing debate in international relations on how international governance affects domestic policy-making, we depart from previous studies by introducing diffusion as a distinct class of convergence mechanisms which has so far been neglected in much of the more traditional comparative politics and international relations literature, but which can be shown to complement the more frequently examined mechanisms of co-operative harmonization and coercive imposition (see Bennett 1991b, for an exception). Diffusion, as we use the term, refers to processes where national policy-makers voluntarily, that is without being formally obliged by international agreements or forced by external actors, adopt a certain policy innovation and in doing so draw on policy models which have been communicated in the international system (Howlett 2000; Rogers 2003). Like Elkins and Simmons we understand diffusion as a class of mechanisms 'characterized by interdependent, but uncoordinated, decision making' where 'governments are independent in the sense that they make their own decisions without cooperation or coercion but interdependent in the sense that they factor in the choices of other governments' (Elkins and Simmons 2005: 35). While this understanding of diffusion as a process rather than an outcome differs from some of the extant literature (including some of the contributions in this special issue) (see Knill 2005), it reflects an emerging consensus among scholars of policy diffusion that more can be gained analytically from treating diffusion as a well-specified set of mechanisms of policy change than from equating it with an all-encompassing notion of spread (see, for example, Busch *et al.* 2005; Elkins and Simmons 2005; Lazer 2005; Levi-Faur 2005; Meseguer and Gilardi 2005; Tews 2005; Jörgens 2004; Simmons and Elkins 2004).

In the first part of the paper, drawing on literature from international relations and comparative political science we develop a typology of three classes of international convergence mechanisms by characterizing the differences between harmonization, imposition and diffusion. Given the abundant studies which have been written on harmonization and imposition, we shift the focus to diffusion which has so far received less attention. In the second part, we use this typology as a framework for the empirical analysis of the international spread of six environmental policy innovations. If convergence is to be conceptualized as an evolution over time (Knill 2005; Holzinger and Knill 2005), it is likely that several distinct mechanisms may have played a role at different points in time (Bennett 1991b: 230–1). Therefore, it is the aim of this article to assess whether, how and to what extent each of these three classes of mechanisms has contributed to policy convergence.

A TYPOLOGY OF CONVERGENCE MECHANISMS

Cross-national policy convergence is often explained by structural changes related to economic globalization or political internationalization. Empirical studies revealed, however, that these structural changes do not necessarily or automatically result in policy convergence (Drezner 2001 provides an overview). In other cases convergence is explained by 'modernizing forces', i.e. a range of social and economic forces produced by industrial development. However, this macro-level explanation bears the risk of obscuring analytically distinct processes that contribute to policy convergence (Bennett 1991b).

While we do not doubt the general explanatory potential of these approaches, in our view economic globalization, political internationalization and 'modernizing forces' should be primarily regarded as driving forces at the macro-level of analysis. In order to fully understand processes of policy change and convergence, one must focus on the distinct political mechanisms by which these structural pressures are 'translated' into policy convergence. As Bennett has put it: '[I]t is not enough to say that comparable conditions produce comparable problems which produce comparable policies. There are also different political mechanisms, . . . through which policies might converge' (Bennett 1991b: 217). In this article, we therefore ask how and through which intermediate mechanisms (causal linkages) the structural changes and the 'modernizing forces' affect domestic policies in such a way that policies converge across countries. In line with a growing interest in mechanism- and process-based accounts in political science which 'explain salient features of episodes, or significant differences among them, by identifying within those episodes robust mechanisms of relatively general scope' (Tilly 2001: 24; see also Hedström and Swedberg 1998) we conceive of mechanisms as 'recurrent processes linking specified initial conditions and a specific outcome' (Mayntz 2004: 241). The mechanisms that eventually may lead to policy change and convergence are numerous. They include such diverse processes as independent but similar domestic responses to similar policy problems, negotiation of and compliance with multilateral agreements, supranational law-making, hegemonic coercion, intergovernmental reinforcement, regulatory competition, persuasion, peer-pressure, learning or imitation, to name just a few. In order to categorize this wide array of possible causes of policy convergence, we propose a typology of three broad classes of mechanisms: (1) the co-operative *harmonization* of domestic practices by means of international legal agreements or supranational law; (2) the coercive *imposition* of political practices by means of economic, political or even military threat, intervention or conditionality; and (3) the interdependent, but un-coordinated *diffusion* of practices by means of cross-national imitation, emulation or learning. These classes of mechanisms are distinct with regard to their mode of operation, the principal motivations of policy-makers to adopt policies and the leeway they grant national policy-makers to influence the content and independently decide on the adoption of a policy. Since we are mostly interested in the international sources of policy convergence, this typology does not include a fourth class of mechanisms, namely independent domestic responses to similar policy problems or functional requirements. However, in our empirical analysis this 'null hypothesis' is always taken into account.

Harmonization

The term harmonization as it is being used here integrates mechanisms such as negotiation, legalization, compliance and enforcement. In international relations, harmonization is conceptualized as a multilateral and state-centred process where international negotiations among sovereign states and subsequent policy formulation lead to domestic implementation and compliance.[1] The same states that create the regulations are also responsible for their implementation. Thus, in processes of harmonization, sources and targets of political decisions are identical.

Harmonization is characterized by highly institutionalized and centralized top-down decision-making procedures in the course of which the co-operating states consent on the international harmonization of their policies. It involves the conscious and negotiated modification of domestic policies by governments committed to cross-national standards which they have had a hand in drafting (Howlett 2000: 308). Of course, harmonization contributes to policy convergence only in so far as the agreed rules prescribe the implementation of similar policies and states comply with these rules.

While nations participate voluntarily in this multilateral decision-making, once an agreement is reached and 'legalized', they are more or less strongly obliged to comply with and to implement it (Abbott and Snidal 2000; Abbott *et al.* 2000). Thus, harmonization involves some sacrifice of national autonomy and sovereignty.

Nations largely share similar motivations when they negotiate and implement international agreements or supranational regulations. They either attempt to improve the management of collective, typically transboundary, problems where unilateral action offers at best unsatisfactory solutions or collective action problems hinder an effective management, or they seek to avoid negative externalities of unilateral action and hope to realize positive gains (Martin and Simmons 1998).

Imposition

Imposition[2] involves a set of mechanisms ranging from forceful coercion to economic and political conditionality. At a lower level of analysis, coercion encompasses further sub-mechanisms like economic sanctions or military intervention. Similarly, conditionality can be disaggregated into the sub-mechanisms of intergovernmental reinforcement by reward, by punishment or by support (Schimmelfennig and Sedelmeier 2004: 663–4). In general terms, imposition occurs when external actors intentionally force nations to adopt policy innovations which they would not have adopted otherwise and do so by exploiting economic or political power asymmetries. Thus, in contrast to harmonization, sources and targets of this mechanism no longer coincide.

In the case of imposition the involved actors differ fundamentally in their principal motivations as well as in their opportunities to shape the content of the adopted policies. Policy-makers in the targeted nations have little or no opportunity to influence the policy content which is determined by the imposing actor. The principal motivation for actors that attempt to impose policies is to export their fundamental values and principles. By contrast, policy-makers in nations on which policies are imposed either simply shy away from superior power or cede to the demands because of expected political or economic benefits which imposing actors offer in exchange for conformity with their demands. These incentives range from access to monetary resources, e.g. development loans, to access to important organizations or institutions, e.g. membership of the European Union (EU).

In sum, imposition eliminates almost any voluntary element in national decisions to adopt a policy innovation. More often than not, nations targeted by imposition cannot afford to defy and resist the political or economic conditionality, although the option to forgo the incentives or face the consequences of non-conformity with external demands exists, at least theoretically.

Diffusion

While processes of harmonization and imposition without any doubt contribute to policy convergence, several studies observed policy convergence even in the absence of these mechanisms. Research on international norm dynamics, for example, has revealed that global norms and principles can become influential without first being spelled out in international agreements (Finnemore 1996; Finnemore and Sikkink 1998). The alternative explanation, that policy convergence results from a more or less accidental accumulation of independent national reactions to economic and political globalization or modernizing forces, falls short of systematically recognizing the growing density of communicative interlinkages among nations. These interlinkages make independent and isolated national policy decisions increasingly unlikely (Lazer 2005). Unsurprisingly, thus, this type of structural explanation has increasingly been challenged (Drezner 2001). Against this background, we argue that diffusion constitutes a third and distinct class of convergence mechanisms which need to be systematically integrated in the analyses of policy convergence. Diffusion processes have for a long time received considerable attention in explaining policy convergence at the national level (Walker 1969; Gray 1973; Berry and Berry 1999). More recently, a growing number of studies have gone beyond anecdotal references and applied this concept systematically to the international level (Jordana and Levi-Faur 2005; Gilardi 2005; Busch and Jörgens 2005a; Busch *et al.* 2005; Way 2005; Simmons and Elkins 2004; Kern *et al.* 2001; Bennett 1988).

In accordance with the existing literature, we define diffusion as a process by which policy innovations are communicated in the international system and adopted voluntarily by an increasing number of countries over time (see Elkins and Simmons 2005; Rogers 2003; Dolowitz and Marsh 2000). Diffusion refers to an international spread of policy innovations driven by information flows rather than by hierarchical or collective decision-making within international institutions. At the micro-level it is triggered by mechanisms of social learning, copying or mimetic emulation (Jörgens 2004; Orenstein 2003). The essential feature of policy diffusion is that it occurs in the absence of formal or contractual obligation. Moreover, diffusion is basically a horizontal process whereby individually adopted policies and programmes add up to a decentralized regulatory structure (see Levi-Faur 2005). Unlike in the case of multilateral legal treaties, which are negotiated centrally between states and subsequently implemented top-down, with diffusion, decision-making procedures are decentralized and remain at the national level. Diffusion becomes manifest only through the accumulation of individual cases of imitation, emulation or learning with respect to one and the same policy item. In the absence of a centralized regulatory regime with highly visible and explicitly stated aims, international policy diffusion may thus result in a 'regulatory revolution by stealth' (Levi-Faur and Jordana 2005: 8).

While our understanding of diffusion follows the predominant use of this concept in the recent literature (for an overview, see Elkins and Simmons 2005; see also Rogers 2003; Howlett 2000; Bennett 1991a, 1997), it contradicts those approaches that view diffusion as an outcome rather than a process. A prominent example for this body of literature is Eyestone's understanding of diffusion as 'any pattern of successive adoptions of a policy innovation' (Eyestone 1977: 441). This understanding of diffusion as the sum of all domestic adoptions of a policy innovation, regardless of the particular causal mechanisms through which these adoptions were brought about, certainly is legitimate. However, its analytical usefulness for the study of policy change and convergence is rather limited. Instead of explaining how policies spread internationally, it merely provides a new linguistic term for the rather trivial observation that policies actually spread from one country to another. Moreover, as Elkins and Simmons convincingly argue, the natural science analogy makes little sense in social or political processes.

> In the natural sciences, diffusion usually refers to the spread of molecules from an area of high concentration to one of low concentration, resulting in a more uniform, and thinned-out, distribution of the molecules. With the spread of social practices, however, this sense of 'thinning-out' is irrelevant, if not altogether wrong. That is, the source or epicenter of diffusion is not necessarily 'depleted' when the practice spreads to another area.
>
> (Elkins and Simmons 2005: 36)

Therefore, political scientists increasingly use diffusion as a 'flagship term for a large class of mechanisms and processes associated with a likely outcome' (Elkins and Simmons 2005: 36). At the most general level, these mechanisms are characterized by interdependent, but uncoordinated, decision-making. Their underlying rationale is that the political choices of one country affect the subsequent choices of other countries, 'but not through any collaboration, imposition, or otherwise programmed effort on the part of any of the actors' (Elkins and Simmons 2005: 38).

National policy-makers are motivated by several reasons to emulate other countries' policies. Firstly, they may act in a rational and problem-oriented manner by looking across national borders for effective solutions to pressing domestic problems (Dolowitz and Marsh 2000; Rose 1991). Secondly, they may be persuaded, but in contrast to imposition not forced, by other actors to adopt policies from abroad (Finnemore 1993; Keck and Sikkink 1998). Thirdly, they may be motivated by norm-driven and legitimacy-oriented considerations. Once a policy innovation has been adopted by a fair number of countries, this will result in increased pressure for conformity. Moreover, it will offer domestic political élites new means for increasing their legitimacy and for enhancing their self-esteem in an international society structured by emerging normative standards of appropriate behaviour (Markus 1987; Finnemore and Sikkink 1998).

Diffusion, harmonization and imposition at a glance

Summarizing the above distinctions, a typology of three distinct classes of convergence mechanisms emerges (Figure 1). The typology has by no means explanatory or theory status. Rather, it provides a heuristic model which serves cognitive purposes and allows for more systematic analysis of the evolution of policy convergence. The three classes of mechanisms are ideal types whose boundaries may to some extent be blurred in the real world.

The typology put forward here is supported by a number of other scholarly efforts to systematize the ways in which international processes have an effect on domestic policy-making and contribute to convergence. Howlett (2000) uses the terms 'harmonization', 'domination' and 'emulation' when reasoning about international influences on policy convergence. Bennett (1991b) distinguishes 'emulation', 'harmonization', 'élite networking' and 'penetration' when accounting for this phenomenon. Both terminologies share a significant conceptual overlap with our distinction. In a similar vein, Dolowitz and Marsh (2000) conceptualize different types of policy transfer along a continuum ranging from voluntary lesson-drawing over obligated transfer to direct imposition. In the field of organizational sociology, DiMaggio and Powell (1983) have argued that institutional isomorphism – that is, the process through which organizations in a given social system grow similar over time – can be either 'coercive', 'mimetic' or 'normative'. Contrary to the model proposed here, DiMaggio and Powell subsume both asymmetric power relationships and legal standard-setting under the heading of coercive isomorphism. In return, both mimetic and normative isomorphism are variants of what is

Class of Mechanisms	Diffusion	Harmonization	Imposition
Mode of operation	Persuasion, emulation and learning Decentralized decision-making	Negotiation, enforcement and monitoring Centralized and joint decision-making	Coercion, political or economic conditionality Decentralized decision-making
Principal motivations of national policy-makers to adopt external policy models	• Search for effective solutions for domestic problems • Gain internal and external legitimacy	• Manage effectively transboundary challenges and at the same time dissatisfaction with solutions to transboundary challenges provided for by unilateral action • Avoid negative externalities (e.g. trade distortions) • Realize positive gains (e.g. access to new markets)	• Export fundamental values and principles as well as policies perceived to be successful • Access to economic and political resources (e.g. join international decision-making bodies or gain financial support) • Avoid negative consequences (e.g. sanctions)
Degree of influence on design of policy innovation and decision to adopt it	high →	→	→ low

Figure 1 Typology of international convergence mechanisms

labelled here 'diffusion'. While these differences are mainly attributable to differences in the subject of analysis – nations, on the one hand, and organizations, on the other – the work of DiMaggio and Powell makes a strong argument for the importance of non-hierarchical emulation and learning, even in those environments where authoritative decision-making is a valid option.

THE INTERNATIONAL SPREAD OF ENVIRONMENTAL POLICY INNOVATIONS

This section analyses the international spread of three different kinds of policy innovations: national environmental policy plans and sustainable development strategies (general policy programmes), environmental ministries and agencies (institutions) as well as feed-in tariffs and quotas for the promotion of renewable electricity (instruments). The country set encompasses forty-three countries which can be divided into two main groups: industrialized countries[3] and Central and Eastern European (CEE) countries.[4] The policy innovations were selected from an empirical study which analyzes the spread of twenty-two environmental policy innovations across these countries from 1945 to 2000.

For eight of these policy innovations our data even cover the worldwide spread (Busch and Jörgens 2005a, 2005b).

The analysis at hand investigates convergence with regard to whether similar policies, institutions and type of instruments had been adopted in different countries. If the number of countries with a similar policy innovation in place, e.g. environmental ministries, increases over time, these countries increasingly grow alike or converge with regard to this policy innovation. We defined for each policy innovation a set of basic characteristics. To be considered as 'adopted' and taken into account in the analysis, these minimum criteria had to be matched by the design of the respective policy, institution or instrument in every country.[5] The minimum criteria, however, tolerate some differences because '[i]n the real world we would never expect a programme to transfer from one government to another without history, culture and institutions being taken into account' (Rose 1991: 21; see Bennett 1991b for a detailed discussion). For example, it would make little sense to consider only environmental ministries as similar which employ identical numbers of civil servants.

National environmental strategies

Environmental strategies are comprehensive governmental programmes of action that are developed with the participation of a wide range of societal actors and that formulate medium- and long-term goals for an economically and socially sound environmental policy (Jänicke and Jörgens 1998). Empirically, two types of strategic approaches can be distinguished: *environmental policy plans* which focus predominantly on environmental problems and view social and economic aspects merely as important constraints, and *sustainable development strategies* which attempt to set separate goals for all the environmental, social and economic dimensions of sustainable development.

Environmental strategies have spread rapidly since the 1980s. By 2003, twenty-three out of twenty-five industrialized and all CEE countries had formulated an environmental strategy (Figure 2). Worldwide, 140 countries had formulated a national environmental strategy by 2003 (Busch and Jörgens 2005b). Although marked differences remain in these plans in respect of both the relevance and the specificity of their goals (Jänicke and Jörgens 1998), all use an approach of targeted, cross-media and – at least in intention – participatory environmental planning.

Within the group of industrialized countries, the main driving force behind the spread of environmental strategies was diffusion. Initially, direct policy transfer played an important role. For example, the Dutch National Environmental Policy Plan of 1989 was rapidly elevated into a widely recognized model. It was imitated by several industrialized countries and served as an important source of inspiration to others (Jörgens 2004). During the 1990s, the diffusion of this policy innovation became increasingly institutionalized at the international level. In 1992 the United Nations Conference on

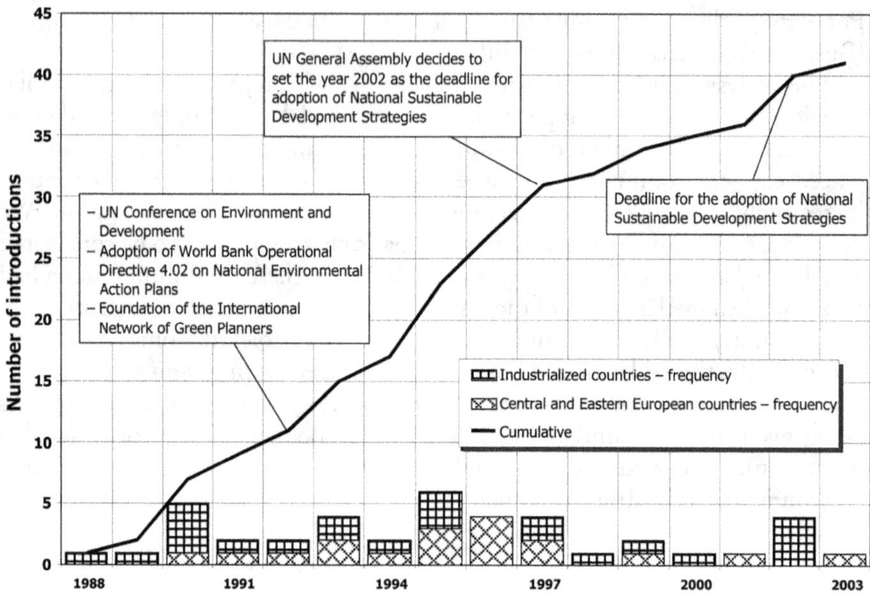

Figure 2 International spread of environmental strategies*
*Only the first adoption of an environmental strategy, either an environmental policy plan or a sustainable development strategy, is counted.
Source: own data.

Environment and Development (UNCED) recommended in Agenda 21 that '[g]overments should adopt a national strategy for sustainable development'. This recommendation was neither legally binding nor specified any point in time by when compliance was expected. Thus, it involved a relatively low degree of formal obligation and left it to policy-makers to decide whether or not to adopt an environmental strategy. Almost all strategies which were adopted between 1992 and 1997 include prominent references to UNCED and Agenda 21. Also in 1992 the EU adopted its Fifth Environmental Action Programme (EAP), which strongly influenced the development of environmental strategies in numerous Western European countries and was itself inspired by the Dutch model (Jörgens 2004). While many European strategies explicitly refer to the EU's EAP, some, like the Austrian National Environmental Plan, went so far as to copy central elements of the EAP (Pleschberger 1999). In these cases, therefore, the Dutch model diffused from the national to the supranational level of the EU and back to the national level of EU member states – a process which Padgett refers to as 'uploading' and 'downloading' (Padgett 2003: 227–8).

Following the UNCED a wide range of domestic or transnational, governmental or non-governmental actors started using the prescriptions of Agenda 21 as a point of reference for their demands. In 1993 the Organization for

Economic Co-operation and Development (OECD) included the implementation of an environmental strategy among the criteria in its Environmental Performance Reviews. In 1992 the International Network of Green Planners was created, which until its termination in 2004 provided a forum for policy-makers to share information, learn from experiences and promote the spread of environmental strategies. At the domestic level, opposition parties as well as non-governmental environment organizations regularly referred to Agenda 21 to exert pressure on governments to adopt an environment strategy. Overall, implementing the international norm of sustainable development through sustainability strategies had become a major manifestation of appropriate government behaviour (Jörgens 2004).

Diffusion processes also occurred in CEE and in the so-called newly independent states (NIS). Again, the EU's Fifth EAP was an important reference point for domestic initiatives. Another driver was the 1993 EAP for CEE. Implementation of this programme, whose main objective was the establishment of environmental strategies in CEE, was to be overseen by a newly created task force which 'brought together national environmental officials from all CEE countries and the NIS'. Its main function 'was to support a mutual effort in "learning by doing" – exchanging experience, identifying "best practices", and stimulating co-operation and support among network members' (OECD 1998: 20).

The dominant mechanism in CEE, however, was the imposition of environmental strategies by means of economic conditionality. The main actor was the World Bank. Its Operational Directive 4.02 from 1992 formally required the preparation of National Environmental Action Plans (NEAPs) as a condition for receiving World Bank loans and effectively made this instrument mandatory for borrower countries. In CEE the adoptions of Albania (1993), Moldova (1995), Macedonia (1997) and Bosnia-Herzegovina (2003) were triggered by World Bank conditionality. In the more developed CEE countries, other organizations took the place of the World Bank as environmental strategies were 'being implemented . . . primarily at the direct instigation of aid donors who have insisted on such planning exercises as a necessary prerequisite to cost-effective environmental investments' (Connolly and Gutner 2002).

Ten years after the first introduction of an environmental strategy and the start of its remarkable spread across 113 countries driven mainly by imposition and diffusion, the UN General Assembly passed a resolution calling all UN members to complete a sustainable development strategy by 2002. While UN declarations and resolutions do not constitute binding international law, by setting a fixed deadline and establishing supervisory mechanisms the resolution contained two important elements which characterize international law and which augmented significantly the pressure on governments to comply with the resolution. It can be argued, therefore, that since 1997 harmonization has increasingly become the dominant driver of the global spread of environmental strategies. Within the group of industrialized countries it replaced imitation and learning as principal mechanisms of spread. In Central and Eastern Europe the situation was different. Owing to the different objects of spread – NEAPs imposed by the World Bank constitute a well-specified sub-type of environmental strategies that is clearly distinct from sustainable development strategies promoted by the United Nations – imposition was not replaced by harmonization, but was merely supplemented by it.

As a result, within the OECD a total of fourteen out of thirty OECD member governments formally adopted a National Strategy for Sustainable Development in the period from 1997 to 2003. Even more interesting is that, in 2002 alone, a total of ten OECD countries either formally adopted their strategy or presented a complete draft. Altogether, twenty out of twenty-five industrialized countries had adopted a sustainable development strategy and twenty-three an environmental policy plan (Figure 3).[6] Only four OECD members – Mexico, New Zealand, Turkey and the United States – had not adopted a National Sustainable Development Strategy or at least announced its publication by the year 2003 (Jörgens 2004). In CEE countries the adoption of environmental action plans and sustainable development strategies varied significantly from the industrialized countries. While all CEE countries had formulated a NEAP by 2003, only ten out of eighteen had adopted a sustainable development strategy.

This observation suggests, first of all, that in CEE the imposition of NEAPs by the World Bank and other donor agencies had stronger effects than the 'soft' harmonization by the UN resolution. Two reasons can be found for this. First, by the

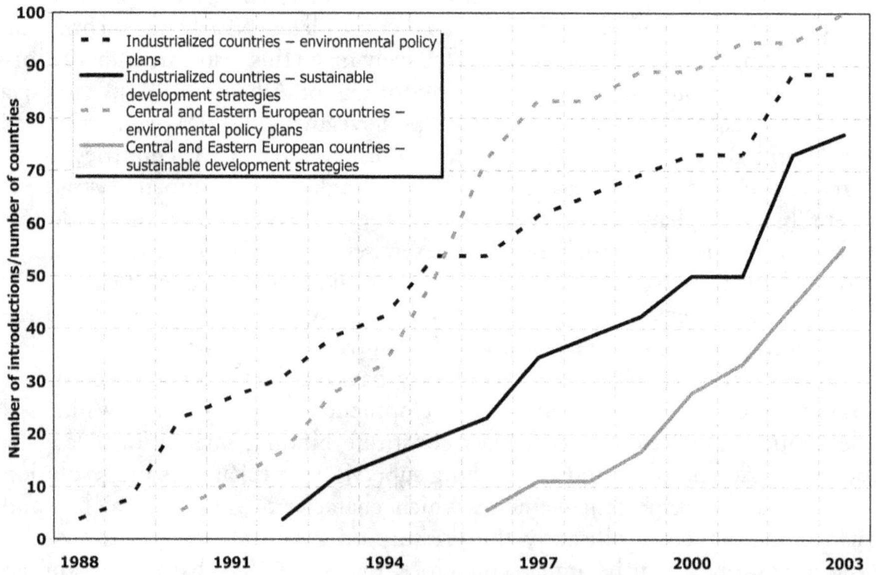

Figure 3 International spread of sustainable development strategies and environmental policy plans
Source: Own data.

time the UN resolution was adopted, a majority of the CEE countries were already engaged in the formulation of NEAPs. These countries simply lacked the political and administrative capacity to start yet another process of reporting and strategy formulation. Second, in the face of limited national capacities for environmental strategy formulation, NEAPs, driven by economic conditionality, were given priority over sustainable development strategies driven by legal but basically unenforceable international agreement. Having to choose between money and reputation, most CEE countries and many more developing countries opted for the former (Busch and Jörgens 2005b; Jörgens 2004).

Environmental institutions

Environmental concerns can be institutionalized in the domestic political system in a number of ways. Governments may create independent environmental ministries or agencies, set up independent advisory institutions, such as scientific expert councils or sustainability commissions, or establish environmental departments in non-environmental ministries. The following section focuses on two of these alternatives by analysing the international spread of environmental ministries and agencies. Both institutions constitute an important step in the creation of national capacities for environmental protection and indicate a country's concern about environmental issues (Jörgens 1996).

Environmental ministries address a broad range of environmental issues. They prepare and implement environment related decisions, regulations and laws; they adopt environmental programmes and represent domestic environmental interests in international policy processes. Except for the US, where only an environmental agency with ministerial competencies exists, all industrialized and CEE countries had established a national ministry for the environment by the year 2003 (Figure 4).

Environmental agencies, by contrast, conduct research, generate and compile data on the state of the environment, inform the public, and advise responsible ministries. Their international spread was slower and less complete with environmental agencies being created in eighteen out of twenty-five industrialized, but only eight out of eighteen CEE, countries (Figure 5).

Neither imposition nor harmonization could be observed during the spread of both environmental ministries and agencies as no binding international laws existed which obliged countries to establish these institutions. Some indications suggest, however, that processes of diffusion contributed significantly to the international proliferation of these institutional innovations.

In both cases the rate of adoption significantly increased above the overall average of annual introductions in the early 1970s and 1990s (Figures 4 and 5). Against this background, the explanatory null hypothesis that the accelerations simply and exclusively resulted from accidental culminations of independent and unconnected national responses to domestic problems appears at best implausible. Environmental challenges did not only emerge in the early 1970s or 1990s, but had already been on domestic policy agendas for several decades.

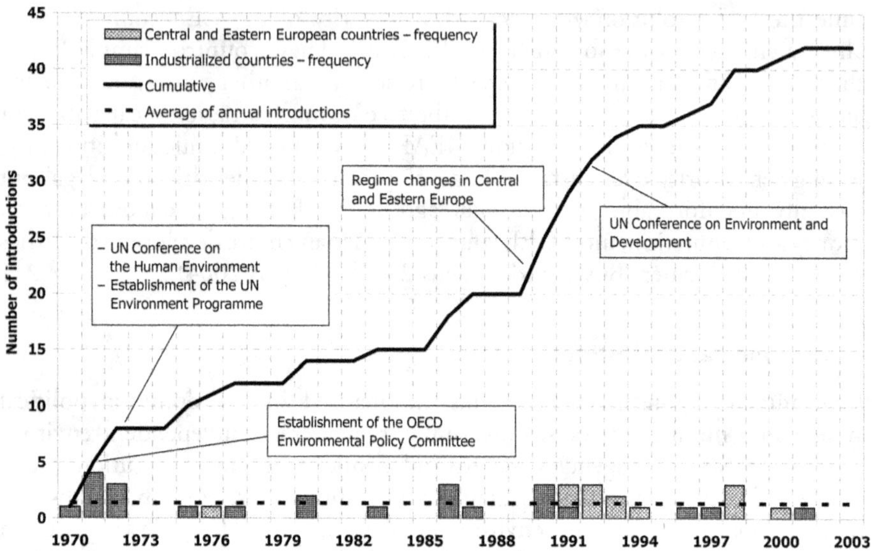

Figure 4 International spread of environmental ministries
Source: Own data.

Nor could a sudden intensification of environmental pressures be observed by that time which could have accounted for the culmination (Meyer *et al.* 1997: 627).

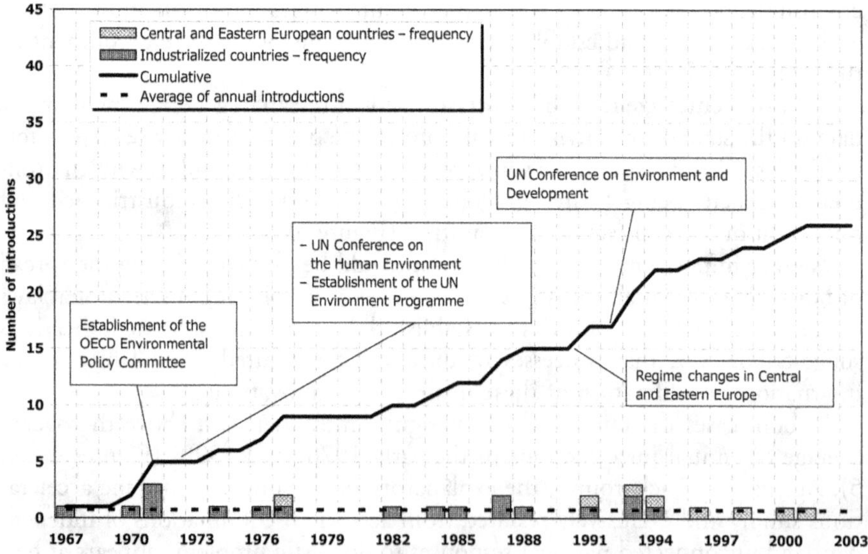

Figure 5 International spread of environmental agencies
Source: Own data.

The accelerations, however, coincided with outstanding international events and policy developments which institutionalized the communication and exchange of experiences among nations on environmental management, including possible institutional responses at country level. Most important in this regard were the UN Conference on the Human Environment (UNCHE) in 1972 in Stockholm and the UNCED in 1992 in Rio de Janeiro as well as the creation of the OECD Environmental Policy Committee in 1970 and of the UN Environment Programme (UNEP) in 1972. This coincidence does not suffice to claim that diffusion was driving the spread of environmental ministries and agencies. But these events indicate a significant rise in international interaction and communication which principally enhances the likelihood of diffusion (Berry and Berry 1999). Thus, they weaken once more the assumption that nations simply responded independently to identical problems without taking note of experiences and approaches communicated in the international system.

Moreover, it is reasonable to assume that these international events and related processes affected the establishment of national environmental institutions in a number of ways (see Haas 2002 for similar arguments). First of all, the variety of preparatory meetings and activities preceding the UN conferences certainly stimulated countries to (re-)consider their existing efforts in managing environmental challenges. Secondly, the widely visible preparatory processes of these high-level intergovernmental conferences on environmental issues prompted governments to ponder ways to effectively represent their national interests at the international level (Küppers *et al.* 1978). An effective way for governments to determine their specific interests in this newly globalizing issue area, and to competently defend these interests at international gatherings, was to create specialized environmental agencies or ministries within the national government. Likewise, well-defined domestic responsibilities facilitate the effective representation of national interests in permanent intergovernmental forums like the OECD's Environmental Policy Committee or UNEP. Meyer *et al.* even argue 'that formalized national ministries arise only when enough international conferences and organizations exist for ministers to attend' (Meyer *et al.* 1997: 639). Finally, Principle 17 of the Stockholm Declaration specifically urged countries to institutionalize environmental concerns at the domestic level: 'Appropriate institutions must be entrusted with the task of planning, managing or controlling the environmental resources of states with a view to enhancing environmental quality.' Tolba *et al.* (1995) argue that this demand can be interpreted as a non-binding commitment of governments to establish environmental institutions. The creation of environmental ministries or agencies enabled governments to respond to these international stimuli. In the early stages of environmental institutionalization ministries and agencies were conceived of as equal alternatives. Governments entrusted either a ministry or an agency with the main responsibility for environment related tasks. Many of the agencies which were founded in the 1970s were vested with executive competencies comparable to those of ministries, namely in Denmark, Sweden, Japan, the US and Switzerland. Later ministries evolved into the principal model for institutionalizing environmental protection. Today, only one country, the US, has failed to set up a federal ministry of the environment and concentrates environmental responsibilities in the hands of its Environmental Protection Agency. By contrast, sixteen countries refrained altogether from establishing an environmental agency.

Against this background, it appears reasonable to claim that diffusion mechanisms contributed to a significant extent to the international spread of environmental ministries and agencies, particularly in the 1970s. International communication and exchange of experiences on how to manage environmental challenges as well as specific demands or incentives for creating environmental institutions affected national decisions to voluntarily set up ministries or agencies. Moreover, Meyer *et al.* (1997) argue that, taken together, developments at the international level since the early 1970s contributed to the emergence of a 'world environment regime'. This regime established environmental protection and its domestic institutionalization as an international norm for modern statehood. The effect of this normative pressure becomes particularly evident when considering that eleven out of eighteen newly independent or created CEE countries chose to establish an environmental ministry within the first three years of national sovereignty (Figure 6).

On the one hand, this surge can apparently be interpreted as a result of the political transformation processes in CEE since 1989. On the other hand, the management of other challenges, such as economic and democratic

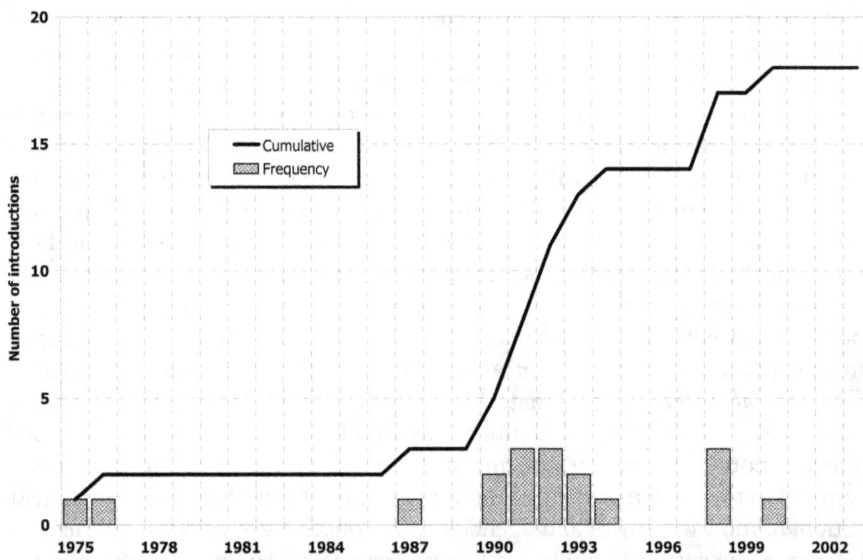

Figure 6 International spread of environmental agencies in CEE countries
Source: Own data.

development, was certainly more urgent by that time. Moreover, financial resources were scarce and many countries lacked the political and administrative capacities for the creation of new bureaucracies. Against this background, it is even more striking that, in a comparably short period of time, a large number of governments in CEE decided to set up environmental ministries. This behaviour suggests that governments in CEE may have felt the need to conform to international normative pressure to address environmental issues. By creating environmental ministries policy-makers evidently signalled to the world that they take environmental challenges seriously and match the normative expectations arising from the world environment regime. Environmental protection, symbolized through the creation of environmental ministries, had become taken for granted as an essential element of responsible governance.

Altogether, the creation of environmental ministries and agencies can thus be attributed to a significant degree to mechanisms of policy diffusion.

The promotion of renewable electricity

Governments utilize a broad range of instruments for increasing the use of renewable energy sources in electricity generation. However, two instruments stand out in the policy debate: feed-in tariffs and quotas. The following analysis compares the international spread of these two instruments.

Feed-in tariffs oblige network operators, energy traders or consumers to buy electricity generated from renewables and to pay a fixed price. By 2003, eighteen European countries had introduced feed-in tariffs, whereas no non-European countries had adopted this policy innovation (Figure 7).

Quotas for renewable electricity predominantly target energy producers by defining a minimum share of electricity to be generated from renewables. National regulators require these actors to acquire a sufficient quantity of certificates which are issued in exchange for a specified amount of renewable electricity. Either energy producers acquire these certificates by actually producing electricity from renewables or they purchase surplus certificates from other energy producers whose production exceeds their minimum share. Non-complying actors with an insufficient number of certificates are fined. By 2003, ten countries had introduced quotas, eight of which were members of the EU (Figure 7).

The international spread of feed-in tariffs and quotas was driven neither by mechanisms of harmonization nor imposition. Rather, the analysis of both processes points to an important role of diffusion mechanisms during the instruments' spread.

In the case of feed-in tariffs, diffusion was mainly restricted to individual cases of horizontal learning and emulation. In particular, the German regulations became a policy model for many other countries. In Switzerland, Austria, France, Greece and the Czech Republic policy-makers were inspired by the German feed-in tariff and drew on this model when designing their own

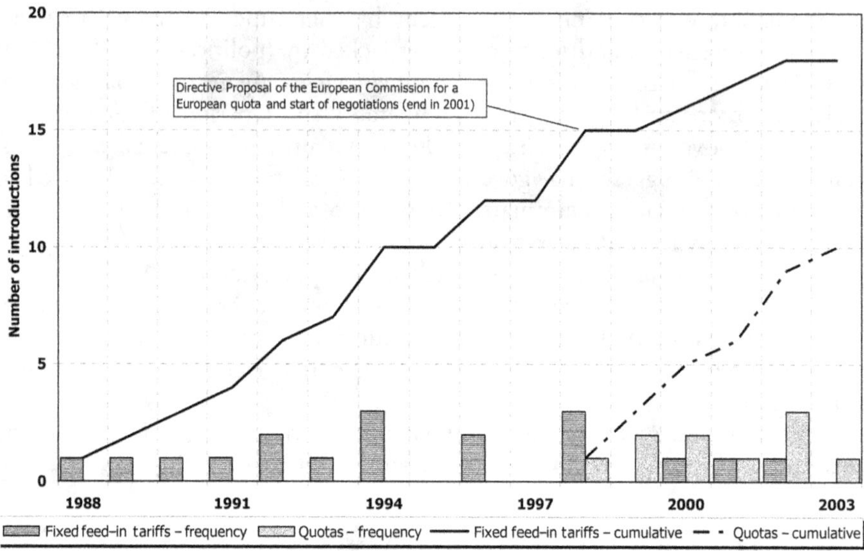

Figure 7 Spread of feed-in tariffs and quotas for renewable electricity
Source: Own data.

national regulations (Busch 2003; Busch and Jörgens 2005b). These governments, as well as others, systematically searched for policies already implemented elsewhere before deciding upon their own ways of promoting the generation of electricity from renewables. The French government, for example, drew on an analysis of various policy instruments for the promotion of renewable electricity in six European countries. The explicit aim of this study commissioned by the French government was to identify successful policies which were transferable to the French context (Cochet 2000).

In the case of quotas, the flow of information about this instrument was institutionalized at the international level. In particular, the intention of the European Commission to harmonize the promotion of renewable electricity contributed to this institutionalization. The Commission made it very clear that it would prefer quotas as a model for harmonizing regulations for the generation of electricity from renewables. In a working paper published in 1998 the Commission writes: '[T]he move from a tariff approach towards one based on trade and competition [i.e. quotas and renewable energy certificates trade] is at some stage inevitable' (European Commission 1998: 17). The Commission, moreover, funded several research projects examining the implications of a European-wide introduction of quotas as well as the conditions for their successful implementation. The Renewable Energy Certificate (REC) System – an organization which aimed to establish an institutional framework that allows for the European-wide introduction and operation of quotas – was financially supported by the Commission (Busch 2003). Accordingly, the European

Commission drafted and presented a directive in 1998 demanding the prohibition of feed-in tariffs and the introduction of quotas.[7] Lauber argues that the Commission's preference affected several national decisions to introduce a quota: '[I]n the preparation of the EU directive, several states prepared ... [quota] systems at the domestic level, on the assumption that this was the best market approach and with the expectation that a European market for RECs would develop in the near future' (Lauber 2001: 8) A concrete example of this strategy is Denmark (see Meyer 2003).

Strikingly, in the very year when the Commission stated its preference and quotas started to spread, the annual average of introductions of feed-in tariffs decreased (1.4 from 1988 to 1998 and 0.6 from 1999 to 2003) (Figure 7). If decisions to abolish feed-in tariffs are taken into account, this decrease is even more significant (Figure 8). Poland and Italy replaced their feed-in tariffs with a quota. Denmark and Sweden plan to abolish their feed-in tariffs once the already adopted quotas are operating properly (Busch and Jörgens 2005b). Denmark made this shift because it expected quotas to become the standard in the EU (Meyer 2003).

These observations suggest that the international institutionalization of information flows driving the spread of quotas may have slowed the spread of the competing instrument of feed-in tariffs which was driven by diffusion as well, but characterized by direct and horizontal processes of emulation and learning between countries. However, institutionalized diffusion and the presentation of a draft harmonization directive by the European Commission alone cannot account for these effects. Other developments at the international level

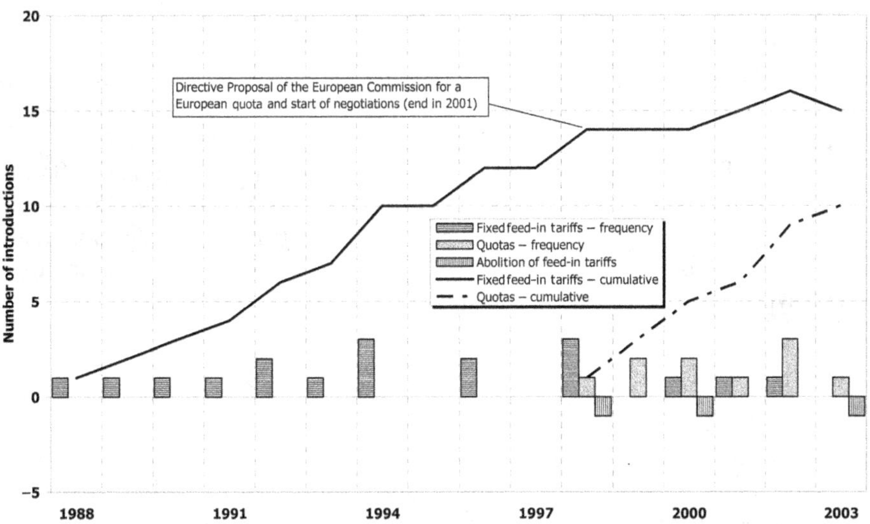

Figure 8 International spread of feed-in tariffs and quotas for renewable electricity
Source: Own data.

created political and legal uncertainties about the future of feed-in tariffs, possibly hampering their spread even more. In 1998, the European Parliament had rejected a Europe-wide introduction of feed-in tariffs. In the same year German energy companies had brought an action against the German feed-in tariff at the European Court of Justice which was eventually decided in 2001. Finally, in Brussels quotas were perceived to better fulfil market and competition rules. With the liberalization of the European internal market for electricity, this assessment increasingly gained importance as an evaluation criterion for national energy policies (Busch and Jörgens 2005b).

CONCLUSIONS

The conceptual distinction and empirical analysis support the claim that diffusion constitutes a class of convergence mechanisms in its own right. When seeking to understand policy convergence conceptually and empirically, neglecting diffusion risks overlooking a distinct and important type of convergence mechanism.

From a conceptual angle, it became evident that diffusion involves processes other than harmonization, imposition or the accidental accumulation of independent domestic reactions to identical problems or structural changes. The empirical findings demonstrate that it is necessary to distinguish between different groups of convergence mechanisms. It could be shown that policy convergence evolves not only as a result of harmonization or imposition. Nor can policy convergence be reduced to an accidental accumulation of independent domestic reactions to identical problems or structural changes. A reduction to these mechanisms and sources in empirical analyses of policy convergence risks overlooking processes of cross-national emulation and learning and their impact on policy convergence. The empirical analysis has thus shown that mechanisms of diffusion were important when accounting for policy convergence and could be observed in all cases.

Addresses for correspondence: Per-Olof Busch, Freie Universität Berlin, Environmental Policy Research Centre, Ihnestraße 22, 14195 Berlin, Germany. Tel: +49 (0) 30 838 544 93. Fax: +49 (0) 30 838 566 85. email: pelle@zedat.fu-berlin.de/Helge Jörgens, The German Advisory Council on the Environment, Reichpietschufer 60, 10785 Berlin, Germany. Tel: +49 (0) 30 263 696 111. Fax: +49 (0) 30 263 696 109. email: helge.joergens@uba.de

ACKNOWLEDGEMENTS

This article is based on findings from a research project on the Diffusion of Environmental Policy Innovations as an Aspect of the Globalization of Environmental Policy which has been financed by the German Volkswagen Foundation. We would like to thank Christoph Knill and Volker Schneider for detailed and very helpful comments on earlier versions of this article. We also thank the participants of the preparatory workshop on 23 and 24 April in Hamburg for their constructive criticism and helpful suggestions.

NOTES

1 The research on harmonization of policies forms an important element in the study of international co-operation and regimes which has been central to international relations (Simmons and Martin 2002; Kratochvil and Ruggie 1986; Rochester 1986; Hasenclever *et al.* 1997; Levy *et al.* 1995; Haggard and Simmons 1987). Within the European context extensive research has been conducted by the European Union (EU) to analyse the impact of supranational regulations on domestic policy-making (Kohler-Koch and Eising 1999; Kohler-Koch, 2003; Scharpf 1999).

2 Other related notions can be found in the literature: Dolowitz and Marsh (2000: 14–15) use the term 'coercive transfer', Bennett's notion of 'penetration' is quite similar to imposition (1991a: 227–9) and Ikenberry speaks of 'external inducement' (1990: 99–101). Imposition has been studied most extensively in the realm of development aid (Keohane and Levy 1996; Nelson 1996; Nelson and Eglinton 1993; Olson 1979; Mosley *et al.* 1995). More recently, an increasing number of studies analyse imposition in connection with the enlargement of the EU to Central and Eastern European (CEE) countries, such as the special issue of the *Journal of European Public Policy* on 'External Governance in the European Union' (see Schimmelfennig and Wagner 2004; Schimmelfenning and Sedelmeier 2004; see also Grabbe 2002; Tews 2002b). For historical examples, see Dolowitz and Marsh (1996, 2000); Stone (1999).

3 Australia, Austria, Belgium, Canada, Denmark, Finland, France, Germany, Greece, Iceland, Ireland, Italy, Japan, Korea, Luxembourg, the Netherlands, New Zealand, Norway, Portugal, Spain, Sweden, Switzerland, Turkey, the United Kingdom and the USA.

4 Albania, Belarus, Bosnia Herzegovina, Bulgaria, Croatia, the Czech Republic, Estonia, Hungary, Latvia, Lithuania, Macedonia, Moldova, Poland, Romania, Russia, the Slovak Republic, Slovenia and Ukraine.

5 The major criteria are that policy innovations have to be of nation-wide scope (i.e. regional or state policies are not counted) and that they have to be adopted formally by governmental or parliamentary decision.

6 The reason why not all adoptions of national sustainable development strategies are reflected in the proliferation curve in Figure 3 is that many countries had already adopted an environmental strategy at an earlier time, and only this first national adoption of an environmental strategy is shown in the graph.

7 Owing to the resistance in particular of the German and Spanish governments this draft was not agreed upon. In September 2001 the European Commission finally adopted a framework directive leaving the decision on which policy should be implemented to the national governments until 2012.

REFERENCES

Abbott, K.W. and Snidal, D. (2000) 'Hard and soft law in international governance', *International Organization* 54(3): 421–56.

Abbott, K.W., Keohane, R.O., Moravcsik, A., Slaughter, A.-M. and Snidal, D. (2000) 'The concept of legislation', *International Organization* 54(3): 401–19.

Bennett, C.J. (1988) 'Different processes, one result: the convergence of data protection policies in Europe and the United States', *Governance: An International Journal of Policy and Administration* 1: 162–83.

Bennett, C.J. (1991a) 'How states utilize foreign evidence', *Journal of Public Policy* 11: 31–54.

Bennett, C.J. (1991b) 'What is policy convergence and what causes it?', *British Journal of Political Science* 21: 215–33.

Bennett, C.J. (1997) 'Understanding ripple effects: the cross-national adoption of policy instruments for bureaucratic accountability', *Governance: An International Journal of Policy and Administration* 10(3): 213–33.

Berry, F.S. and Berry, W.D. (1999) 'Innovation and diffusion models in policy research', in P.A. Sabatier (ed.), *Theories of the Policy Process*, Boulder, CO: Westview Press, pp. 169–200.

Busch, P.-O. (2003) 'Die Diffusion von Einspeisevergütungen und Quotenmodellen: Konkurrenz der Modelle in Europa' [The diffusion of fixed feed-in tariffs and quotas: competition of models in Europe], FFU-report 03–2003, Berlin: Environmental Policy Research Centre.

Busch, P.-O. and Jörgens, H. (2005a) 'International patterns of environmental policy change and convergence', *European Environment* 15(2): 80–101.

Busch, P.-O. and Jörgens, H. (2005b) 'Globale Ausbreitungsmuster umweltpolitischer Innovationen' [Global patterns of the international spread of environmental policy innovations], FFU-report 02–2005, Berlin: Environmental Policy Research Centre.

Busch, P.-O., Jörgens, H. and Tews, K. (2005) 'The global diffusion of regulatory instruments: the making of a new international environmental regime', *The Annals of the American Academy of Political and Social Science* 598 (March 2005): 146–66.

Cochet, Y. (2000) 'Rapport au Premier ministre: Stratégie et moyens de développement de l'efficacité énergétique et des sources d'énergie renouvelables en France', Paris.

Connolly, B. and Gutner, T. (2002) 'Policy networks and process diffusion: organizational innovation within the "Europe for Environment" network'. Unpublished manuscript.

DiMaggio, P.J. and Powell, W.W. (1983) 'The iron cage revisited: institutional isomorphism and collective rationality in organizational fields', *American Sociological Review* 48(2): 147–60.

Dolowitz, D. and Marsh, D. (1996) 'Who learns what from whom: a review of the policy transfer literature', *Political Studies* 44(2): 343–57.

Dolowitz, D. and Marsh, D. (2000) 'Learning from abroad: the role of policy transfer in contemporary policy making', *Governance: An International Journal of Policy and Administration* 13(1): 5–24.

Drezner, D.W. (2001) 'Globalization and policy convergence', *International Studies Review* 3: 53–78.

Elkins, Z. and Simmons, B. (2005) 'On waves, clusters and diffusion: a conceptual framework', *The Annals of the American Academy of Political and Social Science* 598 (March 2005): 33–51.

European Commission (1998) 'Electricity from renewable energy sources and the internal electricity market', Brussels: European Commission.

Eyestone, R. (1977) 'Confusion, diffusion and innovation', *American Political Science Review* 71(2): 441–7.

Finnemore, M. (1993) 'International organizations as teachers of norms. The United Nations Educational, Scientific, and Cultural Organization and science policy', *International Organization* 47(4): 565–97.

Finnemore, M. (1996) 'Norms, culture, and world politics: insights from sociology's institutionalism', *International Organization* 50(2): 325–48.

Finnemore, M. and Sikkink, K. (1998) 'International norm dynamics and political change', *International Organization* 52(4): 887–917.

Gilardi, F. (2005) 'The institutional foundations of regulatory capitalism: the diffusion of independent regulatory agencies in Western Europe', *The Annals of the American Academy of Political and Social Science* 598 (March 2005): 84–101.

Grabbe, H. (2002) 'European conditionality and the *acquis communautaire*', *International Political Science Review* 23(3): 249–68.

Gray, V. (1973) 'Innovations in the state: a diffusion study', *American Political Science Review* 67(4): 1174–85.

Haas, P.M. (2002) 'UN conferences and constructivist governance of the environment', *Global Governance: A Review of Multilateralism and International Organizations* 8: 73–91.

Haggard, S. and Simmons, B.A. (1987) 'Theories of international regimes', *International Organization* 41(3): 491–517.

Hasenclever, A., Mayer, P. and Rittberger, V. (1997) *Theories of International Regimes*, Cambridge, UK: Cambridge University Press.

Hedström, P. and Swedberg, R. (eds) (1998) *Social Mechanisms. An Analytical Approach to Social Theory*, Cambridge: Cambridge University Press.

Heichel, S., Pape, J. and Sommerer, T. (2005) 'Is there convergence in convergence research? An overview of empirical studies on policy convergence', *Journal of European Public Policy* 12(5): 817–40.

Holzinger, K. and Knill, C. (2005) 'Causes and conditions of cross-national policy convergence', *Journal of European Public Policy* 12(5): 775–96.

Howlett, M. (2000) 'Beyond legalism? Policy ideas, implementation styles and emulation based convergence in Canadian and U.S. environmental policy', *Journal of Public Policy* 20(3): 305–29.

Ikenberry, J.G. (1990) 'The international spread of privatization policies: inducement, learning, and policy-bandwaggoning', in E.N. Suleiman and J. Waterbury (eds), *The Political Economy of Public Sector Reform and Privatization*, Boulder, Colo.: Westview Press.

Jänicke, M. and Jörgens, H. (1998) 'National environmental policy planning in OECD countries: preliminary lessons from cross-national comparisons', *Environmental Politics* 7(2): 27–54.

Jordana, J. and Levi-Faur, D. (2005) 'The diffusion of regulatory capitalism in Latin America: sectoral and national channels in the making of a new order', *The Annals of the American Academy of Political and Social Science* 598 (March 2005): 102–24.

Jörgens, H. (1996) 'Die Institutionalisierung von Umweltpolitik im internationalen Vergleich' [The institutionalization of environmental policy: an international comparison], in M. Jänicke (ed.), *Die Umweltpolitik der Industrieländer. Entwicklung – Bilanz – Erfolgsbedingungen. [Environmental Policies in Industrialized Countries]*, Berlin: Edition Sigma, pp. 59–111.

Jörgens, H. (2004) 'Governance by diffusion – implementing global norms through cross-national imitation and learning', in W.M. Lafferty (ed.), *Governance for Sustainable Development. The Challenge of Adapting Form to Function*, Cheltenham: Edward Elgar Publishing, pp. 246–83.

Keck, M.E. and Sikkink, K. (1998) *Activists Beyond Borders*, Ithaca, NY: Cornell University Press.

Keohane, R.O. and Levy, M.A. (eds) (1996) *Institutions for Environmental Aid: Pitfalls and Promise*, Cambridge, Mass.: MIT Press.

Kern, K., Jörgens, H. and Jänicke, M. (2001) 'The diffusion of environmental policy innovations: a contribution to the globalization of environmental policy', WZB Discussion Paper FS II 01–302, Berlin: Social Science Research Centre.

Knill, C. (2005) 'Introduction: Cross-national policy convergence: concepts, approaches and explanatory factors', *Journal of European Public Policy* 12(5): 764–74.

Kohler-Koch, B. (ed.) (2003) *Linking EU and National Governance*, Oxford: Oxford University Press.

Kohler-Koch, B. and Eising, R. (eds) (1999) *The Transformation of Governance in the European Union*, London: Routledge.

Kratochvil, F. and Ruggie, J.G. (1986) 'International organization: a state of the art on an art of state', *International Organization* 40(4): 753–75.

Küppers, G., Lundgreen, P. and Weingart, P. (1978) *Umweltforschung – die gesteuerte Wissenschaft? Eine empirische Studie zum Verhältnis von Wissenschaftsentwicklung und Wissenschaftspolitik*, Frankfurt am Main: Suhrkamp.

Lauber, V. (2001) 'The different concepts of promoting RES-electricity and their political careers', in F. Biermann, R. Brohm and K. Dingwerth (eds), *2001 Berlin Conference on the Human Dimensions of Global Change – Global Environmental Change and the Nation State*, Potsdam: Potsdam Institute for Climate Impact Research, pp. 296–304.

Lazer, D. (2005) 'Regulatory capitalism as a networked order: the international system as an informational network', *The Annals of the American Academy of Political and Social Science* 598 (March 2005): 52–66.

Levi-Faur, D. (2005) 'The global diffusion of regulatory capitalism', *The Annals of the American Academy of Political and Social Science* 598 (March 2005): 12–34.

Levi-Faur, D. and Jordana, J. (2005) 'Preface: The making of a new regulatory order', *The Annals of the American Academy of Political and Social Science* 598 (March 2005): 6–9.

Levy, M.A., Young, O.R. and Zürn, M. (1995) 'The study of international regimes', *European Journal of International Relations* 1(3): 267–330.

Markus, M.L. (1987) 'Towards a "critical mass" theory of interactive media: universal access, interdependence and diffusion', *Communication Research* 14: 491–511.

Martin, L. and Simmons, B. (1998) 'Theories and empirical studies of international institutions', *International Organization* 52(4): 729–57.

Mayntz, R. (2004) 'Mechanisms in the analysis of social macro-phenomena', *Philosophy of the Social Sciences* 34: 237–59.

Meseguer, C. and Gilardi, F. (2005) 'What is new in the study of policy diffusion? A critical review'. Paper presented at the 46th Annual Convention of the International Studies Association, 1–5 March 2005 Honolulu, Hawaii, USA.

Meyer, J.W., Frank, D.J., Hironaka, A., Schofer, E. and Tuma, N.B. (1997) 'The structuring of a world environment regime, 1870–1990', *International Organization* 51(4): 623–51.

Meyer, N.I. (2003) 'European schemes for promoting renewables in liberalised markets', *Energy Policy* 31: 665–76.

Mosley, P., Harrigan, J. and Toye, J. (1995) *Aid and Power: The World Bank and Policy Based Lending*, London and New York: Routledge.

Nelson, J.M. (1996) 'Promoting policy reforms: the twilight of conditionality?', *World Development* 24(9): 1551–9.

Nelson, J.M. and Eglinton, S. (1993) *Global Goals, Contentious Means*, Washington, D.C.: Overseas Development Council.

OECD (1998) 'Evaluation of progress in developing and implementing national environmental action programmes (NEAPs) in Central and Eastern Europe and the new independent states', Paris: OECD.

Olson, R.S. (1979) 'Economic coercion in world politics: with a focus on north-south relations', *World Politics* 31(4): 471–94.

Orenstein, M.A. (2003) 'Mechanisms of diffusion. An interdisciplinary review'. Paper presented to the American Political Science Association Annual Meeting, Philadelphia, 28–31 August 2003.
Padgett, S. (2003) 'Between synthesis and emulation: EU policy transfer in the power sector', *Journal of European Public Policy* 10(2): 227–45.
Pleschberger, W. (1999) 'The national environmental plan of Austria – a lesson to learn in environmental policy?', in P. Glück, G. Oesten, H. Schanz and K.-R. Volz (eds), *Formulation and Implementation of National Forest Programmes: Theoretical Aspects*, Joensu: European Forest Institute, pp. 215–27.
Rochester, J.M. (1986) 'The rise and fall of international organization as a field of study', *International Organization* 40(4): 777–813.
Rogers, E. (2003) *Diffusion of Innovations*, New York: Free Press.
Rose, R. (1991) 'What is lesson-drawing?', *Journal of Public Policy* 11(1): 3–30.
Scharpf, F.W. (1999) *Governing in Europe*, Oxford: Oxford University Press.
Schimmelfennig, F. and Sedelmeier, U. (2004) 'Governance by conditionality: EU rule transfer to the candidate countries of Central and Eastern Europe', *Journal of European Public Policy* 11(4): 661–79.
Schimmelfennig, F. and Wagner, W. (2004) 'Preface: External governance in the European Union', *Journal of European Public Policy* 11(4): 657–60.
Simmons, B. and Elkins, Z. (2004) 'The globalization of liberalization: policy diffusion in the international political economy', *American Political Science Review* 98(1): 171–89.
Simmons, B. and Martin, L.L. (2002) 'International organizations and institutions', in W. Carlsnaes, T. Risse and B. Simmons (eds), *Handbook of International Relations*, London: Sage Publications.
Stone, D. (1999) 'Learning lessons and transferring policy across time, space and disciplines', *Politics* 19(1): 51–9.
Tews, K. (2002) 'Politiktransfer: phänomen zwischen policy-lernen und oktroi. Überlegungen zu unfreiwilligen umweltpolitikimporten am beispiel der EU-osterweiterung', *Zeitschrift für Umweltpolitik & Umweltrecht*, 25(2): 173–201.
Tews, K. (2005) 'The diffusion of environmental policy innovations: cornerstones of an analytical framework', *European Environment* 15(2): 63–79.
Tilly, C. (2001) 'Mechanisms in political processes', *Annual Review of Political Science* 4: 21–41.
Tolba, M., El-Kholy, O.A., El-Hinnawi, E., Holdgate, M.W., McMichael, D.F. and Munn, R.E. (1995) *The World Environment 1972–1992. Two Decades of Challenges*, London: Chapman & Hall.
Walker, J.L. (1969) 'The diffusion of innovations among American states', *American Political Science Review* 63(3): 880–99.
Way, C. (2005) 'Political insecurity and the diffusion of financial market regulation', *The Annals of the American Academy of Political and Social Science* 598 (March 2005): 125–44.

Climate policy convergence in Europe: an assessment based on National Communications to the UNFCCC

Johan Albrecht and Bas Arts

1. INTRODUCTION

The climate change issue is a complex, so-called 'unstructured' policy problem (Dunn 1994). There is disagreement among stakeholders concerning the status of climate science and the underlying values as well as the opportunities for policy intervention. The Intergovernmental Panel on Climate Change (IPCC), the scientific body that supports the current climate change regime, stated in 1996 that the balance of evidence suggests that a human-induced climate change is occurring, although many uncertainties remain. The so-called 'sceptics' challenge this view (Boehmer-Christiansen 1994; IPCC 2001) and focus on the unreliability of climate models, the invalid generalizations and extrapolations of climate data, and alternative theories to explain global warming. In addition, there is wide disagreement on values (Gupta *et al.* 2003). Different stakeholders – industrialized countries, developing countries, industrial groups and non-governmental organizations – start from different 'value systems' on the basis of which they promote or put into critical perspective the need to protect the climate system. The main contradiction in this perspective is the one between economic and ecological values, both mobilized by different interests.

Yet, an impressive international regime on climate change has emerged, involving over 190 countries (Grubb *et al.* 1999; Mintzer and Leonard 1994; UNFCCC 2003). This regime was established by the 1992 United Nations Framework Convention on Climate Change (UNFCCC) and the subsequent Kyoto Protocol of 1997. Although the goal of the Kyoto Protocol was to increase the ecological effectiveness of the existing climate policy, it resulted in a problematic divide. Because of the rejection of the Protocol by the US, as a result of the unanimous acceptance of the Byrd-Hagel resolution by the US Senate which condemned the lack of meaningful participation of developing countries, as well as the lengthy hesitation by Russia, it took eight years for the 1997 Kyoto Protocol to come into force (16 February 2005).

Although the UNFCCC and the Kyoto Protocol are legally binding, a high degree of flexibility is offered to individual countries. Policy-relevant national circumstances can strongly influence greenhouse gas emission patterns and mitigation options, whereas differences in climate change vulnerability will shape future national adaptation strategies. Consequently, significant institutional flexibility with respect to national policy targets, obligations, and policies and measures is essential.

Based on information from three rounds of National Communications of industrialized countries to the UNFCCC, in which they report their climate policy strategies between 1994 and 2002, we present a quantitative analysis of the development of climate policies and measures in European countries. This overview is used to explore different concepts of climate policy convergence among European Union (EU) countries. We clearly distinguish between 'output' and 'outcome' convergence. For the *explanation* of convergence, we adhere to the explanatory scheme in the introduction to this special issue. This scheme consists of international, domestic and policy-specific causes. We focus on the first group – international causes – to assess possible climate policy convergence, especially since climate policy was launched as an international issue right from the start. In addition, we also consider domestic factors, particularly to explain variation and divergence in climate policies and measures.

Introducing an effective climate policy requires the involvement of as many stakeholders as possible and this is clearly a unique policy challenge. Given the essential role of stakeholder interactions in the development of climate policy, we opted to integrate into our analysis Jepperson's (2002) taxonomy of institutional logics in national political systems. This taxonomy explicitly refers to the role of corporations and associations in policy processes.

The paper contains the following sections. In section 2, we present an overview of the international climate change regime. This is followed by a section on the concept, assessment and explanation of policy convergence, as framed in this paper (section 3). Subsequently, we present our results on climate policy convergence in Europe (section 4), after which we finalize the paper with an explanatory and a concluding section (sections 5 and 6 respectively).

2. THE CLIMATE CHANGE REGIME

The climate regime is characterized by a number of core elements. First, Article 2 of the UNFCCC defines the ultimate goal of the climate regime: 'the stabilization of the atmospheric concentration of greenhouse gases at levels which avoid a dangerous interference with the climate system' (UNFCCC 1992). Since this stabilization goal is not yet clearly defined, as scientists disagree on what 'safe levels' of atmospheric greenhouse gas concentrations are, climate policy in developed countries is mainly directed at *mitigation* policies and measures that can slow down the increase of global emissions, in order to delay the increase of atmospheric concentration levels.

The second substantive core element of the climate regime relates to quantitative and binding targets for anthropogenic greenhouse gas emissions in developed countries. The binding targets have been established in Annex B of the Kyoto Protocol (Grubb *et al.* 1999; Oberthür and Ott 1999; Rolfe 1998; UNFCCC 1998). For most Annex B countries, these caps generally imply *reduction* targets compared to the level of emissions in 1990 (for example, −8 per cent for the EU, −7 per cent for the US and −5 per cent for Japan), whereas other countries need to stabilize their emissions at the 1990 level or are even allowed to increase their emissions under the current climate regime (e.g. Australia can increase its emissions by 8 per cent). Annex B countries need to realize their national targets in the commitment period 2008–2012.

Thirdly, the climate regime contains a number of guidelines for the parties to formulate domestic policies and measures (or PAMs). Article 4 of the UNFCCC and Article 2 of the Kyoto Protocol include references to PAMs to mitigate a possible climate change (reductions of greenhouse gas emissions due to increased energy efficiency levels, sustainable energy structures, sustainable agriculture, the elimination of market imperfections and adverse state subsidies) or adapt to the possible consequences of climate change. Although the *design* of climate PAMs is obligatory under the current climate regime, specific types and specific substances of PAMs are not prescribed. Hence, parties are free to select and implement a certain set of PAMs at the national level.

Finally, Article 12 of the UNFCCC states that all parties are obliged to regularly communicate to the Conference of Parties (CoP) – the main institutional body of the regime – detailed information on their national climate policy. This includes, according to the reporting guidelines, a national inventory of anthropogenic emissions and a description of steps taken or planned by the party to comply with the commitments under the UNFCCC. In addition, industrialized countries – or *Annex I countries* – should provide a detailed description of PAMs, together with a specific estimate of the effects of these.

3. POLICY CONVERGENCE: CONCEPT, ASSESSMENT, EXPLANATION

Concept

Internationalization processes, such as globalization and Europeanization, are often assumed to imply processes of convergence among countries, although not by definition (Drezner 2001; Knill 2001). Nor can we speak of a *general* phenomenon, as countries remain different in several characteristics as well, despite the globalized world we live in. Yet different national political, economic and social institutions may become more similar over time, due to mechanisms such as adaptation pressure from international organizations and agreements, market integration, transnational communication, transboundary diffusion of ideas and mutual learning (Holzinger and Knill 2005; Jordan and Liefferink 2004). These observations also hold for policy-making, including environmental policy (Bennett 1991; Weale 1992). Policy convergence is generally defined as 'the tendency of policies to grow more alike, in the form of increasing similarity in structures, processes and performances' (Kerr, cited in Drezner 2001: 53). 'Structures' in this definition refer to administrative organizations and rules, 'processes' to agenda-setting and policy-making, and 'performances' to policy outputs and policy outcomes. All three dimensions – structures, processes, performances – may be more or less subject to convergence processes.

This paper presents an analysis based on National Communications (NCs) to the UNFCCC and focuses on the last dimension, namely convergence in *performance.* Obviously, national policies are formulated as a national response to the obligations of the international climate policy regime.

In dealing with policy performances, we make the commonly used distinction between 'policy outputs' and 'policy outcomes' (based on Dunn 1994; Knill and Lenschow 2000; Van Steertegem 2003). *Outputs* cover the launching of PAMs as well as the organization and mobilization of resources to execute these. *Outcomes,* on the other hand, refer to the effects of these PAMs in terms of goal-achievement. As stated in the above, both outputs and outcomes – as aspects of policy performance – can be subject to convergence. Then 'output convergence', as we call it, refers to the extent to which (climate) PAMs as well as (climate) policy instruments of different countries grow more alike over time, and 'outcome convergence' refers to the extent to which these PAMs of different countries produce ever more similar effects in terms of goal-achievement and problem-solving (see Table 1).

Table 1 Conceptual framework of this paper

Concept	*Dimensions*
Output convergence	Policies and measures: similarity grows over time
Outcome convergence	Effects of policies and measures: similarity grows over time

It should be noted that we are able to present an *ex-post* analysis of output convergence in this paper, as countries started to adopt PAMs in about 1994 (when the UNFCCC entered into force). However, with respect to outcome convergence, this is not possible, as the *effects* of these PAMs will only be known by the end of the commitment period 2008–2012. Hence, we are dealing with *future projections* of policy effects over here. Such *ex-ante* analyses are characterized by many uncertainties. Moreover, countries have used different methodologies to calculate their emission projections and the future effects of their PAMs. Also, most of them negotiated as soft targets for themselves as possible. In other words, we are dealing with self-selected targets and self-projected future emissions and policy effects in the case of outcome convergence in this paper, so we should be careful not to draw too easy conclusions.

Assessment

Now that we have defined the key concepts, the question is how to operationalize these. Firstly, the (possible) increase of similarity among PAMs – output convergence – will be assessed on the basis of the reported PAMs in different sectors (like transport, industry and energy) in the three NCs which each country involved published over time. Secondly, the (possible) increase of similarity in the *effects* of PAMs – outcome convergence – will be assessed on the basis of: (a) checking whether ever more countries foresee being able to realize their mitigation targets over time, and (b) calculating the 'policy gap' for each country, on the basis of their Kyoto target and projected future emissions, including the effects of their (additional) PAMs. As already mentioned, our assessment of outcome convergence is restricted to an *ex-ante* analysis based on self-selected targets and self-projected future emissions and policy effects, which will put our conclusions on outcome convergence in a certain perspective (see next section). In total, the NCs of twenty-three European countries were analysed (listed in Table 5). However, not every European country published three NCs.

Explanation

With respect to policy convergence, we apply the explanatory scheme of the introduction to this special issue (see also Bennett 1991; Drezner 2001;

Holzinger and Knill 2005; Jordan and Liefferink 2004). This scheme consists of international causes, domestic causes and policy-specific causes for policy convergence. As climate policy is of international origin, we will concentrate on the first category of international causes below. Within this category, four mechanisms to understand policy convergence are distinguished: *imposition* (forced by states or international organizations on other states), *international harmonization* (binding international and supranational law), *regulatory competition* (adaptation of regulation into a similar direction due to international market pressure) and *transnational communication* (collective learning in international organizations). However, this paper also touches upon *outcome* convergence. To explain this type of convergence, one cannot make use of the same explanatory scheme as for output convergence, because – as Holzinger and Knill (2005) note – outcomes are only *indirectly* related to outputs. Outputs are poor predictors of outcomes, as any implementation process is affected by many intervening variables.

For in so far as the international mechanisms to explain *output* convergence fall short, we will focus on domestic factors too. It should be stressed that we are dealing with a heterogeneous group of European countries in our sample. Institutionally, these countries differ widely. To theorize about a wide group of countries, we use Jepperson's (2002) taxonomy of institutional logics in national political systems.

This taxonomy is based on two dimensions: 'collective action' and 'organization of society'. The first dimension distinguishes between 'society-centric' and 'state-centric' collective agency. In state-centric societies, governments steer and guide society 'from above', while deriving authority from the state. Such a government may even decide to build a new nuclear plant, while an overwhelming majority of the population is strongly against it. In society-centric politics, citizens and action groups have much more access to decision-makers and well-organized action groups can launch new policy issues quite easily. For example, the unexpected problems with genetically modified organisms (GMOs) in Europe are the result of effective campaigning by interest groups in open societies such as the United Kingdom. It is not a coincidence that mainly in the US the scientific uncertainties with respect to climate change dominate the public debate. Several well-structured interest groups did elaborate and diffuse this issue of scientific uncertainty in a fragmented issue-focused political landscape.

With respect to the 'organization of society', Jepperson (2002) distinguishes between 'associational' and 'corporatist' dimensions. In associational societies, new partnerships might suddenly emerge to reflect new interests. A typical example of an associational organization in the context of climate policy is a new federation of small producers of renewable energy which presents its views to decision-makers. Corporatism, in contrast, construes collective action on an inclusive basis among functionally and hierarchically defined groups. With corporatism, the same federation of renewable energy will face high barriers around decision-makers. This taxonomy, based on Jepperson (2002), is presented in Table 2. For comparable taxonomies, we refer to Self (1985), Van Esch (2001) and Van Tatenhove *et al.* (2000).

This taxonomy is of great relevance for climate policy. Climate policy convergence ultimately deals with convergence patterns in the reorganization of societies. This type of reorganization/transformation takes a long time before it can be observed. Climate policy requires the definition and implementation of a clear and future-oriented low-carbon societal project. This goal touches upon many different interests and the interaction between states, industries, decision-makers and interest groups will shape the evolution of climate policy. The taxonomy shows that the chances for a strong take-off of climate policy depend most of all on the ability to organize interest groups in favour of climate policy. Once these interest groups are legitimized by the state – a process that will take some time – the prospect of developing climate policy becomes more attractive, especially when the state acts as a facilitator. However, once enough interest groups defend the transition to a low-carbon society in liberal-pluralist societies with an adaptive policy process, a general consensus can suddenly emerge to tackle the climate challenge. Of crucial importance, of course, is the commitment by government to safeguard

Table 2 National political institutions

Organization of society/collective action	*Societal*	*Statist*
Corporate	*Social-corporatist* Interactions among formally organized interests; government is a partner and facilitator; effectiveness and transparency of policy is important. *Example*: Sweden, Denmark	*State-corporatist* Centralized and bureaucratic approach; state legitimizes new societal groups and interests; high state capacity to implement policies. *Example*: Germany, Japan
Associational	*Liberal-pluralist* Dynamic issue-focused policy orientation; weak state and competition among interest groups; open and adaptive political environment. *Example*: US, UK	*State-nation* Co-operation between state and private interests as well as citizens; high state capacity; focus on consensus and risk-minimization. *Example*: France

Source: Based on Jepperson (2002).

vested interests. The recent decision of the British government to set a 60 per cent reduction target for greenhouse gas emissions by the year 2050 is illustrative in this context (DTI 2003). Acceptance of new societal interests can take longer in statist societies, but the presence of a strong state with the ability *and* political will to effectively implement ambitious policies can yield impressive results in the short term.

4. CLIMATE POLICY CONVERGENCE IN EUROPE: RESULTS

Policies and measures

Given the institutional economic constraints on drastic reductions of emissions, national climate policies should consist of measures with immediate, medium-term and long-term impact. After all, the climate policy process does not end with the commitment period of the Kyoto Protocol (2008–2012). The design and development of long-term measures – e.g. changes in energy and electricity structures – are of vital economic interest for each country and hence require careful consideration. We can assume that long-term greenhouse gas mitigation measures fall mainly in the category of planned measures, whereas short-term mitigation measures can already be implemented. In the NCs, *implemented* PAMs, according to the reporting guidelines, need to be distinguished and reported next to *planned* PAMs. However, these guidelines do not distinguish between short-, medium- and long-term PAMs.

The changing nature and development of climate policy can be deduced from a longitudinal analysis of the NCs. Table 3 presents such information, on PAMs as well as on their preconditions. To start with the latter, we find that the number of countries which consider themselves vulnerable to the consequences of climate change increased from twelve in the first NC to nineteen in the third NC. These self-assessments should in principle be reflected in more efforts to implement PAMs to reduce greenhouse gas emissions or to prepare an optimal adaptation to the changing climate. The number of countries which associate an economic cost with the changing climate also increased, from seven in the first round of NCs to thirteen in the third round. The presence of economic costs links financial benefits to national efforts to mitigate greenhouse gas emissions. This implies a more positive cost–benefit assessment of climate PAMs. The fact that ever more countries consider themselves vulnerable to climate change and foresee economic costs as a consequence of climate change could be interpreted as the diffusion of a 'sense of urgency regarding climate change' among the countries involved. Such a 'sense of urgency' is an important precondition for the development of policy.

Table 3 also presents a general overview of the PAMs in the three NCs of the twenty-three European countries in our analysis. The average number of implemented PAMs did increase from eighteen in the first NC to twenty-nine

Table 3 Policies and measures in the National Communications

	NC 1	*NC 2*	*NC 3*
Countries which consider themselves vulnerable to consequences of climate change	12	13	19
Countries which foresee economic costs from climate change	7	7	13
All PAMs (average (standard deviation))	18 (32)	29 (31)	26 (18)
Energy: number of PAMs (average (standard deviation))	7 (17)	11 (18)	9 (12)
Energy: number of *planned* PAMs (average (standard deviation))	10 (14)	9 (13)	6 (6)
Countries distinguishing most important energy PAMs	3 (BUL, GRE, NOR)	6 (POR, FRA, GRE, NOR, SLO, UK)	9 (POR, BUL, EST, FRA, GER, NET, POL, CZE, SLO)
Industry: number of PAMs (average (standard deviation))	3 (5)	3 (5)	4 (4)
Industry: number of *planned* PAMs (average (standard deviation))	3 (3)	4 (4)	4 (4)
Countries distinguishing most important industry PAMs	1 (GRE)	4 (BUL, FRA, GRE, SLO)	8 (POR, FRA, GER, GRE, NET, NOR, POL, CZE)
Transport: number of PAMs (average (standard deviation))	4 (7)	6 (7)	5 (5)
Transport: number of *planned* PAMs (average (standard deviation))	7 (14)	10 (15)	6 (6)
Countries distinguishing most important transport PAMs	2 (GRE, FRA)	5 (BUL, FRA, GRE, SLO, NET)	9 (POR, FRA, GER, GRE, NET, SWI, UK, NOR, POL)

and twenty-six in the second and the third NC respectively. However, the standard deviation for the total number of PAMs is much lower for the third NC, which refers to more emphasis on fewer measures by the countries. A selection process took place in most countries. This can be interpreted as an indication of output convergence based on similar patterns – here selection after the initial exploration of many possible PAMs – in the development of climate PAMs. The countries with the greatest reduction in the number of PAMs between the second and third NCs are Belgium, Germany, Ireland, Slovenia, the Czech Republic, Poland and Sweden. Over the same period, the number of PAMs increased in Bulgaria, Hungary, France, Greece and Switzerland. However, the last three countries reported a low number of PAMs in their second NC, so the increase should be interpreted as moving towards the average number of PAMs.

In addition to this selection process, output convergence is also expressed by the growing similarity of PAMs in sectors like energy, industry and transport. The most important PAMs – fuel switches, energy-efficiency improvements, an increasing reliance on renewable energy, the development of new technologies – are considered by all European countries. What matters, of course, is the real effort to successfully develop these new measures. The NCs, however, provide too little information to assess the latter. The focus on fuel switches and renewable energy should not be a big surprise. The EU goals with respect to the promotion of renewable energy and the increasing share of gas in total energy use have obvious implications for the EU member states.

Table 3 shows that most climate PAMs are taken in the energy sector; on average seven in the first NC, eleven in the second NC and nine in the third NC. The number of planned policies and measures for the energy sector is reduced from ten to six on average. The standard deviation for the planned energy PAMs was fourteen for the first NC, but only six for the third NC. Here again, we touch upon the phenomenon of output convergence, namely the selection of a limited set of key measures, which will be further elaborated on in the future. An important point, however, is that some countries do not distinguish clearly between implemented and planned measures, although this is demanded by the reporting guidelines. According to the guidelines, priority should be given to those PAMs which have the most significant impact. Countries should, therefore, select a set of most important measures. We consider this as an essential requirement and competency, since it is easy to publish an impressive list of PAMs, whereas it is difficult to prioritize and mobilize consensus regarding a core set of PAMs. Therefore, we consider this ability as typical for countries with a relatively high state capacity.

However, Table 3 shows that most countries do not distinguish the most important measures from the less important ones (although their number is increasing over time). Furthermore, when this distinction is made, countries only present very basic descriptions of PAMs, without attaching precise implementation plans and time-frames. The countries which do distinguish, however, are listed in Table 3. It is striking that most of these are 'state-centric' countries, as expected, and several economies in transition are found in this group. The latter are typically not considered as climate policy pioneers, but economic transition also includes modernization of energy structures. Thus, the connection between economic transition and climate policy is obvious for these countries. Bulgaria, for example, lists the reduction of subsidies and the modernization of the electricity sector as the most important energy measures in its third NC. In Estonia, a fuel switch from coal to gas is the most important energy measure. Measures with respect to coal mining and coal-powered plants are a priority for Poland, while the Czech and Slovak Republics focus on energy efficiency and an increase in the installed capacity of renewable energy. The most important energy measures in the third NC of France are additional nuclear investments and investments in co-generation. For Germany, an increase in renewable capacity is top priority. A further diversification of energy structures is the first priority in Portugal, whereas Greece wants to increase the share of natural gas in the energy mix. The Netherlands lists some measures with respect to coal-fired power plants.

The average number of implemented and planned PAMs for industry is surprisingly low in all countries and in all NCs. The low standard deviation suggests that there are no countries with long lists of industrial PAMs. In the third NC, Germany refers to the voluntary agreements with industry as the most important measure. Comprehensive voluntary agreements with strict enforcement procedures are typical of state-corporatist societies. France also mentions voluntary commitments, whereas in Greece and Poland the restructuring of heavy industries is presented as the most important measure. The Czech Republic refers to the implementation of the Integrated Pollution and Prevention Control Directive of the EU as the most important measure.

The average number of implemented PAMs for transport is slightly higher and there are also more PAMs planned for this sector. France foresees technical inspections for light vehicles in its third NC, whereas several countries consider fiscal instruments (Portugal, Germany, Switzerland and the UK). The promotion of public transport is another obvious option and is emphasized by Greece, the UK and the Netherlands. The reduction of implemented and planned PAMs from the second to the third NC can be, again, an indication of a set of 'core' measures, selected for further elaboration in the transport sector. The much lower standard deviation for the number of planned transport PAMs confirms this assumption.

Overall, European countries seem to converge with regard to the selection of a set of 'core' PAMs for energy and transport, the two sectors with relatively low capital–turnover ratios. This selection and prioritization process has mainly taken place in the so-called statist countries. As predicted by theory, these countries have the ability to launch policy initiatives quickly, overruling domestic protest if necessary. However, a comprehensive policy package with respect to industry seems to be much more difficult to establish. This can be the result of differing industrial structures that require country- or group-specific PAMs.

Table 4 National Communications – information on scenarios

	NC 1	*NC 2*	*NC 3*
Countries that include a reference scenario for emissions in their projections	7	12	13
Countries that present all hypotheses and key variables used in the projection models	7	10	13
Countries that include a 'with measures' scenario for emissions in their projections	11	17	16
Countries that include a 'with additional measures' scenario for emissions in their projections	1	5	11
Countries that foresee achieving their mitigation target	11	12	16

Projected effects of policies and measures

In order to assess the future effects of PAMs, information is needed on projected emissions and the models used for these projections by the countries involved. Table 4 includes such information. The number of countries presenting projections for a reference scenario – i.e. a projection of emissions if no climate PAMs are taken or a *business-as-usual scenario* – did increase over the three NCs, but is still rather low. A similar development is observable for the number of countries that present the used hypotheses and key variables in the economic models for the projections. Without this information, it is impossible to assess the quality of the projections of emissions and the adequacy of the PAMs. We also found that the number of countries which present 'with measures' projections and 'with additional measures' projections is increasing from, respectively, eleven and one countries in the first round of NCs to, respectively, sixteen and eleven countries in the third round.[1] More countries clearly follow the UNFCCC guidelines to present a 'with measures' projection. In addition, the increase in 'with additional measures' projections – not an obligation under the UNFCCC guidelines – indicates that the quality of long-term assessments of the impact of possible PAMs is improving. Otherwise, it would not be possible to distinguish the effects of already planned and implemented measures from the effects of a reserve set of additional measures.

Table 4 also contains some general information on *outcome* convergence – again, based on data and targets as negotiated, assessed and projected by the countries themselves. The table shows that more countries foresee that they will be able to realize their mitigation target, from eleven in 1994 to sixteen in 2002. We will return to this subject below.

Table 5 Greenhouse gas projections (expressed in CO_2 equivalents) in the third National Communication and the Kyoto Protocol target

Country	*Tg CO_2 equiv. emission in 1990*	*WM projected by 2010 (%)*	*WM projected by 2020 (%)*	*WAM projected by 2010 (%)*	*WAM projected by 2020 (%)*	*KP reduced target (%)*	*WM–KP gap (% 2010 emission)*
Austria	77.39	11.2	15.4	−7.5	−10.9	−13	21.8
Belgium	144.50	18.5	–	6.3	–	−7.5	22
Bulgaria	157.09	−14.8	−1.3	−20.1	−7.0	−8	–
Czech Republic	192.02	−33.2	−36.9	−36.5	−40.2	−8	–
Estonia	43.50	−56.6	−58.8	−59.9	−64.4	−8	–
Finland	77.09	16.6	23.7	−1.7	–	0	14.3
France	549.34	6.0	18.8	−4.6	−2.2	0	5.7
Germany	1,222.76	−33.6	–	–	–	−21	–
Greece	104.89	40.3	59.9	26.7	–	25	11
Hungary	84.47	−22.0	−20.5	–	–	−6	–
Italy	520.58	3.7	–	−4.7	–	−6.5	9.9
Latvia	31.06	−58.8	−50.3	–	–	−8	–
Netherlands	217.00	18.0	31.3	6.0	–	−6.5	20.8
Norway	51.96	21.6	–	11.4	–	1	17
Poland	463.05	−14.9	−5.2	–	–	−6	–
Portugal	64.96	99.7	113.2	95.1	105.5	27	8.3
Russia	2,360.00	−11.1	14.1	–	–	0	–
Slovakia	72.94	−27.1	–	−34.0	–	−8	–
Slovenia	20.18	9.8	12.7	−1.4	−1.6	−8	16.3
Spain	208.92	47.1	–	27.0	–	15	21.9
Sweden	70.56	0.5	3.2	–	–	4	–
Switzerland	53.24	−1.0	−3.8	−5.9	−10.5	−8	7
UK	742.50	−15.1	−11	−23.9	−23	−12.5	–

Table 5 presents an overview of the gaps between the (self-)projected emissions and the (self-)negotiated Kyoto Protocol reduction targets for our set of countries. In the second column, emissions data for 1990 are presented in carbon dioxide (CO_2) equivalent Tg (one tera-gram = one million metric tons), the baseline for the Kyoto targets. The guidelines for the NCs require projections 'with measures' (WM), but countries are free to include projections 'with additional measures' (WAM). For the projected scenarios, the change in percentages always refers to the level of emissions in 1990. The last column presents the gap between the projected emissions under the WM scenario and the allowed emissions under the Kyoto Protocol. This gap is expressed as a percentage of projected emissions for 2010. However, not all European countries present WAM projections in their latest NC.

Given the figures in Table 5, eleven countries will not meet their Kyoto Protocol emissions target under the WM projections. With additional measures, Finland and France project meeting the Kyoto Protocol target, whereas countries like Greece, Italy and Switzerland will almost meet their target. This is not the case for six countries – Austria, Belgium, the Netherlands, Norway, Slovenia and Spain – as their PAMs, additional or not, will always fall short. Therefore, these countries will need the flexible instruments under the Kyoto Protocol to meet a part of their quantitative reduction targets abroad.

It is difficult to draw conclusions on outcome convergence from Table 5. The gap between projected emissions and the national reduction target depends not only on the effectiveness of short-term climate policies, but also on the ability of national negotiators to secure achievable reduction targets. When comparing Table 3 with Table 5, we find that most countries, those which clearly selected a core set of the most important PAMs, face fewer problems in meeting their reduction targets. But again, this could be the result of relatively softer reduction targets compared to other countries. Furthermore, emission inventories and especially projections of emissions are subject to different methodologies and to frequent revisions. After 2012, a comparison of emissions to projected emissions will yield interesting results with respect to the ability to forecast the impact of climate policy measures.

5. EXPLAINING CLIMATE POLICY CONVERGENCE

As already mentioned in the theoretical section of this paper, we apply the explanatory scheme introduced in this special issue in order to seek an explanation for the extent of climate policy convergence which we found. Given our analysis in the above, we cannot confirm the mechanism of international harmonization on the basis of binding international law and legal compliance, as countries are not legally bound to design climate PAMs in a particular way. 'Imposition' is even less likely than harmonization, as neither the UNFCCC regime nor individual parties can force others to adopt certain PAMs. The mechanism of 'regulatory competition' does not explain output convergence in our case. Climate policy, in particular, imposes future restrictions with only limited current costs. Hence, an endangering of the competitiveness of countries and companies by climate PAMs has so far remained a vague future threat. However, we observed that, with respect to industrial PAMs, no set of core measures is emerging in most countries. This is probably related to regulatory competition. In its second NC Germany proposed concrete options for fiscal measures at the European level, i.e. the implementation of an EU-wide CO_2 tax[2] and the increase of minimal excise duties on mineral oils. Hence, the mechanism of 'regulatory competition' can explain a different pattern in industry when compared to the selection process that took place in the energy and transportation sectors.

Instead of binding harmonization, imposition or regulatory composition, the mechanism of 'transnational communication' best explains climate policy output convergence. Holzinger and Knill (2005) distinguish four sub-mechanisms: (1) *lesson-drawing* (e.g. country X experiences a similar problem as country Y and adopts a successful policy from Y); (2) *transnational problem-solving* (a group of countries experience a similar policy problem, and design and adopt a common policy model); (3) *emulation* (a country copies a widely used model, in search of policy conformity with other countries); and (4) *international policy promotion* (international organizations recommend certain policy models to address certain problems and, as a result, several countries adopt these policies). Of these sub-mechanisms, (2) and (4) seem particularly relevant as the climate change regime has been a common effort to address a shared policy problem (sub-mechanism (2)). Furthermore, it functions as an international institution that promotes certain policy models today (sub-mechanism (4)). For example, the UNFCCC, the Kyoto Protocol and many CoP decisions refer to concrete (sets of) domestic PAMs in addition to the use of international flexibility instruments. The same holds for the recommendations and decisions of other international institutions, such as the EU and the Organization for Economic Co-operation and Development. The other sub-mechanisms are of less relevance here, as the climate change issue is a *global* issue, so countries began an international policy process right from the start. *Individual* learning and copying from other countries have therefore hardly played any role, an exception being the late 1980s when some countries started to formulate national targets to reduce greenhouse gas emissions, a route which was followed by others (O'Riordon and Jäger 1996). Soon after, however, international target-setting took over the initiative.

Besides international mechanisms, domestic factors should be considered in an analysis of policy convergence. As our analysis shows, there are striking differences with respect to the development of climate policy among country groups with different political-institutional settings (see the Jepperson taxonomy). For example, the selection of core sets of measures took place mainly in the two groups of statist countries. To a large extent, these core sets are growing more similar over time and focus on energy efficiency and low-carbon policies. Of course, given the very different nature of the countries in our analysis, country-specific circumstances can be reflected in the set of core measures (for example, the restructuring of energy-intensive sectors in economies in transition). As a consequence, each type of convergence analysis is conditional.

6. CONCLUSION

Climate PAMs in European countries have developed in a particular way in the period 1994–2002. Whereas the number of PAMs has increased in general, certain 'core sets' of PAMs have been formulated in certain sectors – notably energy and transport (and surprisingly not in a sector such as industry) – and by countries characterized by (relatively) strong states. With that, our analysis and results show *some* climate policy *output* convergence in Europe. Besides the tradition of 'statism', this convergence can be best explained by transnational communication in, and policy promotion by, international institutions. The different situation with respect to industrial PAMs is probably related to the mechanism of regulatory competition.

Contrary to output convergence, we did not find climate policy *outcome* convergence. Although ever more countries believe they will be able to realize their mitigation targets in the future, thus complying with the Kyoto Protocol, a more detailed analysis shows both huge differences among countries and many cases of (potential) non-compliance. Nonetheless, any conclusion on (or lack of) outcome convergence of this sort should be put in perspective, given the highly political nature of the setting of national emission reduction targets, on the one hand, and the future projections of domestic greenhouse gas emissions and national policy effects, on the other. In such a situation, future compliance prospects can be more the result of good negotiation and creative scenario-building skills and less the effect of 'real' PAMs.

Address for correspondence: Bas Arts, Department of Political Sciences of the Environment, Nijmegen School of Management, Radboud University Nijmegen, PO Box 9108, 6500 HK Nijmegen, The Netherlands. Tel: ++31-(0)24-3612103. Fax: ++31-(0)24-3611841. email: B.Arts@fm.ru.nl

ACKNOWLEDGEMENTS

The authors wish to thank Christoph Knill, two anonymous reviewers and the participants in the Hamburg workshop on *Policy Convergence in Europe* (24–25 April 2004) for their very useful comments and suggestions for improving the paper.

NOTES

1 'Additional measures' are considered for implementation when the initial 'with measures' did not meet the mitigation targets.
2 Several other countries also suggested that new energy taxes should not be introduced unilaterally but be considered at the international level.

REFERENCES

Bennett, C. (1991) 'What is policy convergence and what causes it?', *British Journal of Political Science* 21(2): 215–33.

Boehmer-Christiansen, S. (1994) 'Scientific uncertainty and power politics: the Framework Convention on Climate Change and the role of scientific advice', in B. Spector, G. Sjöstedt and I. Zartman (eds), *Negotiating International Regimes. Lessons Learned from the United Nations Conference on Environment and Development*, London: Graham & Trotham/Martinus Nijhoff, pp. 171–80.

Drezner, D. (2001) 'Globalization and policy convergence', *The International Studies Review* 3(1): 53–78.

DTI (2003) *Our Energy Future – Creating a Low-Carbon Economy*, London: DTI Energy White Paper.

Dunn, W.N. (1994) *Public Policy Analysis. An Introduction*, 2nd edn, Englewood Cliffs: Prentice-Hall.

Grubb, M., Vrolijk, C. and Brack, D. (1999) *The Kyoto Protocol: A Guide and Assessment*, London: RIIA.

Gupta J., van Ierland, E. and Kok, M. (eds) (2003) *Issues in International Climate Policy. Theory and Policy*, Cheltenham: Edward Elgar.

Holzinger, K. and Knill, C. (2005) 'Causes and conditions of cross-national policy convergence', *Journal of European Public Policy* 12(5): 775–96.

IPCC (2001) *Climate Change 2001 Synthesis Report – Summary for Policy Makers*, Geneva: IPCC.

Jepperson, R.L. (2002) 'Political modernities: disentangling two underlying dimensions of institutional differentiation', *Sociological Theory* 20(1): 61–85.

Jordan, A. and Liefferink, D. (eds) (2004) *Environmental Policy in Europe. The Europeanization of National Environmental Policy*, London: Routledge.

Knill, C. (2001) *The Europeanisation of National Administrations. Patterns of Institutional Change and Persistence*, Cambridge: Cambridge University Press.

Knill, C. and Lenschow, A. (2000) *Implementing EU Environmental Policy. New Directions and Old Problems*, Manchester: Manchester University Press.

Mintzer, I.M. and Leonard, J.A. (eds) (1994) *Negotiating Climate Change. The Inside Story of the Rio Convention*, Cambridge: Cambridge University Press.

Oberthür, S. and Ott, H.E. (1999) *The Kyoto Protocol: International Climate Change Policy for the 21st Century*, Berlin/Heidelberg/New York: Springer.

O'Riordon, T. and Jäger, J. (1996) *Politics of Climate Change. A European Perspective*, London: Routledge.

Rolfe, C. (1998) *Kyoto Protocol to the UNFCCC: A Guide to the Protocol and Analysis of its Effectiveness*, West Coast Environmental Law Association.

Self, P. (1985) *Political Theories of Modern Government*, London: Allen & Unwin.

UNFCCC (1992) *United Nations Framework Convention on Climate Change: Text*, Geneva: UNEP/WMO Information Unit on Climate Change.

UNFCCC (1998) *United Nations Framework Convention on Climate Change: Text of the Kyoto Protocol*, Geneva: UNEP/WMO Information Unit on Climate Change.

UNFCCC (2003) *Compilation and Synthesis of Third National Communications* (FCCC/SBI/2003/7).

Van Esch, F. (2001) 'Defining national preferences: the influence of international non-state actors', in B. Arts, M. Noortmann and B. Reinalda (eds), *Non-state Actors in International Relations*, Aldershot: Ashgate, pp. 109–26.

Van Steertegem, M. (ed.) (2003) *Milieu- en natuurrapport Vlaanderen: beleidsevaluatie*, Vlaamse Milieu-maatschappij.

Van Tatenhove, J., Arts, B. and Leroy, P. (eds) (2000) *Political Modernization and the Environment. The Renewal of Policy Arrangements*, Dordrecht: Kluwer.

Weale, A. (1992) *The New Politics of Pollution*, Manchester: Manchester University Press.

Central banks on the move

Martin Marcussen

I. THE BASIC PATTERNS OF CONVERGENCE

> If the fundamental, evolutionary criterion of success is that an organization should reproduce and multiply over the world, and successfully mutate to meet the emerging challenges of time, then central banks have been conspicuously successful.
>
> (Capie *et al.* 1994: 91)

Almost all sovereign states today have a central bank of their own and, since the beginning of the 1990s, the majority of these central banks have gone through statutory reforms granting them legal independence. Figure 1 depicts the total number of central banks from year to year in the period 1870–2003. It also illustrates the number of central banks that have gone through reforms with the explicit purpose of making the bank more independent from political interference.

One of the two diffusion tracks on which I focus concerns the worldwide spread of the 'central bank' as a distinct organizational structure. During the twentieth century the number of central banks rose from 19 in 1900 to 175 by 2003. Some parts of Figure 1 almost speak for themselves. The earliest central banks (Sveriges Riksbank, 1668; the Bank of England, 1694) were

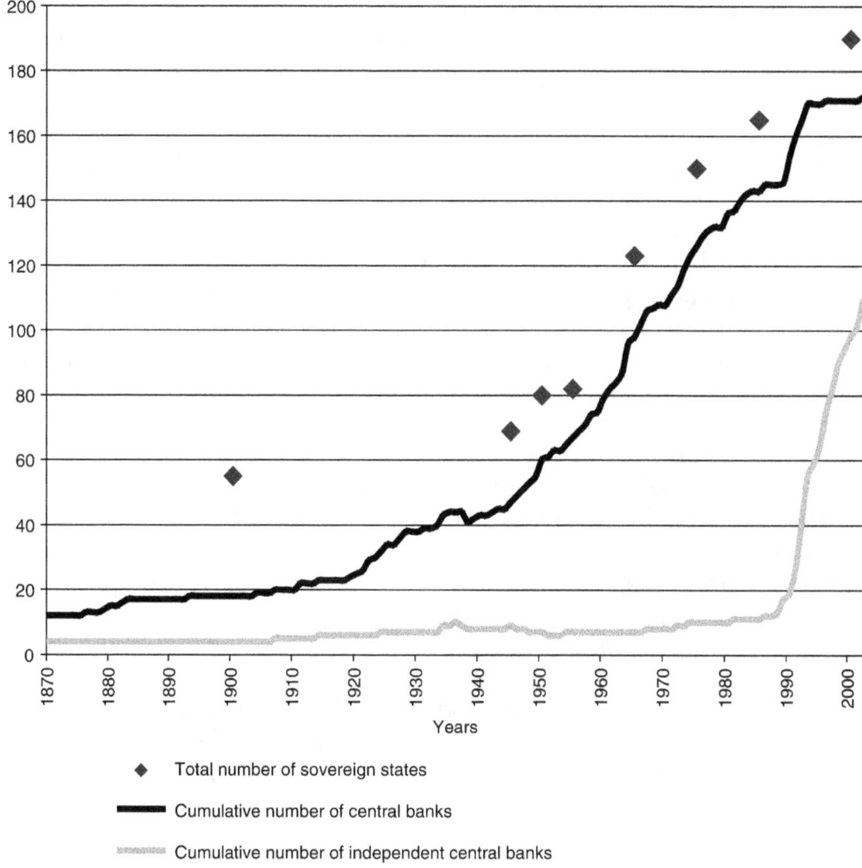

Figure 1 Sovereign states and central banks, 1870–2003
Sources: For central banks: The Morgan Stanley Central Bank Directory 2004, www.centralbanknet.com. For central bank independence: Cukierman *et al.* (1992); Jácome (2001); Maliszewski (2000); Maxfield (1997); McNamara (2002), www.centralbanknet.com; national central bank legislation.

created in the seventeenth century and for many decades, until the middle of the eighteenth century, the number of central banks was fairly stable. However, from the 1920s onwards, the total number of central banks seemed to grow exponentially. Today more than 90 per cent of all existing states have established central banks.

Another part of Figure 1 concerns the track that illustrates the diffusion of central bank independence as a legal standard. Here we see a slightly different pattern. There seems to be a radical increase in legal central bank independence during the 1990s. However, it is in relation to this track that I definitely have the weakest data. A major weakness concerns the fact that the data for legal central bank independence are not based on one single definition of legal central bank independence. The data are collected from a series of independent sources that have been compiled with a view to studying central bank constitutional reform in many different ways. Nevertheless, it seems to me that the data, despite their different origins and basis, are valid because they converge to a large extent. Taken individually, the data series all show a sharp upward slope from the end of the 1980s onwards.

Figure 1 raises the question as to whether it is possible to trace a tendency towards global convergence when it comes to the existence of central banks and their statutory position. To see this, the relevant measure is not the absolute number of central banks, but rather the number of central banks as a proportion of the total population of sovereign states.

Indeed, Figure 2 confirms that there has been a tendency towards increasing convergence with regard to the number of central banks in the world. An increasing portion of the world's sovereign states have installed a central bank. The curve has a clear upward slope.

The central banks which have achieved some degree of statutory independence in relation to the total number of central banks show a very different pattern. Figure 3 illustrates that central banks created up to 1990 tended, as a rule, not to be statutorily independent from their governments. From 1990 onwards, the situation changed and a veritable wave of independence flushed over the world of central banking.

In the next section, I will discuss what a central bank is and how we should understand the concept of legal independence. In the third section, I will then go into some detail to explain the identified tendencies of convergence. Finally, I will conclude the article by asking the question 'So what?' Why should we care about convergence processes in general and why is the case of central banking particularly interesting?

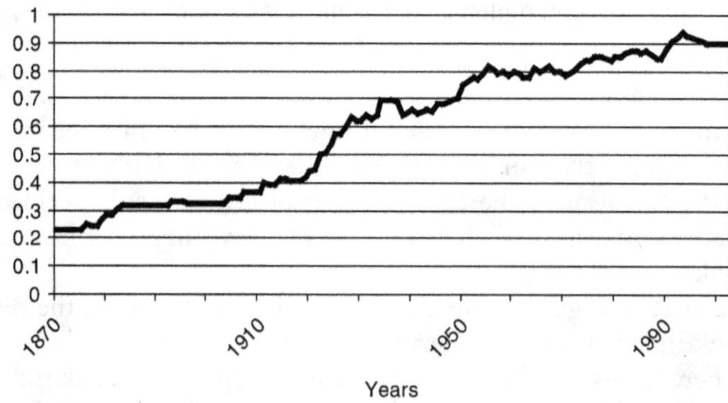

Figure 2 Proportion of sovereign states with central banks, 1870–2003

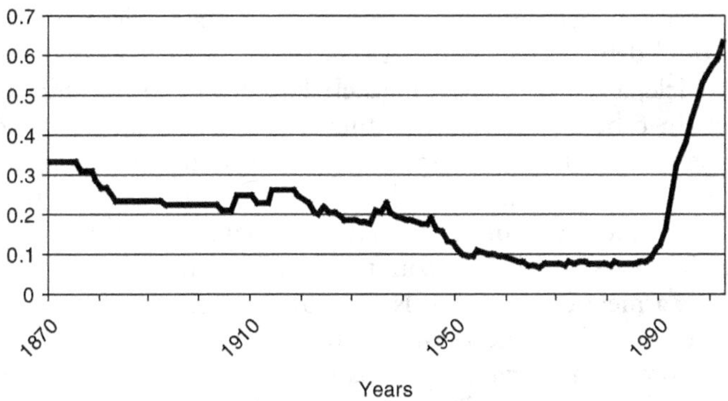

Figure 3 Proportion of central banks with legal independence, 1870–2003

II. WHAT IS CONVERGENCE?

Defining central banking is problematic. In one sense we recognize it when we see it (Capie *et al.* 1994: 5). To various degrees central banks are characterized by the fact that they have a monopoly over the issuing of notes, they are the lenders of last resort for private bankers and other financial institutions, they implement their governments' monetary policies, and sometimes they also supervise the entire financial system. Article 56 of the Statutes of the Bank for International Settlements (BIS) stipulates that a 'central bank means the bank or banking system in any country to which has been entrusted the duty of regulating the volume of currency and credit in that country'.

It is difficult to say that central banks *strictu sensu* existed prior to the Classical Gold Standard (1873–1914). Sveriges Riksbank, the oldest in the world, was a privately owned bank which was reorganized as a state bank in 1668. However, it was the Bank of England, founded in 1694, which was the first to get a monopoly over the issue of money in 1844. The Riksbank achieved the same function only in 1897. The function as a lender of last resort was added much later. The Bank of England was again a first mover since it had already been entrusted with that function in 1870. In 1873 Walter Bagehot (English economic journalist, 1826–1877) published *Lombard Street: A Description of the Money Market* which could be seen as a textbook on how to run a central bank in a crisis. For Walter Bagehot the main, if not the sole, criterion of a central bank's level of modernity is its function as lender of last resort. The Banque de France followed suit in 1880 and Sveriges Riksbank in 1890.

The legendary Governor of the Bank of England, Montagu Norman (governor 1920–1944), was among those central bankers who made an effort to define central banking back in 1921 (Sayers 1976: appendices: 74–5). His list of central bank functions still defines modern central banking to a large extent. Modern central banking, therefore, is a fairly recent phenomenon, and many central banks developed only slowly from commercially oriented institutions to what we would define today as classical central banks (de Kock 1974).

In this article, a central bank is registered according to the official date of its foundation. In other words, disregarding its functions, an institution is considered to be a central bank as soon as it and others call it a central bank. Therefore, when I trace the central bank as an organizational structure that has travelled worldwide, I do not imply that this organizational structure manifests itself in similar ways in different countries. The central bank, as understood in this article, is a meta-concept that is attributed different meanings in different contexts, and, over time, the meaning attached to this very special concept is being reinterpreted and typically expanded. Still, it stays the same meta-concept. Thus, the question that interests me here is why a large majority of sovereign states argue that they have something called a central bank.

Like the concept of a central bank, the concept of legal central bank independence is difficult to define. Legal or statutory central bank independence is, of course, not a binominal either/or phenomenon. Detailed scales of legal central bank independence have been developed (see, for instance, Cukierman *et al.* 1992). For the purpose of this paper, however, it is necessary to distinguish legal independence from behavioural independence (Maxfield 1997). Whereas legal independence is formally derived from the constitution of the central bank and concerns its prescribed relationship to the central government, behavioural independence concerns the question of whether a central bank in day-to-day practice really has a great deal of discretion to pursue a defined objective. Nowadays, legal and behavioural independence seem to coincide. However, in earlier periods, this was not so.

In short, this paper defines a central bank to be legally independent once it has gone through an institutional reform whose explicit purpose was to grant it more autonomy from the government in its pursuance of a stated objective. This is a very broad and inclusive definition of legal independence, which emphasizes that a concrete reform has taken place to change the statutes of the central bank. Thus, an actor with the necessary reform capacity and will has explicitly stated that it is desirable that the central bank is legally independent, and has actually carried through a reform of the statutes of the central bank in question.

Again, there are many ways in which a central bank can be reformed, and no two central banks have undergone the same kind of reform. Also, nothing is implied about the effects of the reform. It is not assumed that the concerned central bank is, in its day-to-day behaviour, actually independent from national politicians and governments. What interests me here is the fact that some politicians have tried to adopt the idea of central bank independence and reformed the central bank accordingly. Strictly speaking, the convergence processes that I trace and analyse in this article can help us to understand why the meta-concepts of 'central bank' and 'legal independence' have spread so widely around the world. A study like this requires that attention is directed towards the mechanisms that have helped these meta-concepts/ideas on their journey across the globe.

III. EXPLAINING CENTRAL BANKS AND CENTRAL BANK INDEPENDENCE CONVERGENCE

Parallel problem pressure

Functionalist explanations of why the central bank as an organizational structure and independence as a legal standard became so popular all over the world will tend to focus on the explicit domestic demand for these structures and standards (Finnemore 1996: 39; Holzinger and Knill 2005). The popular version of such a demand-driven explanation will run like this: 'We have these structures and standards because they have proved to be effective in solving our immediate problems.' According to this argument, a set of problems has been identified (lack of credibility, high inflation, malfunctioning or non-existent commercial banking, etc.) and the perfect set of solutions has been chosen to solve these problems. Consequently, if central banks and legal independence actually help states to solve their problems, these practices will be demanded in places where there is no independent central banking. The success of particular triumphant central bank institutions will be evaluated and compared to the success of alternative organizational set-ups. If a central bank institution is chosen, it is because the decision-makers decided that central banking for them really is the optimal solution. Hence, if there is no relationship between the existence of central banks and their legal independence, on the one hand, and solutions to the identified problems, on the other hand, then central banks, where existing, will be dissolved. Long-lived dysfunctional institutions are assumed away in such a framework.

As has been shown by other researchers, demand-driven explanations have been useful in explaining some stages of central bank diffusion. It has been argued that central banks were the only institutions that could provide governments with the credibility they needed to attract money to finance major wars. It has also been argued that, for some countries, the creation of a central bank was the only way to create the public good of a well-functioning and stable financial system (Broz 1998). At the end of the Napoleonic wars a series of central banks were founded, for instance, those of Austria-Hungary, Norway, Denmark, and the Second Bank of the United States, because the states had generated very high inflation through excessive issue of government paper currency to meet their wartime expenditures (Capie *et al.* 1994: 4–5). By establishing a central bank these states could achieve credibility and thereby attract finances from abroad, which could be repaid over a long time horizon.

One could ask why not all states that were engaged in war had established a central bank right away or, alternatively, why it took so long before Switzerland (1905), Australia (1911), the United States (1913), and Canada (1935) got their central banks. The early establishers like Sweden (1668), Great Britain (1694), France (1800), Finland (1811), the Netherlands (1814), Austria (1816), Norway (1816,) Denmark (1818), Portugal (1846), Belgium (1850), Spain (1874), and Germany (1876) were all centralized or semi-centralized countries with few institutional veto-points and therefore possessed greater decision-making capacity. The latecomers, on the contrary, seemed to be organized according to a federal principle which supposedly increases the number of veto-points in decision-making (Broz 1998: 242).

In this article I do not raise objections against the dominant explanation for the origin of central banks. In explaining why central banks were founded outside Europe in later periods, I do, however, want to highlight that we will need to supplement the classical demand-based explanation with supply-side explanations. To understand the increasing popularity of the central bank structure around the world, it seems to be necessary to distinguish between at least four different waves of convergence – the European wave, the inter-war wave, the post-colonial wave and the post-Cold War wave – each of which may require specific explanations (see Figure 4).

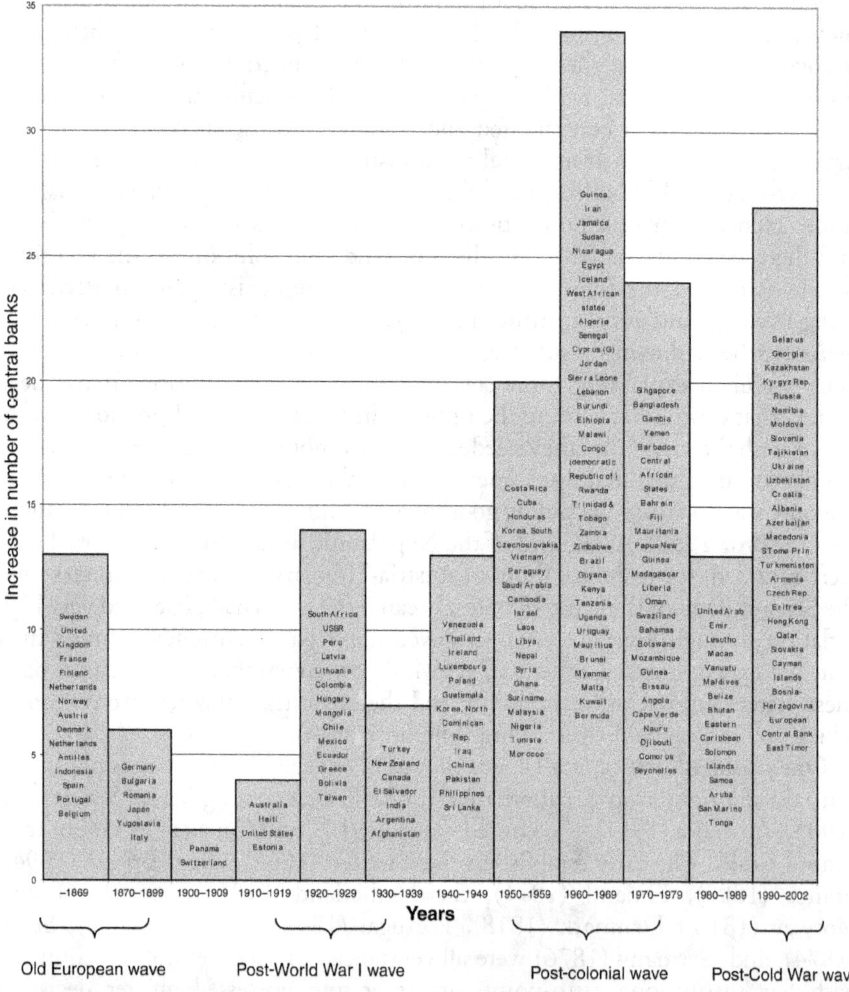

Figure 4 New central banks per decade

We do not know much about why central bank independence has become a mantra across the world in places as different as India, Chile and Sweden. A classical demand-driven explanation will argue that states reform their central bank towards more independence because a credibility problem has arisen (Rogoff 1985). In this view, central bankers are seen as conservative inflation-fighters. With an eye on the chances of getting re-elected, the nature of any government is to focus on the short time-span. By its nature the government will exploit its power over the central bank and require excessive expansionary monetary policies in order to boost the economy. This will result in inflationary tendencies, which, according to such a reasoning, would be a wrong signal to send to the financial markets. Dependent central banking thus means that foreign capital owners will not only avoid investing money in the country, they will also sell their stocks of the national currency. The case for central bank independence is closely related to the desire to re-establish the fiscal and monetary discipline that we know from the Classical Gold Standard. An independent central bank is seen as much more credible than elected politicians, particularly if the bank is given an inflation-fighting mandate.

The empirical evidence in support of the classical explanation has its flaws (Hayo and Hefeker 2002). One puzzle is that central bank independence has also been introduced in countries which have not experienced hyperinflation at all (Beyeler 2002), and that many central banks were granted legal independence *after* inflation had been reduced rather than before (Cobham *et al.* 2000). In order to understand why countries like Belgium (1993), Japan (1995) and Luxembourg (1998), which were not confronted with a virulent inflation spiral, undertook central bank reforms, we will have to include other supply-driven explanations. Also, to understand why central bank reform took place everywhere in Europe, despite the fact that low inflation had been achieved through other means prior to the reforms, we will have to look at additional explanations.

Another puzzle is that a direct negative correlation between central bank independence and inflation can be identified when the sample includes developing countries and countries in transition (Cukierman *et al.* 1992; de Haan and Kooi 2000). Other studies have even found a direct positive correlation between the level of inflation and legal central bank independence in these countries (Hillman 1999). Yet others have concluded that if there is a positive relationship between central bank independence and low inflation, there is a high price to pay. Since central bank independence seems to be positively associated with lower growth and higher unemployment there is no such thing as a 'free lunch' (Down 2004).

Finally, another branch of research has further emphasized that central banks will be quite inefficient without a series of supporting embedding institutions such as well-functioning corporatist arrangements (Iversen 1998) and a developed anti-inflation stability culture (de Jong 2002). The extent to which legal independence sends the right and credible signals to the financial markets depends on many contextual factors including the overall administrative and political culture of the country, the general institutional configuration of the polity, bargaining patterns, actor constellations, etc. (Posen 1993).

Therefore, it seems to be necessary to supplement the classical demand-driven explanations with some supply-driven explanations (Finnemore 1996: 47). Supply-driven explanations introduce more agency in an account of diffusion processes. People, organizations and states are introduced as ideational entrepreneurs and promoters of organizational structures and legal standards. Additionally, a central element in a supply-driven explanation is to investigate whether states have adopted certain organizational structures and legal standards because, in world society, these structures and standards are considered as examples of modernity, progress, civilization and excellence (Meyer and Rowan 1991). In other words, it may be that the emulation of a central bank structure takes place when states that do not have a central bank desire to be considered as integral parts of world society. This logic follows the dictum: 'If you want to belong to our group, and have what we have, you must be like us!'

Supply-driven approaches do not assume that the diffused structures or standards are necessarily the functionally optimal ones. Nor do they assume that dysfunctional structures and standards are automatically dismantled and left behind. Rather, we need supply-driven explanations to understand diffusion in cases where there is no obvious reason to believe that the adopted structures and standards are the only ones that can meet the challenges of the day. Table 1 lists a set of both demand- and supply-side mechanisms that seem to have been decisive in an explanation of why convergence in terms of central bank structures and standards has taken place.

The post-World War I wave: imposition and international model promotion

In the inter-war period, the 'European model' soon became diffused to other parts of the world. The experience of central banks in continental Europe led to a common opinion on how a central bank should be established and run. The way in which central banks were constructed before World War I had after the war become the common and standardized model for others to copy in the industrialized countries. Its very existence, its main functions and operational techniques were generally accepted and taken for granted. To understand why central banks were so frequently established in the inter-war period, it is necessary to take into account the political pressure that was put on the countries founding central bank institutions as well as the extensive transnational communication that took place at the level of monetary élites.

Protagonists in the process of diffusing central banking worldwide were the American Federal Reserve Governor Benjamin Strong (in office 1914–1928) and his counterpart from the Bank of England, Montagu Norman (in office 1920–1944). Strong has been described as a true believer in 'internationalism' and central bank co-operation. He was personally devoted to the Allies' cause during World War I, he believed that Americans had a special responsibility

Table 1 Mechanisms of convergence

The central bank as an organizational form		*Central bank independence as a legal standard*	
Demand-based explanations	*Supply-side explanations*	*Demand-side explanations*	*Supply-side explanations*
18th–19th century: **Parallel problem pressure** The central bank as a credibility-enhancing device on the financial markets → Government's bank → Bankers' bank			Administered countries (Germany and Austria): **Imposition** Penetration
	Inter-war period: **Imposition and international model promotion** Conditionality + socialization (League of Nations) Conditionality + persuasion (Norman and Strong) Conditionality + technical assistance (Kemmerer missions)	New Zealand (1989): **Parallel problem pressure**	Asia, Africa, CEECs and NICs (1990s): **Imposition and international model promotion** IMF technical assistance and conditionality Personal training and deliberation
1960s–1970s: **Emulation** Newly independent colonies 1990s: **Emulation** Newly independent countries in Central and Eastern Europe and the former Soviet Union		Eager EMU reformers (early 1990s): **Emulation**	Acquiescent EMU reformers (late 1990s): **Harmonization through international legal obligations**

to foster co-operation during and after the war, and he promoted strong Anglo-American co-operation in order to prepare for the post-war international order. Indeed, 'his internationalist activities served as a near-religious faith for him' (Roberts 2000: 65). At the same time, he was a true believer in the Gold Standard principles of sound finances and stable prices (Chandler 1958: 183). This was a belief he shared with British Central Bank Governor Montagu Norman. As a consequence of their shared belief in stability-oriented macro-economic policy they both rejected Keynes' views which at the time were regarded with considerable suspicion in central bank circles. The following passage describes the shared worldview of Norman and Strong and how this view was formulated and practised as a common political project:

> Norman and Strong had in common many things that predisposed them to congenial and effective cooperation. Both were bankers with long and responsible experience in the greatest financial centers of their respective countries. Both shared a banker's conservatism, distrust of 'politicians', and impatience with 'theory' that seemed inapplicable to 'practice.' They were not routine administrators; they were innovators with grandly conceived projects ... Three other convictions shared by Norman and Strong deserve special attention: (1) Central banks should be 'independent' of 'political control' ... (2) Central banks should not deal with foreign governments but only with foreign central banks ... (3) International cooperation on monetary matters should be largely entrusted to central banks.
>
> (Chandler 1958: 260–1)

The two were entirely committed to establish central bank co-operation to rebuild Europe and it has been argued that international central banking as we know it today was mainly their invention (Cottrell 1995: 139). The first international meeting that involved many central bankers took place within the framework of the League of Nations (a so-called 'International Financial Conference') in Brussels from 24 September to 8 October 1920. It attracted central bankers and finance ministers from thirty-nine countries (Sayers 1976: 153–63). The European central bankers were just getting on speaking terms with each other. However, with a remarkably broad consensus it was agreed to call for every country to have a central bank; that this central bank should be independent; and that governments and central banks should return to the policy goals of the pre-war era. The secretariat of the League of Nations was asked to write a report about the ways in which the participating countries actually responded to the recommendations. Thus, the League of Nations engaged in multilateral surveillance to ensure compliance with the agreed macro-economic governance principles.

The conclusions of the Brussels conference were spelled out in detail at the Genoa conference (the so-called 'International Economic Conference') in April 1922. One of the three adopted reports, the Financial Commission of the League of Nations, primarily constituted by central bankers, repeated the recommendations that central banks should be created and the Gold Standard restored, and the principles of independent central banking and economic conservatism were underlined.

In the inter-war years, the League of Nations assisted in economic restructuring in Central Europe by channelling cheap loans. To these loans were attached conditions about the countries' macro-economic governance structures, like the existence of a central bank. Norman and Strong continuously emphasized these conditions when they were in contact with their neighbours, colonies and allies:

> Though there were some differences from case to case, Strong and Norman usually insisted that countries seeking to resume gold payments should meet all the following conditions: (1) balance the government budget ... (2) ... free the central bank ... from the needs of the Treasury ... (3) adopt noninflationary monetary policy ... (4) assure the independence of the central bank ... Strong and Norman could refuse credits to the country's central bank until both the central bank and its government met the conditions they laid down.
>
> (Chandler 1958: 281, 285)

Additionally, Norman and Strong crusaded through Central and South America and the Commonwealth countries to spread the message. For his part, Norman simply refused to visit countries which had not already established a central bank or were planning to do so. Only in 1922, the year of the Genoa conference, Norman sent a letter to a dozen countries in Central and Eastern Europe and the British dominions in order to set up a meeting to discuss further co-operation:

> Among the few deliberate policies consistently followed by the Bank [of England] throughout the inter-war years was its encouragement of the foundation of central banks in what may be called the Dominions ... The Bank of England – and not only its Governor – exerted itself to give the movement an impetus, to shape the new central banks in its own image.
>
> (Sayers 1976: 201)

In Latin America, Benjamin Strong and Princeton professor Edwin Walter Kemmerer were spreading the gospel of central banking (Capie *et al.* 1994: 21). Kemmerer's career as 'money doctor' led him to a long series of Central and South American countries either representing the Federal Reserve directly or accompanied by Fed personnel. Kemmerer himself was an ardent exponent of the Gold Standard and laissez-faire, and an important element of the Kemmerer missions was to establish independent central banks that could function as lenders-of-last-resort. On the web-sites of El Banco de la República de Colombia, El Banco Central de Chile, El Banco de Reserva del Peru, Banco Central del Ecuador, El Banco Central de Bolivia, etc., it is described how Kemmerer during successive visits engaged actively in the economic life of these countries. The proposed central banks were typically modelled according to the Federal Reserve system (Drake 1989).

Of today's central banks twenty-one were created during the inter-war years but not much came out of the plea for independent central banking (Deane and Pringle 1994: 58; Sayers 1976: 159). The economic catastrophe of the 1930s completely overthrew the earlier dominant ideology and a series of central banks were nationalized. However, as the 1920s ended, central bank co-operation was to be institutionalized in the BIS. This organization in neutral Switzerland should above all foster co-operation among central banks. In reality, a central bankers' club had thus been created.

In sum, two types of ideational entrepreneur helped to diffuse the central bank as an organizational form through transnational communication: the League of Nations and central bank governors. The League helped to diffuse the central bank through conditional lending and through socialization in international conferences throughout the 1920s. Among the central bank governors, Benjamin Strong and associated money doctors as well as Montagu Norman stand out as internationalists with a strong belief in the Gold Standard and in central bank co-operation.

The colonial independence wave and the post-Cold War wave: emulation

Since World War II, eighty-five former colonies have gained political independence from their colonizers. Most states gained independence during the 1960s (forty-six former colonies) and the 1970s (twenty). After only five years of independence 54 per cent (forty-six states) had established a central bank. Today, 92 per cent (seventy-eight states) of the newly independent states have established central banks either on their own or in monetary unions (eight states in the Central Bank of West African States, six states in the Bank of Central African States, and eight states in the Eastern Caribbean Central Bank).

In the former Soviet Union and Central and Eastern Europe, central banks, where they had existed, were abolished with the communist take-over at the beginning of the century and their owners and managers were executed or driven abroad (Deane and Pringle 1994: 291–306). With the dissolution of the Soviet Union, however, a second (post-Cold War) wave of central bank diffusion materialized. Thus, between 1990 and 1992, all the newly independent states of the former Soviet Union established their own central banks.

It seems as if the pattern of convergence that we can identify from the 1960s to the present day has its own self-enforcing logic. Thus, it can be argued that once international fads and norms have passed a certain threshold or tipping point the social practice – in this case the central bank as an organizational form – spreads almost by itself. Concretely, in the period after World War II, a tipping point had been reached and it had become less a question of convincing and persuading the new states to adopt these rationalized elements of world culture and more a question of self-induced adaptation. Although many scientific experts, private consultants, international non-governmental organizations and international economic organizations assist the new states in their transformation to become members of a world society, the states and élites therein will themselves to a large extent be major drivers behind the reforms.

In order to understand the most recent diffusion processes we must therefore supplement the mechanisms we have studied so far (parallel problem pressure resulting from wars and banking panics, and transnational communication via ideational entrepreneurs and central bank conferences) with the idea that sometimes states simply adopt a certain organizational structure such as a central bank because the act in itself will classify the state as being modern and developed and thereby a legitimate actor in world society. States will even skip earlier, relatively well-functioning arrangements such as currency boards to introduce the world standard. Furthermore, facing economic collapse, state élites will start to verbally rationalize the typically dysfunctional new structures. This can be referred to as a demand-driven explanation, although of a completely different kind than the functionalist one discussed earlier. For the two most recent stages in central bank convergence it is argued that in addition to the supply of appropriate central bank structures from diverse international and national agencies, transition élites themselves emulate these very same structures for mainly symbolic reasons.

What we have learned so far is, first, that the central bank institution has spread in various waves and has now become a common organizational structure for an extremely large percentage of sovereign states. Second, to explain why the central bank institution has become so successful, we need to focus not only on the classical demand-driven and functionalist explanations that tend to rationalize the central bank institution as the most optimal institutional constellation in the case of parallel problem pressure. Ideational entrepreneurs, either as international economic organizations or as individual personalities, have helped the central bank fad on its way worldwide through transnational communication. At the same time, the spread of central bank institutions has obtained an almost self-reinforcing dynamic evidenced by the fact that many state élites themselves are eagerly engaged in emulating central bank structure as a sign of statehood. Thus diverse supply- and demand-driven explanations supplement each other.

In the following I will look at the dynamics that seem to have been decisive for the diffusion of a standard such as the legal independence of central banks.

Legal central bank independence in one go

How can we understand the very steep upward slope of the legal independence curve in Figure 1? Countries in the less developed as well as in the highly developed parts of the world undertook profound central bank reform in the 1990s. Governments from both the right wing and the left wing took the initiative for such reforms. It is worth remembering that we are in fact talking about a veritable collective endeavour on a worldwide scale.

A first factor concerns the efforts of *international financial institutions* to require domestic reforms of national financial structures through political pressure and technical assistance so that these structures correspond to the prevailing monetary ideology of the time. What has elsewhere been referred to as a 'Washington Consensus' (Williamson 2000) is essentially expressing the idea that sound finances, sound money and sound institutions are considered to be desirable objectives by themselves. Sound finances in this terminology mean that public budgets should ideally be in surplus and that foreign debts should be reduced at all costs. Sound money means low interest rates and low inflation, and sound institutions mean little state interference in the economy, privatization and independent central banking.

The International Monetary Fund (IMF) and the World Bank are now described as 'the new missionary institutions, through which these ideas were pushed on the reluctant poor countries that often needed their loans and grants' (Stiglitz 2002: 13). The institution has changed markedly since the days when John Maynard Keynes and others formulated the objectives of the IMF. The IMF was 'founded on the belief that markets often worked badly, it now champions market supremacy with ideological fervour' (Stiglitz 2002: 12). In a sense, the IMF lost its *raison d'être* with the collapse of the Bretton Woods fixed exchange rate system, but it soon found new roles. Indeed, the IMF does engage in large-scale institutional reform in its member countries from the Middle East, Africa, South and Central America, Central and Eastern Europe and in the former Soviet Union. Under the heading of 'technical assistance' IMF experts 'contribute to the development of the productive resources of member countries by enhancing the effectiveness of economic policy and financial management' (www.imf.org, 17 February 2005). This includes scrutiny of central banking practices and central bank legislation in the concerned countries. Throughout the 1990s the IMF organized 'technical assistance missions' to no less than seventy-one countries from all parts of the world to reform central bank legislation (Jácome 2001: 33). As an example, IMF technical assistance to South Korea can be mentioned. The conditions attached to the loans granted to Korea in the midst of the 1997 'Korean crisis' included a change in the statutes of the Bank of Korea to make it legally independent. Thus, the Bank of Korea was told to become more independent from commercial banking and from the Korean government as well as to focus exclusively on inflation. At the time, Korea had never had a problem with inflation. However, as part of a standard 'technical assistance procedure' preceding an IMF loan, the Bank of Korea was decisively told to become independent. For Korea this amounted to a huge reform which represented a revolutionary break with the system on which modern Korea was built (Kirk 1999: 122).

The IMF and the World Bank are not, of course, the only international economic institutions that promulgate central bank independence. The African Development Bank, the Asian Development Bank, the European Bank for Reconstruction and Development (EBRD), the BIS, the Organization for

Economic Co-operation and Development (OECD), etc. are all actively talking the 'sound policy discourse'.

Thus, both imposition through conditional lending practices and international model promotion through technical assistance, with the purpose of reconstructing the central bank infrastructure of developing and transitional economies around the world, constitute elements that can help us to understand the rapid diffusion of legal central bank independence during the 1990s. Another technique that was applied immediately after the end of the Cold War relates to lesson drawing. By undertaking the *personal training of central bankers* in the transition economies from Central and Eastern Europe as well as from the countries of the former Soviet Union, the objective of European and American central banks was to foster a sound central bank culture in these countries. Central bankers from the transition economies were invited to European and American central banks to participate in conferences and in central bank training placements, and new training centres were established that offered a long list of courses on all aspects of central bank practice. At the Bank of England, a Centre for Central Banking Studies was founded in 1990 and throughout the 1990s it hosted courses attended by several hundreds of central bankers each year. Since 1992, five of the most important international financial organizations – the BIS, the IMF, the World Bank, the OECD and the EBRD – have collectively financed the Joint Vienna Institute with the purpose of fertilizing the ground for a genuine transnational central bank culture. Courses were organized in Vienna as well as in the transition economies, and teaching material and manuals were produced and disseminated. The German Bundesbank has undertaken similar training activities since the mid-1990s. Thus, it seems to be the case that central bankers in the so-called Western economies engaged in a veritable collective process of knowledge dissemination and ideational learning to incorporate new central bankers in the existing transnational central bank community. A set of techniques, arguments, procedures and structures was established in these transition economies and common central bank terminology and language (English) developed.

With regard to the central bank reforms that took place among the members of the European Union (EU) in the 1990s, the story is quite different (Marcussen 2000). By the end of the 1980s, central bankers were invited by the heads of state and government to formulate the basic principles for European economic and monetary union (EMU). The sound money, finances and institutions doctrine was amply developed in the concluding Delors report which formed the basis for the legal and institutional set-up of EMU and its convergence criteria.

Thus, in Western Europe a clear *legal obligation* was established that demanded profound central bank reform in a series of EU member states such as Finland (1999), Luxembourg (1999) and Ireland (1999). In other European countries, international legal constraints in the form of EMU convergence criteria cannot entirely explain the eagerness of national politicians with regard to central bank reform. In Great Britain, France and Sweden, for instance, central bank reform were undertaken way ahead of time (in the case of

France), even though no real legal requirement existed (in the case of Great Britain), and even though national politicians had publicly argued that they did not feel obliged by EMU's convergence criteria (in the case of Sweden). In the 1980s, in all three of these countries, central bank independence was considered to be completely 'un-British', 'un-French' and 'un-Swedish' by national parliamentarians. However, early in the 1990s, four years before it was actually required, the Banque de France had already been reformed in preparation for full participation in the third and final stage of EMU. Now central bank reform was depicted in the Assemblée Nationale as being a way for France to play a proactive role in the EU and in the European System of Central Banks (ESCB). Great Britain had obtained a formal opt-out from the third stage of EMU. However, despite the fact that no legal pressures were forcing British politicians to initiate central bank reform, the Bank of England was reformed in the first week after the Labour government came to power in 1997. Labour politicians now defended the reform by referring to earlier periods of greatness where the independent Bank of England stood as the guarantor of British financial hegemony. Sweden had not obtained an opt-out from EMU since the country was a newcomer to the EU. However, on joining the EU in 1995 Swedish politicians said publicly and wrote that they did not feel obliged to fulfil the EMU's convergence criteria. They underlined that only a public referendum in favour of EMU could force Swedish politicians to adapt to the EMU sound policy standard. Yet, in 1997–1998 the Swedish Riksbank was fundamentally reformed. This was now considered to be in full convergence with Swedish administrative and political culture and tradition.

To explain these sudden shifts in behaviour, we will need to understand that political authorities, although not necessarily under economic and legal pressure, were exposed to ideational pressure in the EU and from their own central bank governors. Thus, by the end of the 1980s and beginning of the 1990s, the central bank stability dogma had become so widely accepted and internalized among European macro-economic élites that it came to characterize the ideational foundation of the European macro-economic institutional field. This spilled over into national political debates and caused institutional reforms. Central bank researchers have gone so far as to suggest that the power of ideas can actually best explain the ups and downs of independent central banking:

> The switch to Keynesian principles of 'managed money' after World War II, the adoption of floating exchange rates and then monetary targets in the 1970s, and now the enthusiasm for central bank independence, all have owed much of their force to academic ideas whose time had arrived.
>
> (Capie *et al.* 1994: 80)

What we have learned in this section strengthens the lessons drawn from studying the diffusion of central banking: there is a case for supplementing demand-driven explanations with supply-driven explanations. With regard to the diffusion of the legal independence standard in the 1990s, it becomes important to systematically study the role of political pressure from international financial institutions (the IMF and others), individual central bankers (in the Delors committee and elsewhere) as well as forums for transnational communication, learning and deliberation (the Joint Vienna Institute and other training arrangements). These entrepreneurs and the ways in which they applied deliberative as well as indirect coercive learning techniques have actively helped the independence standard on its way in its worldwide journey.

IV. SO WHAT?

Why should we care about patterns of convergence? Overall, the purpose of studying convergence processes is not to conclude that differences between institutions, ideas, identities, interests and instruments are becoming increasingly insignificant. Nor is it the intention to completely ignore important processes and patterns of divergence. Convergence and divergence are the two flip sides of the same coin. From the 1950s to the present day, convergence studies have developed from discussing whether convergence is a relevant term in a multidimensional and multifaceted but also increasingly interconnected world, to empirically identifying processes of convergence and divergence, and to theoretically developing tools that can help us to understand these processes and their expressions in social life. One important reason why we should care about convergence studies is that they help us to transcend established analytical categories and frontiers; for instance, those between 'the national' and 'the international', between 'public' and 'private', between 'politics' and 'economics', etc. The study of convergence and divergence points to institutional and social processes and dynamics that can hardly be grasped within the framework of state-centred theories of governance (Rosenau 1997).

In that regard, the central bank case is interesting. It spells out quite clearly how patterns of convergence go together with patterns of divergence. It also illustrates how different patterns of convergence at different levels are interlinked in a complicated manner. As the state form has developed from the seventeenth century onwards to becoming the one and only legitimate way of organizing public authority, it is clear that state convergence at a generalized level can be identified. Of course, there are still not, and there will probably never be, two states that resemble each other in an accurate way. In the twentieth century, the state form increasingly goes together with standardized organizational forms such as a central bank. Therefore, one pattern of convergence is apparently following and closely linked to another pattern of convergence. Again, there are no two central banks that are completely identical. Central banks differ in regard to transparency and communication, they work with different objectives, their territorial organization is different and their relationships to external actors also differ. Despite these differences, most states today would argue that they indeed have a central bank. At the end of the twentieth century, we see a third pattern of convergence developing: legal central bank independence. Compared to the first two patterns of convergence, this one has developed over a very short time span. States have developed over centuries, central banks over the twentieth century, and central bank independence over the last decade. Again, however, convergence goes together with divergence. Legal independence is not implemented in the same way anywhere, and legal or statutory independence is far from being the same as behavioural or real independence. In sum, therefore, the case of central banking is good at illustrating that patterns of convergence processes are interlinked in many and complicated ways, that convergence can and does take place at many different levels of abstraction and precision, and that convergence at some level or some dimension always goes together with divergence.

An additional conclusion that can be drawn from the case of central banking concerns the ways in which we try to explain convergence. It does not seem to be sufficient to rely on classical demand-driven explanations when studying central bank convergence. A case has been made in support of supply-driven explanations. Convergence of the central bank institution has taken place over various decades and in many waves. Each of these waves has its own logic and dynamic. The earliest waves were driven forward by wars and by panic among commercial bankers. The inter-war wave included a large amount of political entrepreneurship, either in the context of international organizations such as the League of Nations or by individual central bankers and so-called money doctors. Such political entrepreneurship seems to have been easier in the 1960s and 1990s than in the inter-war period. Since World War II, central banking has become an integral element of statehood in world society as a result of which central bank convergence in the 1960s and 1990s was characterized by its own logic. Any new state that wishes to act and to be considered as a sovereign player in world society needs to acquire some basic features – among these a classical central bank institution is of primary importance.

The convergence of legal independence has been much faster. Although behavioural independence has gone up and down over the last two to three hundred years, widespread legal independence is actually quite a new phenomenon. Again, we need to include supply-driven explanations, and consequently integrate the active political strategies of international organizations and individual central bankers. Among them, the roles of the Washington-based organizations in particular have been mentioned but many others have prompted central bank reform. I have mentioned the group of central bankers in the Delors committee who formulated the basic principles of European EMU, but individual central bankers have played a part as well. Both deliberative as well as semi-coercive techniques of convergence building based on conditionality have been applied in the process. An important point, therefore, is that the creation and functioning of monetary institutions is a highly politicized endeavour and should be studied accordingly.

Address for correspondence: Martin Marcussen, International Centre for Business and Politics, Copenhagen Business School, Steen Blichers Vej 22, DK-2000 Frederiksberg, Denmark. Tel: +45 3815 3595. e-mail: mm.cbp@cbs.dk

ACKNOWLEDGEMENTS

Thanks for encouragement and excellent comments from Michelle Beyeler, Orfeo Fioretos, Christoph Knill, Hans Peter Olsen, and two anonymous reviewers.

REFERENCES

Beyeler, M. (2002) 'The resiliency of macroeconomic policy regimes – a comparative analysis of central bank reform'. Paper prepared for the 30th ECPR Joint Session of Workshops, Turin, 22–27 March.

Broz, J.L. (1998) 'The origins of central banking: solutions to the free-rider problem', *International Organization* 52(2): 231–68.

Capie, F., Goodhart, C., Fisher, S. and Schnadt, N. (1994) *The Future of Central Banking – The Tercentenary Symposium of the Bank of England*, Cambridge: Cambridge University Press.

Chandler, L.V. (1958) *Benjamin Strong, Central Banker*, Washington, DC: The Brookings Institution.

Cobham, D., Cosc, S., Mattesini, F. and Serre, J.-M. (2000) 'The nature and relevance of central bank independence: an analysis of three European countries', *Discussion Paper Series*, no. 0017, University of St Andrews: Department of Economics.

Cottrell, P.L. (1995) 'The Bank of England in its international setting, 1918–1972', in R. Roberts and D. Kynaston (eds), *The Bank of England. Money, Power and Influence 1694–1994*, Oxford: Clarendon Press, pp. 83–139.

Cukierman, A., Webb, S.B. and Neyapti, B. (1992) 'Measuring the independence of central banks and its effects on policy outcome', *The World Bank Economic Review* 6(3): 353–98.

de Haan, J. and Kooi, W.J. (2000) 'Does central bank independence really matter? New evidence for developing countries using a new indicator', *Journal of Banking and Finance* 24: 643–64.

de Jong, E. (2002) 'Why are price stability and statutory independence of central banks negatively correlated? The role of culture', *European Journal of Political Economy* 18(4): 675–94.

de Kock, M.H. (1974) *Central Banking*, London: Crosby Lockwood Staples.

Deane, M. and Pringle, R. (1994) *The Central Banks*, London: Hamish Hamilton.

Down, I. (2004) 'Central bank independence, disinflations, and the sacrifice ratio', *Comparative Political Studies* 37(4): 399–434.

Drake, P.W. (1989) *The Money Doctor in the Andes: The Kemmerer Missions, 1923–1933*, Durham: Duke University Press.

Finnemore, M. (1996) *National Interests in International Society*, Ithaca: Cornell University Press.

Hayo, B. and Hefeker, C. (2002) 'Reconsidering central bank independence', *European Journal of Political Economy* 18(4): 653–74.

Hillman, A.L. (1999) 'Political culture and the political economy of central bank independence', in M.I. Blejer and M. Skreb (eds), *Major Issues in Central Banking, Monetary Policy and Implications for Transition Economies*, Amsterdam: Kluwer Academic Publishers, pp. 73–86.

Holzinger, K. and Knill, C. (2005) 'Causes and conditions of cross-national policy convergence', *Journal of European Public Policy* 12(5): 775–96.

Iversen, T. (1998) 'Wage bargaining, central bank independence, and the real effects of money', *International Organization* 52(3): 469–504.

Jácome, H.L.I. (2001) 'Legal central bank independence and inflation in Latin America during the 1990s', *IMF Working Paper* WP/01/212, Washington: International Monetary Fund.

Kirk, D. (1999) *Korean Crisis – Unraveling of the Miracle in the IMF Era*, New York: Palgrave.

Maliszewski, W.S. (2000) 'Central bank independence in transition economies', Centre for Social and Economic Research (CASE), London School of Economics and Political Science, September.

Marcussen, M. (2000) *Ideas and Elites: The Social Construction of Economic and Monetary Union*, Aalborg: Aalborg University Press.

Maxfield, S. (1997) *Gatekeepers of Growth: The International Political Economy of Central Banking in Developing Countries*, Princeton: Princeton University Press.

McNamara, K. (2002) 'Rational fictions: central bank independence and the social logic of delegation', *West European Politics* 25(1): 47–76.

Meyer, J.W. and Rowan, B. (1991) 'Institutionalized organizations: formal structure as myth and ceremony', in W.W. Powell, and P.J. DiMaggio (eds), *The New Institutionalism in Organizational Analysis*, Chicago: University of Chicago Press, pp. 41–62.

Posen, A.S. (1993) 'Why central bank independence does not cause low inflation: there is no institutional fix for politics', in R. O'Brien (ed.), *Finance and the International Economy*, Oxford: Oxford University Press, pp. 40–65.

Roberts, P. (2000) 'Benjamin Strong, the Federal Reserve, and the limits to interwar American nationalism', Federal Reserve Bank of Richmond, *Economic Quarterly* 86(2): 61–98.

Rogoff, K. (1985) 'The optimal degree of commitment to an intermediary monetary target', *The Quarterly Journal of Economics* 100(4): 1169–89.

Rosenau, J.N. (1997) *Along the Domestic–Foreign Frontier – Exploring Governance in a Turbulent World*, Cambridge: Cambridge University Press.

Sayers, R.S. (1976) *The Bank of England 1891–1944*, Cambridge: Cambridge University Press, plus appendices.

Stiglitz, J. (2002) *Globalization and Its Discontents*, London: Allen Lane.

Williamson, J. (2000) 'What should the World Bank think about the Washington consensus?', *The World Bank Research Observer* 15(2): 251–64.

Diffusion without convergence: how political context shapes the adoption of regulatory impact assessment

Claudio M. Radaelli

INTRODUCTION

It is often argued that the shift from 'economic interventionism' to regulation as the main policy type is the product of changing governance paradigms (Majone 1996). Although there is a lively debate on whether this process has created a new mode of governance focused on the efficiency of markets (OECD 2002) or, instead, a more subtle form of economic interventionism (as argued by Moran 2003 in his account of British regulation), empirical evidence on regulatory policies across Europe shows that the differences of national styles of regulation have not disappeared (Héritier *et al.* 2001).

A focus on diffusion can provide a convenient lens for the analysis of the different worlds of regulation. Explanations of diffusion relax the assumption that there is an efficient logic in the rise of the regulatory state. Whilst Majone provides a rationale for the adoption of new regulatory tools and institutions based on credibility and the necessity to deliver in terms of efficient markets, diffusion studies explain the growing popularity of new regulatory tools and institutions by using a wider set of variables, including coercion, normative pressure, and mimetism (Pollitt *et al.* 2000; Radaelli 2000). The editor of this special issue makes specific reference to the notion of transnational communication to cover mechanisms of diffusion based on 'lesson-drawing . . ., joint problem-solving activities within transnational élite networks or epistemic communities, the promotion of policy models by international organizations with the objective of accelerating and facilitating cross-national policy transfer as well as the emulation of policy models' (Knill 2005: 770).

The adoption of a diffusion angle shows that efficiency is not the only logic at work. Governments may decide to adopt new institutions and organizations to increase their legitimacy. If more than one logic is at work in the European regulatory state, it becomes easier to account for different results.

This article draws on the diffusion perspective and shows one case of diffusion without convergence by looking at the adoption of regulatory impact assessment (RIA) in Europe. This introductory section provides some essential information on RIA and the research design adopted here. Most European governments are investing in programmes for 'better regulation' and 'good regulatory governance' (OECD 2002). RIA is the cornerstone of these programmes, often in combination with other tools, such as consultation, simplification, codes of conduct on legislative drafting, and initiatives to improve on the access to regulation. It is one of the focal points of the Lisbon strategy to make Europe the most competitive knowledge-based society of the world by 2010. On 26 January 2004, four finance ministers from Ireland, the Netherlands, Luxembourg, and the UK committed four successive European Union (EU) Presidencies to 'further enhance the quality of impact assessments' at the EU level and introduce 'effective systems of impact assessment for new legislation and simplification programmes' at member state level.[1]

The pivotal position of RIA stems from the fact that it provides standards for the whole process of policy formulation, by showing how consultation, the socio-economic costs and benefits, and the major trade-offs in policy choice have been taken into account in the assessment of regulatory proposals or in the analysis of existing legislation.[2] Box 1 presents the main elements of an ideal-typical format of impact assessment.

1 Problem definition
2 Elaboration of different options
3 Consultation
4 Choice of a method to analyse options
5 Analysis of options
6 Special tests (i.e. small and medium enterprises, competition tests, gender impact tests)
7 Criteria of choice among options and regulatory choice suggested to the policy-maker
8 Monitoring regulation and reporting

Box 1 Components of regulatory impact assessment

Specifically, RIA draws on the following elements:

- The definition of the problem (in terms of risk, needs, opportunities for improvement on the status quo).
- An approach to governance based on a transparent, accountable process of formulation of rules, with special emphasis on consultation, the use of empirical evidence in the preparation of legislation, and standards for the validation of natural and social sciences in the regulatory process.
- The explicit consideration of multiple options, including the zero option of not intervening, market-friendly alternatives to regulation, soft law, voluntary agreements, and traditional 'command and control' regulation.
- Specific methodologies for the analysis of different regulatory options, such as cost–benefit analysis, multi-criteria analysis, and comparative risk assessment.
- A commitment to ex-post monitoring and review of regulations.

The question is: what does the diffusion of RIA in Europe really mean? Certainly, RIA is an idea whose time has come. The fact that ideas and policy fads travel across the world is well known. However, to adopt the same idea does not mean convergence in actual action. A new 'bottle' may contain either old or new wine, or, in cases of symbolic politics, even no wine at all. As shown by Hahn and Litan (2004), the diffusion of RIA across the two sides of the Atlantic has not brought about similarities in the process of policy formulation. Transnational communication has produced a community of discourse and has stimulated the introduction of some regulatory policy tools that are labelled 'impact assessment'. But in some cases these tools only exist on paper, and in others disguise different practices under the same label. This stands in contrast to the dominant discourse in policy-maker circles – examined in detail by Radaelli (2004) – that RIA can be designed (and its quality measured) in a decontextualized manner by using checklists and benchmarking tools.

What does the article explain and what is the research design? I am not trying to explain the process of diffusion. Rather, I start from the point made by the literature on diffusion that governments engage in transnational communication and decide to transfer policies for different reasons (such as efficiency, but also mimetism, coercion, or pressure coming from new ideas and discourses formulated by communities of experts). I then move on to explain what happens when governments decide to adopt an instrument like RIA. The dependent variable is the degree of convergence after the decision to adopt RIA has been taken. Convergence can be measured at the level of (a) discourse (that is, governments using the same language of impact assessment to describe their procedures of policy formulation); (b) adoption of guides and regulations on impact assessment; (c) content of impact assessment performed in different countries; and (d) embeddedness of RIA in regulatory policy processes. Roughly speaking, (a) and (b) are bottles, but in terms of activities and output what matters is the wine of (c) and (d). As the wine is very different and in some cases entirely missing, there is diffusion without convergence.

Specifically, I draw on neo-institutional theory and explain diffusion without convergence by using the variables at work in domestic political contexts. The argument here is not that 'context matters', but *how* political context matters. Hence, 'political context' is broken down into the following dimensions: type of bureaucracy, government's capacity to process distributional conflict, characteristics of the policy process, and RIA actors.[3] By doing so, the article seeks to provide a bridge between decontextualized and idiosyncratic approaches, by looking at scope conditions under which a constellation of contextual variables impact on the content and quality of RIA.

In terms of research design, the article compares the US (the country of origin of impact assessment) with the member states of the EU, specifically Denmark, France, Germany, Italy, the Netherlands, and the UK. Extensive information on RIA in the EU is available in two recent studies (FORMEZ 2004; DG Enterprise 2004), hence I will use selective empirical information on EU member states.

Finally, let me illustrate the organization of the article. The next section makes the point about diffusion and lack of convergence, showing that – somewhat paradoxically – it is easier to adopt new policy ideas than to converge on the implementation of policy instruments. The following section – informed by institutional analysis – explains the lack of convergence. The other sections explore the specific dimensions of context. The final two sections link these dimensions and explain why legitimacy and the embeddedness of RIA in the wider process of policy formulation are more important than the quality of economic analysis in impact assessment.

1. EMPIRICAL EVIDENCE ON DIFFUSION

The diffusion of RIA has been remarkable. The major agent of transnational communication at the international level is the Organization for Economic Co-operation and Development (OECD) (1997). In the EU, there are specific bodies engaged with diffusion, such as the Mandelkern Group[4] – its report prepared for the EU Laeken Summit of the European Council provided a formidable forum for socialization of top member states' policy-makers; see Mandelkern Group 2001 – the informal group of directors of better regulation programmes and the 'High-Level Group on Competitiveness' within the Competitiveness Council.[5] Outside the EU, the Sigma agency – a joint initiative of the OECD and the EU, although eminently funded by Brussels – has promoted the adoption of impact assessment in countries willing to join the EU (Sigma 2001).

Transnational communication has been intense. The official rhetoric about the usefulness of impact assessment, and the 'celebration' of RIA (in the Mandelkern report and in several national plans for better regulation), may give the false impression that impact assessment has now become a fairly common tool of regulatory governance with relatively standardized properties across member states. But the process is one of diffusion without convergence. In political science, it is common to distinguish between 'policy diffusion' (in which the analytical focus is on the process of international diffusion of policy ideas and the dependent variable is the pattern of adoption of the same policy across countries) and 'policy convergence' (focused on the effects of diffusion and with similarity or lack of as the dependent variable).

Evidence shows that diffusion has taken place. According to a recent report prepared for the Italian, Dutch, and Irish Presidencies of the EU, before 2001 RIA existed only in a few EU member states: 'RIA was almost unknown not only to laymen, but also to most of the people directly involved in policy formulation and adoption' (FORMEZ 2004: 5). By contrast, in 2004 RIA was officially recognized in the large majority of the EU-15, and even in new member states like Hungary and Poland (Formez 2004: 5). In 2003 a study for the Hellenic Presidency of the EU on thirteen of the then fifteen member states (France and Portugal were not included in the sample) reported on the existence of RIA in seven member states, whilst the other six member states had at least pilot projects (Hellenic Presidency 2003: 8). Thus, all the countries surveyed by the Hellenic Presidency's report claim some experience of RIA.[6] A questionnaire sent in May 2004 to fourteen 'old' EU member states[7] plus the Czech Republic, Estonia, Latvia, Hungary, Poland, Bulgaria, and Norway (in the context of a project on indicators of regulatory quality funded by Directorate General (DG) Enterprise of the Commission) produced the following result: 100 per cent of the sixteen respondents to a question on the importance of impact assessment in better regulation programmes noted that 'the importance of RIA has increased' (DG Enterprise 2004).

Having established that there is a process of diffusion, let us see why there is no convergence. RIA pursues different goals across the EU. Similarity at the level of discourse ('better regulation' principles) and the adoption of some commitments to some type of assessment of impacts (variously defined) of proposed regulation should not be confused with convergence at the level of use of instruments, not to mention convergence of results (achieved via the use of instruments). This is somewhat paradoxical if one considers Peter Hall's argument that major policy ideas and policy paradigms represent the most sophisticated (and most difficult to achieve) type of policy change (Hall 1993). According to Hall, if the whole paradigm upon which policy is built has changed, this will produce wide-ranging changes at the level of policy.

According to the OECD (2002) and the Mandelkern report (2001), RIA is the essential component of a new paradigm dubbed 'regulatory governance' (as opposed to 'economic interventionism'). However, RIA ideas have travelled quite lightly. The fact that a country has a formal description of the role of RIA does not necessarily mean that ministers use RIA in the preparation of new legislation. It does not even mean that – when they use it – ministers broadly follow the steps described in Box 1 above. Let us look at some more evidence. First, there are four clusters of member states in the EU. These clusters have been detected by the DG Enterprise study by using the following criteria: content of impact assessment, presence or absence of indicators of regulatory quality, and quality assurance systems. For some governments impact assessment does not go much further than compliance cost assessment; in other member states it does not stretch beyond a handful of pilot RIAs; in a third cluster, RIA is merely a checklist process; finally, in a few cases there appears to be a consistent effort to assess a wide range of costs and benefits in an integrated process (details in DG Enterprise 2004: ch. 7).

Second, only in a minority of EU member states do impact assessments demonstrate that the benefits of a proposed regulatory option justify the costs. The UK and Italy fall in this category. However, to continue with this example, although the 'net benefit principle' features both in the UK guide to better regulation and in the Italian law on impact assessment (introduced in 1999), rarely does RIA accompany proposals for legislation in the Italian Council of Ministers. By contrast, in the UK impact assessment is used routinely in the formulation of legislation proposed by the government.

Third, when asked about the importance of regulatory quality tools in the policy-making process on a scale from 1 (lowest importance) to 5 (highest importance), RIA was given scores of 1 or 2 by Austria, Luxembourg, and the Netherlands. Greece, Ireland, and the UK were the only 'old' EU member states with a score of 5 for impact assessment (DG Enterprise 2004). Accordingly, the enthusiasm for RIA should be qualified.

Fourth, in a garbage-can fashion, RIA is a solution to different problems. In Germany, Sweden, and Italy RIA is perceived as a possible solution to the problem of simplification, in the Netherlands it is associated with the issue of competitiveness, in Denmark and Belgium the link is between RIA and the quality of the business environment. At the EU level, RIA is perceived as a response to the problem of legitimacy deficit in the Community's regulatory system (Radaelli 2004).

So, having established that the bottle of RIA is new, what type of wine is inside? For the UK, we can talk of relatively new wine (although the UK has been experimenting with RIA since the 1980s) in new bottles. For Belgium, the Netherlands, and Sweden the wine is the old 'compliance cost assessment' and 'reduction of the administrative burdens of enterprises' rebranded as

'RIA'. These member states do not place major emphasis on the assessment of benefits, especially wide societal benefits. Their policy is all about reducing administrative burdens on firms. This is not the same goal as the one of creating the maximum net benefits of regulatory measures. In the DG Enterprise study, only two respondents opted for the latter, whilst ten indicated either 'minimization of regulatory burdens' or 'achieving regulatory goals at the smallest possible cost for business and society' as the main goal of better regulation policy. Finally, in some member states there is no systematic use of RIA, no matter what the formal rules for the formulation of legislation may say. Italy, France, and Austria – to mention three examples – fall in this category of 'new bottles with no wine inside'. Note that both France and Italy have detailed laws on how impact assessment should be done.

To sum up then, the language of RIA has produced a community of discourse for policy-makers and has stimulated the introduction of some instruments which are labelled 'impact assessment' but which in some cases exist only on paper, and in other cases disguise different practice under the same label. Diffusion at the level of 'talk' has not yielded convergence in 'actions' and 'results' – to use the classic terms suggested by Brunsson (1989) and, more recently, Pollitt (2001). Interestingly, no EU government has opposed RIA, for example by arguing that ministers should not be constrained by economic calculations when they make law. In this sense, RIA is a hegemonic discourse – everyone wants to have a bottle of this wine at home. But this discourse is empirically flawed when it argues (as it often does) that there is a one-size-fits-all RIA 'wine'. It is also conceptually flawed when it tries to make the point that the quality of RIA can be measured in a decontextualized manner – a point we will explore later. Let us now examine the role of context in the diffusion process.

2. HOW DOMESTIC POLITICAL CONTEXT MATTERS

How can one possibly explain diffusion without convergence? Institutional analysis of various types (Weaver and Rockman 1993; Hall and Taylor 1996) has persuasively demonstrated that political context matters – especially in the historical-institutionalist version (Steinmo *et al.* 1992). Context matters in processes of diffusion and policy transfer because 'the other conditions are not equal' (Rose 2002). However, this does not mean that only individual explanations can be provided. Rather, it is useful to explore scope conditions and avoid the 'black and white' tension between idiosyncratic explanations and covering laws. If one decides to go beyond the historical-institutionalist point that 'context matters', one has to show *how* it matters.

Drawing on new institutionalism in political science, one can reason that institutions play a role with respect to how RIA is embedded in policy processes, which actors are in a pivotal position in policy formulation, and the concepts of regulatory legitimacy which dominate in each country. Specifically:

(a) Institutional theories (Weaver and Rockman 1993; Hall and Taylor 1996) predict that institutions shape the behaviour of actors and the use of policy tools. Thinking of RIA, the key variables are the bureaucratic context and government's capacity to deal with distributional conflict.

(b) In its original approach (OECD 1997), RIA is supposed to work in a rational, orderly policy process where problems are defined, alternative solutions are probed, and decisions are finally taken by unitary actors. However, theories of the policy process (Sabatier 1999) provide a continuum from rational synoptic models to garbage cans where solutions, actors, and problems are somewhat independent and constantly modified. In between the two extremes, one can find cases of limited structuration of the policy process – as shown by Lindblom's partisan mutual adjustment (Lindblom 1959; Lindblom and Woodhouse 1963), Sabatier's advocacy coalitions framework (Sabatier 1999: ch. 6), and Kingdon's multiple streams model (Kingdon 1984; Zahariadis 1999).

(c) Politico-economic models and pressure group theory (Bernauer and Caduff 2004) suggest that different actors (one can dub them 'RIA stakeholders') will try to use impact assessment for their own goals. Actors have different preferences regarding RIA. For the politician, RIA has to deliver in terms of consensus and political rents. For the bureaucrat, high-quality RIA means respect of formal procedures that define the legitimate activities of the civil service. For the citizen, the test of good RIA is its real-world outcome (whether it produces regulation that delivers a high level of protection and enables the citizen to carry on with socio-economic activities without dissipating the economic and environmental resources of the community). For the firm, different approaches alternatively stipulate that companies try to secure regulation that protects them from new entrants and guarantees rents, or regulation fostering a better business environment.

(d) Finally, the literature on regulatory legitimacy (Majone 1996: ch. 13) suggests that the Achilles heel of RIA may be legitimacy. When policy tools lack credibility, they become at best bureaucratic tick-the-box routines, and at worst they are highly contested. RIA legitimacy may also be connected to risk cultures. In some countries, the legitimacy of science and rationality makes cost–benefit analysis more acceptable than in countries where the culture of risk regulation is not grounded in evidence-based policy.

In consequence, in the remainder of the paper I show how political context matters by breaking it down into different dimensions well known to neo-institutional analysis. Later I will discuss the implications for regulatory legitimacy.

3. BUREAUCRACIES AND IMPACT ASSESSMENT

In its original institutional context – that is the US (see Hahn and Litan 2004) – impact assessment is produced by independent regulatory agencies monitored by the Office of Management and Budget via the Office of

Information and Regulatory Affairs (OIRA). This is a regulatory context characterized by the delegation of regulatory powers to non-majoritarian institutions. The institutional context is based on sector-level, specialized policy-making. RIA is an instrument for discussions at the level of sectoral policy networks (environment, health and safety, food regulation, etc.). The legitimacy of the regulatory process is not based on parliamentary control over the government but on the credibility of executive agencies. The bureaucratic context is one in which agencies and OIRA are well staffed in terms of professional economists. The dominant criterion is efficiency and the main logic is technical. Negotiation and standard operating procedures are not absent, but they are not overwhelming. Indeed, when negotiation among agencies, regulated firms, and committees in Congress has historically become the dominant logic, this has been seen as the pathology of the system – and referred to as 'agency capture'.

In the EU's member states, the bureaucratic contexts are quite different. RIA is still a document for technical discussions at the level of sectoral policy networks, but, most importantly, it is a communication tool between the government and the parliament, and between government and affected interests. The 'regulator' performing RIA is not an independent agency, but a minister reporting to the executive or the Prime Minister. Most independent regulators in Europe have not even been requested to perform impact assessment. Only very recently did countries like the UK introduce RIA as a duty of independent economic regulators.

The European bureaucratic context is one characterized by generalist civil servants or bureaucrats trained in public law. Efficiency still comes second to formal respect of legitimate procedures in the list of criteria used by bureaucracies in countries like Austria, France, Germany, and Italy. Almost invariably, they 'read' RIA in terms of formal (as opposed to substantial) legal logic and conformity to other rules and processes. Not only does the logic of negotiation dominate the behaviour of ministers engaged in impact assessment, it also characterizes the interactions between public administration and pressure groups, and between civil servants and politicians (with the minister, for example, and her or his *cabinets*).

4. GOVERNMENT'S CAPACITY

The capacity of institutions to handle and process conflict is also decisive. The more distributional problems play an important role, the more RIA becomes political because it goes beyond Pareto-efficiency. True, distributional weights can be used to address distributional problems in a transparent manner. But the political problems simply shift to the issue of who sets the weights, how, and why should the process be considered legitimate by all stakeholders.

EU member states have different capacities to deal with distributional problems, depending on whether they are majoritarian or consociational political systems, or, to use Schmidt's typology, simple or compound democracies (Schmidt 2002). In majoritarian democracies like the UK, RIA is used by the core executive to co-ordinate policy. As such, it becomes a component of the discourse within the executive. Schmidt has shown that this discourse is relatively 'thin' in terms of actors and negotiations – hence there are not many distributional problems. The minister draws on RIA to show that the policy choice is being made in the common interest and that the benefits justify the costs. Distributional conflicts kick in when RIA is used outside the executive, in the context of the overall broad argumentation used by the government to persuade the parliament, affected interests, and public opinion.

In consociational democracies like Denmark, policy formulation is multi-actor and 'thick'. Accordingly, RIA is eminently a tool used by socio-economic and governmental élites to define the content of policy. Distributional problems are addressed directly at the stage of policy formulation. It is at this stage that the various checklists and partial estimates of costs and benefits are used (by civil servants, ministers, economic élites, and unions) to articulate a discourse leading to the formulation of regulatory proposals. This is where most of the conflicts arising out of the distributional impact of regulation are settled. Accordingly, RIA in compound democracies may not lead to a final estimate of costs and benefits for a single preferred option. Instead, different partial estimates are available to the stakeholders for the co-ordination of discourse and negotiation before proposed rules are adopted by the government. There is not much evidence of large debates on RIA and its distributional effects at the level of public opinion. Indeed, the very visibility of impact assessment in the public opinion (for example, in the context of debates in the quality press on policy reforms under way) is scarce.

5. POLICY PROCESSES

Institutions provide the riverbeds for policy processes – our second dimension of political context.[8] As originally formulated in the US (OECD 1997), impact assessment is contingent on an orderly policy process with unitary actor and limited information gaps – a model close to the pole of rational-synoptic policy-making mentioned above. In this model, policy decisions are based on the systematic use of empirical evidence. The quality of RIA is measured in terms of the quality of the economic analysis contained therein.

The rational-synoptic model breaks down under conditions of bounded rationality and policy controversies where actors conflict over problem definition and filter the same evidence by using radically different cognitive 'frames'. Additionally, to draw systematically on empirical evidence provided by impact assessment is almost impossible in garbage-can policy processes where problems are constantly reformulated by different political actors, solutions are changed frequently, and the competences of different departments are reshuffled or unclear. In countries like Germany and Italy, the regulatory process is highly fragmented, with multiple points of contact between politics and administration, and between different logics and criteria.

The variability of policy processes explains why some countries like Italy have formally adopted impact assessment, including specific rules on how and when it should be performed, but cannot use it in the ordinary formulation of policy. The problem is the clash between a rather chaotic process of formulation of new legislation (different ministers respond to their political parties more than to the Prime Minister, and often table proposals for new legislation that are not contemplated in the coalition agreement) and an idealistic rational-synoptic process portrayed in the guide to impact assessment. The Italian guide to RIA is contingent on a process of policy formulation that does not exist in that country.

In France, the nature of the policy process kicks in in a different manner. In comparison to Italy, there is more co-ordination at the level of the executive and consequently more coherence at the level of policy formulation. But co-ordination and coherence are achieved politically. Once political agreement has been achieved, RIA is produced (in a few cases and not systematically, as noted above) in haste and superficially, to legitimize choices that have already been taken. Therefore, impact assessment plays a post-decisional role, rather than informing the decision-making process.

In the UK, the annual reports of the National Audit Office (NAO) show that RIA is associated to different policy processes. The NAO 2005 report shows various 'types' of RIA in the British political system. In some regulatory processes, when political pressure to reach one specific decision is high, RIA is used in a post-decisional mode to justify a political choice. The fact that impact assessment was produced according to high or low standards of economic analysis does not affect the final choice made by the government.

In other cases, RIA starts early, when more than one option is still available politically, collects evidence from a variety of sources, including the stakeholders, and engages those who will take the final decision. Put differently, the timing of RIA and the time of political decisions are well integrated. This is a rather exceptional circumstance. Not only may politicans be tempted to decide quickly to respond to public opinion pressures, they may also have already agreed to introduce policy rules in their electoral manifesto, or they may have already instructed commissions of inquiry and produced white papers which backdate the start of a given RIA.

Finally, the NAO 2005 report notes that there are still cases of bureaucratic 'tick the box' attitude to RIA, in which the main goal is to fill in the forms rather than to learn from evidence and explore alternatives to traditional regulation.

These findings show that not only does policy formulation vary across nations, but that even within a single country one can find different types of impact assessment. The more general implication is that the results of impact assessment are contingent on the type of policy process in which RIA works. There are cases in which the process described in RIA guides is rational-synoptic and entirely evidence-based, but decisions are taken in a garbage-can fashion or exclusively on political grounds. The clash leads to the non-use of RIA or to its post-decisional use. Even when the description provided by the guide to impact assessment is not too different from the reality of decision-making, the NAO report shows that there may be easier or more difficult hurdles for the usage of RIA, depending on regulatory sectors, departments in charge of policy, and the vicissitudes of policy formulation.

6. RIA FOR WHOM? THE ROLE OF ACTORS

Institutions provide differential empowerment of actors. As the logic, preferences, and criteria used by the actors involved in policy formulation are not the same, different institutional contexts explain the variability in terms of who is 'in charge' of impact assessment across countries and how the notion of 'RIA quality' is approached.

Drawing on a classic study of decision-making in international politics, Graham Allison's *Essence of Decision* (1971), Farrow and Copeland (2003) argue that RIA can be interpreted in three different (yet not mutually exclusive) ways. They argue that there are at least three RIA 'stakeholders' (political scientists would prefer to stick to 'actors'), i.e. the 'expert', the 'civil servant', and the 'politician'. It is useful to add a fourth important actor, the 'citizen'. And, finally, a fifth ideal-typical actor is the 'corporation' (more precisely, the firm at the micro level and business organizations at a more aggregate level).

Different actors bring into RIA diverse logics, criteria, and quality assurance mechanisms. More fundamentally, better regulation programmes around the EU 'weigh' actors' preferences differently. This is the result of institutional settings and more specific characteristics of the adoption process. Let us first examine the different actors in terms of criteria, logic, and definition of 'successful' RIA, and then move on to illustrate divergence and how institutions and the adoption process explain it.

To begin with, one may legitimately ask the question whether impact assessment programmes are based on the assumption that politicians are rent-seeking – hence RIA should target this problem and empower Weberian civil servants. Or do they make the assumption that policy-makers regulate in the public interest, for example because they want to be re-elected and good quality regulation may increase their popularity? To what extent do the preferences of independent agencies differ from the preferences of elected officials and with what impact on the efficiency and credibility of impact assessment?

The literature on the political economy of regulation is vast. One result is that although elected regulators respond to pressure groups and re-election incentives, they are also driven by their own ideological preferences (Kalt and Zupan 1984). Turning to agencies, in an analysis of Environmental Protection Agency (EPA) decisions, Cropper *et al.* (1992) show that regulators take into account both private interests and diffuse interests (such as the general welfare of the community) when they set environmental standards.

These results come with several qualifications, but the empirical and theoretical literature on how to model actors' preferences should be the starting point of any meaningful RIA system. Without a model that specifies the preferences of policy-makers (be they politicians or civil servants) it is impossible to say what

RIA should do. A 'good RIA design' means different things depending on whether one makes the assumption that civil servants have a preference for regulatory expansion, or are captured by powerful pressure groups, or regulate in the public interest.

Other questions arise from the firms' models in regulatory policy. What do corporate actors want from regulation? Do they seek efficiency or protection? Indeed, the literature suggests very different approaches to the preferences of firms:

- In the public interest theory of regulation, regulators provide rules for the common good and therefore firms should not be necessarily hostile to regulation. One may expect that regulators acting for the common good care about quality and that regulatory efficiency is a component of this.
- In positive political economy, however, firms use regulation as a shelter from competition and new entrants. They try to capture regulators and secure protection. The implication is that dominant companies in a sector would prefer 'low quality', inefficient regulation. A classic paper by Buchanan and Tullock (1975) shows that companies prefer inefficient direct regulation to cost-effective instruments such as environmental taxes because quotas that restrict entry to a market originate scarcity rents.
- In some modern forms of regulatory theories, high levels of environmental and health and safety protection can be a comparative advantage in open markets. Firms may form coalitions with green groups and advocate high levels of protection (Vogel 1995). Using different arguments, Porter (1990) argues that regulation can stimulate innovation and produce competitiveness. One should therefore expect that competitive firms support this type of regulation, whereas marginal firms object to it.
- Finally, another strand of regulatory analysis, this time more focused on empirical studies, has reached the conclusion that the locational choices of companies are not systematically influenced by the presence or absence of high labour and environmental standards (Jaffe *et al.* 1995). This conclusion has been attacked by those who claim that 'good regulatory governance matters' in terms of productivity, better regulatory environment, and ultimately growth (Kaufmann *et al.* 2003).

The problem is compounded by the fact that firms differ in size, sector, and exposure to international trade. Recent models of the firm in regulatory policy break down the notion of the corporate sector as unitary actor and show how different companies join different coalitions in the regulatory game (Bernauer and Caduff 2004).

The result is that one has to clarify the issue 'RIA for whom' before one can design RIA and measure its quality with indicators and benchmarking tools. Overall, the *notion* of 'good RIA' means different things to different stakeholders. Moreover, the *criteria* used to evaluate success differ markedly (Table 1). Let us illustrate this with a simple five-actor approach. Imagine that one can settle the issue of the models of actors by deciding that experts

Table 1 How different stakeholders look at RIA

	Expert	*Civil servant*	*Politician*	*Firm*	*Citizen*
Criteria	Efficiency	Conformity to rules	Consensus	Cost minimization	Cost-effective protection from risk
Success of RIA	Achieving goals in terms of real-world impact	Following legitimate procedures	Outcome of negotiation	Profit	Enabling regulation
Logic of action	Social sciences	Standard operating procedures	Negotiation	Logic of influence	Participation

are neutral and rational actors, bureaucrats are all Weberian civil servants, politicians are best described by public choice theory, citizens are attentive and want to participate, and the firm's utility function does not deviate too much from the neo-classical model (this means that profit maximization is the overriding goal, but we do not say whether firms want to reach it via protectionist regulation or via the reduction of red tape). Consequently, one can reason that:

- The economist (the classic 'expert' in RIA programmes) is concerned about efficiency.
- Civil servants approach RIA by following proper and legitimate procedures in the regulatory process. This actor will use conformity to rules as the main criterion.
- For the politician, RIA may well mean responsiveness to pressure groups, or the median voter, or even responsiveness to external pressure created by the EU, the International Monetary Fund, and so on. Let us assume that the politician uses consensus as the main criterion and success is evaluated in terms of the outcome of negotiations.
- The firm perceives the opportunities of RIA in terms of minimization of costs and defines success in terms of profit.
- The citizens use yet another criterion, the effective protection from risk.

The criteria to establish whether RIA is good or bad vary considerably. They are not necessarily mutually exclusive, though. Regulation produced via proper and legitimate procedures can result in efficient and fair regulation. But one cannot establish a sort of mechanical equivalence of every criterion used by different stakeholders. The idea that RIA should be approached and evaluated only in terms of the quality of its economic analysis is based on institutions and policy processes that give a weight of 100 per cent to one actor, that is, the expert. This looks more like a technocratic dystopia than a realistic description of how actors' preferences are weighted by real-world better regulation programmes.

The *logic of action* is also different. The civil servant follows the logic of standard operating procedures, the politician uses negotiation, and the expert draws on the logic of the social sciences. The citizen's behaviour, instead, is informed by the logic of participation. Finally, the firm draws on the logic of influence.

Institutions provide an opportunity structure which empowers RIA actors differently. Depending on the constellation of logics and criteria, and on the stakeholders in charge of the policy process, RIA programmes go in different directions and pursue different goals. In a context where the logic of formal respect of procedures predominates, RIA is performed by governmental departments to show how the various steps in policy formulation were handled. If the context is one of administrative co-operation, RIA is also shaped by inter-administrative co-operation. It is a tool that enables different departments to manage co-operation (this is to some extent the case in Denmark and the Netherlands). Contrast this with the Westminster model of the UK, where the cabinet office is in charge of RIA and communicates directly with departments about the content of impact assessment. In this case the logic is more 'vertical' than 'horizontal'.

Beyond public administration, the real issue is about the institutional effects on policy styles and their persistence (Unger and van Waarden 1995). A prevailing corporatist style has shaped the Danish RIA, where impact assessment is used by policy-makers in a 'governance mode' that is more 'negotiation' than 'technical analysis of options'. In Italy, where unions and employers' federations were involved in the formulation of policy for most of the 1990s, the initial steps towards the adoption of RIA were marked by an emphasis on consultation and participation of the affected interests.

However, institutional variables (consociational versus majoritarian models) do not tell the entire story. Different governments in the same country try to steer impact assessment in one political direction or another. Consequently, the constellation of dominant actors in the RIA process changes over time. The early RIA approach of the UK (a programme for compliance cost assessment introduced by the Conservative governments in the 1980s) was based on the assumptions that regulatory reform is the solution to the problem of excessive bureaucratic power, that firms are too often excluded from the regulatory process and do not seek protectionist rules, and that policy-makers do not regulate in the public interest, but seek bureaucratic expansion. The adoption of RIA was therefore a component of a political effort to re-balance power in policy-making processes and provide more political opportunities to the business community. With Blair, the opportunity structure for actors involved in impact assessment has changed, with no privileged position granted to corporate actors and an emphasis on a balanced approach to the assessment of a wide spectrum of costs and benefits.

By contrast, in the 1990s, the adoption of RIA in the Netherlands was the solution to the problem of a regulatory process dominated by 'corporatist triangles' (of policy-makers, employers' organizations, and unions). The assumptions were that the regulatory process was not open enough to diffuse interests, that policy-makers tended to coalesce with powerful pressure groups to the detriment of the public interest, and that without a deliberate effort to open up the process (via consultation and impact assessment) the formulation of regulations would become an opaque, unaccountable process. Hence RIA was used by the government to alter the opportunity structure and to provide more power to diffuse interests.

7. REGULATORY LEGITIMACY

What are the implications of our institutionalist account of RIA for regulatory legitimacy? As averred, there are different criteria used by different actors to approach and evaluate RIA. Accurate economic analysis is obviously a cornerstone for the credibility of impact assessment, but it should present the decision-makers with some important issues that *they* have to address – rather than pretending that impact analysis 'silences' the debate by providing a 'scientific' solution to political problems.

If questions are at least as important as answers, then legitimacy is a strong criterion to evaluate RIA. Cross-national experience shows that when impact assessment is built around only one support constituency (such as the business community) the problems of legitimacy become insurmountable (Radaelli 2004). The Italian case (La Spina 2002) is another example of legitimacy problems. RIA was introduced in this country under pressure from the OECD by a small group of policy advisers and a motivated minister. This looks like a case in which the foundations of the system were built by an embryonic epistemic community supported by an entrepreneurial minister. But neither the Italian business community, nor the civil society were really interested in this new tool. The result was that the momentum for RIA was lost.

These points on legitimacy shed a different light on what is a 'good RIA'. The current hegemonic discourse in policy circles has emphasized the importance of good economic analysis. But legitimacy is even more important. It leads to a definition of 'good RIA' (and consequently to a benchmark for its evaluation) based on embeddedness. A 'good RIA' is embedded in the wider regulatory policy process. As argued by DG Enterprise project:

> In a sense, even if impact assessment is impeccable in terms of economic analysis, this is not a sufficient condition for quality. The latter is achieved when better regulation tools change the way regulators think about public policy, inform ministerial decisions, and when they change the way organized interests, firms and citizens engage in the policy-making process, understand and accept the regulatory framework.
>
> (DG Enterprise 2004: 5)

8. CONCLUSIONS

Although a community of discourse has emerged around better regulation programmes and RIA, impact assessment differs markedly throughout the EU. The problem is how to explain the rise of a common discourse, the spread of RIA across Europe, and divergence of content. One common argument in the historical institutionalist literature is that context matters. This article has made an effort to show how political context matters. The institutional elements to control for are the bureaucratic context, how governments handle conflict, the policy process, and the preferences of actors.

Institutions are the riverbeds in which regulatory processes flow. US and European riverbeds are quite different. Within the EU there are several institutional models. Further, RIA is not a tool operating in a vacuum. It is situated in an often-implicit theory of the policy process. In some cases RIA has been imported in EU countries with largely unrealistic models of the policy process. The result has been new bottles with poor wine, or no wine at all.

The point about legitimacy brings us to argue that the plurality of voices and actors in RIA is a precondition for regulatory legitimacy. Arguably, the lesson to be learnt about the diffusion of impact assessment is that social legitimacy is much more important than efficiency. The two are intertwined, of course, as an efficient RIA is more credible than wrong economic analysis of regulatory proposals. But the point is that credibility is the Achilles heel of impact assessment. RIA actors are interested in how their views are incorporated in the regulatory process, how science is validated and by whom, and how the government produces its own numbers. When they think that RIA is tilted towards one actor's preferences to the detriment of others, there is no economic analysis that can compensate for the credibility deficit. If impact assessment is there to 'make institutions think'[9] contextual variables should be taken seriously.

Address for correspondence: Claudio M. Radaelli, Department of Politics, University of Exeter, Exeter EX4 4RJ, UK. email: C.Radaelli@exeter.ac.uk

ACKNOWLEDGEMENTS

I would like to thank an anonymous reviewer, Bas Arts, Fabrizio De Francesco, Robert Hahn, Chris Knill, John Peterson, Francesco Sarpi, Vivien Schmidt, and Kent Weaver for their comments on an early draft, presented at the 2004 Annual Meeting of the American Political Science Association (Chicago, 2–5 September 2004). The usual disclaimer applies.

NOTES

1 http://www.hm-treasury.gov.uk/media/47C54/jirf_0104.pdf.
2 Impact assessment is mostly used ex ante, at the stage of policy formulation, but it can also assist simplification programmes and thus can be used ex post.

3 Hood *et al.* (2001) examine the context of risk regulation regimes by using the three variables of interest-driven pressures, public opinion, and 'market failure' pressures. By contrast, the framework presented in this article pays more attention to institutions.
4 The Mandelkern Group was formed by a Resolution of the Ministers of Public Administration which gave it the 'mandate to develop a common method of evaluating the quality of regulation'.
5 The apparently simple question of who does what in the EU institutions on better regulation opens up the Pandora's box of several units, task forces, committees, high-level groups, and complex organization charts. The Secretariat General of the European Commission (2004) has produced a detailed map.
6 France (not included in the sample) adopted RIA on bills and decrees of the Conseil d'Etat in 1998 (*circulaire*, 26 January 1998). Portugal has a limited form of fiscal analysis.
7 Portugal not included in the sample.
8 The metaphor of institutions as riverbeds appears in Mucciaroni (1992: 466).
9 This is a slogan used by the OECD in its publications on RIA on several occasions.

REFERENCES

Allison, G.T. (1971) *Essence of Decision: Explaining the Cuban Missile Crisis*, Boston: Little, Brown & Co.

Bernauer, T. and Caduff, L. (2004) 'In whose interest? Pressure group politics, economic competition, and environmental regulation', *Journal of Public Policy* 24(1): 99–126.

Brunsson, N. (1989) *The Organization of Hypocrisy. Talk, Decisions and Actions in Organizations*, Chichester and New York: John Wiley & Sons.

Buchanan, J.M. and Tullock, G. (1975) 'Polluters' profits and political response: direct controls versus taxes', *American Economic Review* 65: 139–47.

Cropper, M.L., Evans, W.N., Berardi, S.J., Ducla-Soares, M.M. and Portney, P.R. (1992) 'The determinants of pesticide regulation. A statistical analysis of EPA decision-making', *Journal of Political Economy* 100: 175–87.

DG Enterprise (2004) *Indicators of Regulatory Quality*, Centre for European Studies, University of Bradford.

European Commission (2004) 'Who is doing what on better regulation at EU level – organization charts', *Commission Working Document compiled by the Secretariat General TFAU-2 (Task Force Future of Union)*, Brussels, 1 June.

Farrow, S. and Copeland, C. (2003) 'Evaluating central regulatory institutions'. Paper presented to the OECD Expert Meeting on Regulatory Performance: Ex-post Evaluation of Regulatory Policies, OECD, Paris, 22 September 2003.

FORMEZ (2004) 'A comparative analysis of RIA in ten EU countries'. Report prepared for the Directors of Better Regulation, Dublin, May 2004, http://www.betterregulation.ie.

Hahn, R.W. and Litan, R.E. (2004) 'Counting regulatory benefits and costs: lessons for the US and Europe', AEI–Brooking Joint Center for Regulatory Studies, Working Paper 04/07, October 2004.

Hall, P. (1993) 'Policy paradigms, social learning and the state. The case of economic policy-making in Britain', *Comparative Politics* 25(3) 275–96.

Hall, P. and Taylor, R. (1996) 'Political science and the three new institutionalisms', *Political Studies* 44(5): 936–57.

Hellenic Presidency of the EU, Ad Hoc Group of Experts on Better Regulation (2003) 'Report to the Ministers responsible for Public Administration', Mimeo, Athens, May.

Héritier, A., Kerwer, D., Knill, C., Lehmkuhl, D., Teutsch, M. and Douillet, A.-C. (2001) *Differential Europe. The European Union Impact on National Policymaking*, Lanham, MD: Rowman & Littlefield.
Hood, C., Rothstein, H. and Baldwin, R. (2001) *The Government of Risk. Understanding Risk Regulation Regimes*, Oxford: Oxford University Press.
Jaffe, A.B., Peterson, S., Portney, P.R. and Stavins, R.N. (1995) 'Environmental regulation and the competitiveness of US manufacturing: what does the evidence tell us?', *Journal of Economic Literature* 33: 132–63.
Kalt, J.P. and Zupan, M.A. (1984) 'Capture and ideology in the economic theory of politics', *American Economic Review* 74: 279–300.
Kaufmann, D., Kraay, A. and Mastruzzi, M. (2003) *Governance Matters III: Governance Indicators for 1996–2002*, World Bank. http://www.worldbank.org/wbi/governance/pubs/govmatters3.html.
Kingdon, J.W. (1984) *Agendas, Alternatives and Public Policies*, New York: HarperCollins.
Knill, C. (2005) 'Introduction: Cross-national policy convergence: concepts, approaches and explanatory factors', *Journal of European Public Policy* 12(5): 764–74.
La Spina, A. (2002) 'Expectations, process and outcome in the transfer of RIA: the Italian case'. Paper delivered to the Workshop on RIA in Comparative Perspective, ESRC and Carr-LSE, London, 1 March 2002.
Lindblom, C.E. (1959) 'The science of muddling through', *Public Administration Review* 19: 79–88.
Lindblom, C. E. and Woodhouse, E.J. (1963) *The Policy-Making Process*, New York: Prentice-Hall.
Majone, G. (1996) *Regulating Europe*, London: Routledge.
Mandelkern Group Report (2001) *Final Report*, Brussels, 13 November.
Moran, M. (2003) *The British Regulatory State. High Modernism and Hyper-Innovation*, Oxford: Oxford University Press.
Mucciaroni, G. (1992) 'The garbage can model and the study of policy making: a critique', *Polity* 24(3): 459–82.
National Audit Office (2005) *Evaluation of Regulatory Impact Assessments: Compendium Report 2004–2005*, London: NAO.
OECD (1997) *Regulatory Impact Analysis. Best Practices in OECD Countries*, Paris: OECD Publications.
OECD (2002) *Regulatory Policies in OECD Countries: From Interventionism to Regulatory Governance*, Paris: OECD Publications.
Pollitt, C. (2001) 'Convergence: the useful myth?', *Public Administration* 79(4): 933–47.
Pollitt, C. *et al.* (2000) 'Agency fever? Analysis of an international policy fashion', *Journal of Comparative Policy Analysis* 3(3): 271–90.
Porter, M. (1990) *The Competitive Advantage of Nations*, New York: Free Press.
Radaelli, C.M. (2000) 'Policy transfer in the European Union', *Governance* 13(1): 25–43.
Radaelli, C.M. (2004) 'The diffusion of regulatory impact analysis: best-practice or lesson-drawing?', *European Journal of Political Research* 43(5): 723–47.
Rose, R. (2002) 'When all other conditions are not equal: the context for drawing lessons', in C. Jones Finer (ed.), *Social Policy Reform in Socialist Market China: Lessons for and from Abroad*, Aldershot: Ashgate.
Sabatier, P. (ed.) (1999) *Theories of the Policy Process*, Boulder, CO: Westview Press.
Schmidt, V.A. (2002) *The Futures of European Capitalism*, Oxford: Oxford University Press.

Sigma (2001) 'Improving policy instruments through impact assessment', Sigma Paper No. 31, Paris.

Steinmo, S., Thelen, K. and Longstreth, F. (eds) (1992) *Structuring Politics: Historical Institutionalism in Comparative Analysis*, Cambridge: Cambridge University Press.

Unger, B. and van Waarden, F. (eds) (1995) *Convergence or Diversity? Internationalization and Economic Policy Response*, Aldershot: Avebury Press–Ashgate.

Vogel, D. (1995) *Trading Up. Consumer and Environmental Regulation in a Global Economy*, Cambridge: Harvard University Press.

Weaver, R.K. and Rockman, B.A. (eds) (1993) *Do Institutions Matter?*, Washington, DC: Brookings Institution.

Zahariadis, N. (1999) 'Ambiguity, time, and multiple streams', in P.A. Sabatier (ed.), *Theories of the Policy Process*, Boulder, CO: Westview Press.

COMMENTARY

Policy convergence: a passing fad or a new integrating focus in European Union studies?

Andrew Jordan

According to the *Oxford English Dictionary*, a 'fad' is a craze or something that is enthusiastically, but briefly, taken up by a group of people. Evidently, academia is just as prone to faddish thinking as any other area of social life. New terms, new concepts and new organizing devices seem to come and then go with increasing regularity as the pressure on researchers to 'make their mark' grows. It is against this backdrop that Christoph Knill has assembled this special issue, whose aim is to 'improve our understanding of policy convergence and its causes' (Knill 2005: 765). This is a challenging and thought-provoking question that deserves a wider airing, not least in the European Union (EU) literature. I would like to congratulate Christoph for attempting to raise the profile of this important but under-appreciated topic among the readers of this journal. I would also like to thank him for giving me the opportunity to offer my own comments and suggestions on how the study of policy convergence in the EU can be taken forward.

Knill has, of course, played a very large part in both popularizing and enriching the related concept of Europeanization. His growing interest in understanding how, where, why and when European policies converge is a logical and obvious extension of this earlier work. The broad question that I would like to address in this short commentary is to what extent does this special issue succeed in developing policy convergence research into a similarly enduring focus of EU scholarship? This may seem like an unfairly stern test to apply. To be fair, Knill certainly makes no great claims about what he and his collaborators seek to bring to EU studies. Nevertheless, I strongly suspect that many EU scholars will (at least implicitly) have this question at the back of their minds when they start to read the papers.

In some respects, the portents are very good. Policy convergence has been described as 'one of, if not the, central questions[s] addressed by comparative policy studies' (Howlett 2000: 307). Judging by the contents of one well-known review of public policy analysis (Sabatier 1999), convergence and the debates around closely related concepts, such as policy innovation, diffusion and transfer, are already well-established topics, at least within American circles. However, in other respects, European scholars are not – it has to be said – nearly as accustomed to using the concepts and methods of policy convergence research. The topic of convergence is, for instance, largely neglected in some of the most well-known European textbooks on public policy (e.g. Ham and Hill 1993; Parsons 1995; John 1998). In spite of early claims that it was a natural focal point for EU scholars (for no other reason than that harmonization is the EU's 'core business') (Bennett 1991: 215), the term still does not excite much sustained interest. Scan the indexes of recent texts espousing what could be termed a 'public policy' approach to the EU (e.g. Richardson 2001; Peterson and Bomberg 1999) or even those summarizing EU theorizing (e.g. Wiener and Diez 2004; Rosamond 2000), and the concept is conspicuous by its virtual absence.

In his editorial introduction, Knill concedes that some of the blame for this has to be born by those advocating and practising convergence research. In spite of recent attempts to introduce some order (Bennett 1991; Unger and van Waarden 1995), Holzinger and Knill (2005: 775) admit that it remains a 'rather heterogeneous research field'. Heichel *et al.*'s (2005) comprehensive summary paper substantiates this point very effectively. They conclude that 'A general judgement on the degree of policy convergence . . . is impossible, as there is not enough *common ground* [in the empirical literature] with respect to research designs, concepts and operationalizations' (Heichel *et al.* 2005: 835) (emphasis added). If anything, over the last twenty years the rate of divergence in the convergence literature has continued to grow, at least as far as the use of key terms and concepts is concerned (Heichel *et al.* 2005). Holzinger and Knill (2005: 775) are therefore driven to concede that 'we still have a limited understanding of the causes and conditions of policy convergence.'

On the face of it, frank confessions like these are unlikely to win the advocates of a policy convergence perspective many new followers. In order to avoid this, those advocating convergence research in the EU (which, I presume, includes all the contributors to this volume) urgently need to identify the 'common ground' noted above, in order to provide a launch pad for a more coherent and enduring programme of future work. I would like to argue that this is more likely to happen when: (1) key terms are clearly defined; (2) explanatory variables are accurately identified and defined; (3) credible attempts are made to deal with the vexed issue of causality (i.e. precisely what causes policies to converge?); and (4) advocates relate their work to prevailing debates and analytical frameworks within EU studies. Of these, I suspect that the fourth is likely to be most immediately important to readers of this particular journal. To put it more bluntly, 'what's in [this new concept] for EU researchers' (Radaelli 2000: 132)?

In the remainder of this commentary, I will use these points to try to arrive at an overall assessment of what this special issue is likely to contribute to EU scholarship in the medium to long term.

DEFINING TERMS: WHAT IS POLICY CONVERGENCE?

In his editorial introduction, Knill rightly underscores the importance of working with clearly defined terms. He then offers the following generic definition of policy convergence:

> any increase in the similarity between one or more characteristics of a certain policy . . . across a given set of political jurisdictions . . . over a given period of time. Policy convergence thus describes the *end result* of a process of policy change over time towards some common point, regardless of the causal processes.
>
> (Knill 2005: 768; emphasis added)

This is a good deal fuller than that offered by Bennett (1991) in his widely quoted review article. The opening papers also usefully emphasize that policy convergence is not a static concept, i.e. because policies are the same at a given point in time, does not necessarily confirm that policy convergence has occurred: they could just as easily have emerged independently but in similar forms. According to Bennett, convergence is:

> a process of 'becoming' rather than a condition of 'being' more alike. 'Convergence means moving from different positions towards some common point. To know that countries are alike, tells us nothing about convergence. *There must be movement over time towards some common point.*' In comparative research, therefore, the essential theoretical dimension is *temporal* rather than spatial.
>
> (Bennett 1991: 19; emphasis added)

The opening papers also successfully demarcate policy convergence from a number of other closely related concepts such as diffusion, isomorphism and policy transfer, etc. Finally, Heichel *et al.*'s (2005) distinction between the four different forms in which convergence can occur is immensely useful, as are the various indicators for measuring it (Holzinger and Knill 2005: table 1).

However, the more empirically focused papers in this collection demonstrate the difficulties that arise when these apparently clear analytical distinctions are used in practice. Thus, the papers by Drezner (2005), Radaelli (2005), and Albrecht and Arts (2005) are all clearly concerned with measuring and accounting for the policy convergence (i.e. 'effects' as listed by Knill (2005: table 1), or the 'result' used in the definition above) that has occurred in their respective fields. By contrast, many of the others seem to be as – if not more – concerned with the diffusion (or transmission) of particular innovations over time (i.e. those listed as 'process' by Knill (2005: table 1)).

These and other differences in approach and perspective are not, as Knill makes clear in his editorial introduction, necessarily bad. To some extent, they are inevitable given the complex genealogy of this research area and its deep interconnections with cognate fields. However, at best they might also give unkind critics the impression that the field is not internally coherent or fully formed enough to warrant their sustained attention. At worst, they may suggest that the findings produced by convergence researchers thus far could in large part be accounted for by the different approaches and methods used.

Be that as it may, the striking point which clearly emerges from this particular collection of studies is just how little policy convergence there is in a world which is often presumed to be globalized (and thus increasingly standardized). Of those who are most explicitly concerned with convergence, Drezner (2005) finds evidence of 'bifurcated' policy convergence around two poles; and Albrecht and Arts (2005) demonstrate significantly stronger convergence in terms of policy outputs than policy outcomes. These findings resonate powerfully with what Heichel *et al.* (2005: 817) find in the existing literature, which is 'no homogenous picture of policy convergence'.

Therefore, in the short term the main challenge is to find ways of employing the detailed concepts identified by Knill in a much more consistent and finely grained manner. This, in turn, may require more focused research questions than simply 'is policy in this sector converging?' It is notable that most of the articles in this special issue focus on σ-convergence. Is this an accurate reflection of reality or simply the difficulty of researching the other (three) sub-types? Similarly, *which* aspects of policy are most (or least) likely to converge, etc.? This takes us neatly on to the next issue – the need to specify variables clearly enough.

IDENTIFYING EXPLANATORY VARIABLES

In his editorial introduction, Knill (2005: 764) makes another important point when he argues that 'we still have a rather limited understanding of the phenomenon of policy convergence'. He then shows how the existing literature handles different variables, although he devotes noticeably more space to discussing the independent ones than the dependent ones. The dependent variable tries to capture the aspect(s) of policy under investigation. The early literature on convergence identified a number of promising candidates (Bennett 1988: 418), which Bennett (1991: 218) subsequently boiled down to just five, namely the goals, content (i.e. statutes, rules, etc.), instruments (i.e. the institutional and organizational hardware of the state), outcomes (i.e. the overall effects) and style of policy-making.

Dependent variables

Knill (2005: table 2) arranges the papers in this volume according to different causes of convergence, but he could just as well have used the way they conceptualize the dependent variable. These differences are worthy of further discussion and analysis, as there is a definite bias towards some dimensions of policy than others (although in some of the papers the exact empirical focus is not as clearly specified as perhaps it could be). There are three papers in particular which make a conscious effort to define the dependent variable(s), namely Lenschow *et al.* (2005) Busch and Jörgens (2005); Albrecht and Arts (2005); and Radaelli (2005). It may only be a coincidence, but these four are – to a greater or lesser extent – all interested in the content and the instruments of policy.

This observation begs at least two questions which deserve further scrutiny. First, are these *a priori* the most 'convergent' dimensions of national policy, or are they just the dimensions that can be tracked most easily across time and space? Second, to say that these dimensions are convergent begs the question of whether they are truly functionally equivalent across the cases being examined. In other words, does the mere fact that two countries employ a particular policy instrument (something, presumably, that can be quantified) mean that they use it in precisely the same way? Radaelli's paper, which looks at something as apparently clear-cut as regulatory impact assessment, is highly revealing in this respect as it shows how different actors discursively (re)construct the reality of (non)convergence. Evidently, future research needs to be sensitive to these possibilities. One way might be to harness a mixture of qualitative and larger-n quantitative methods.

Independent variables

If pinning down the dependent variable is problematic, dealing with independent variables in a way which uncovers the underlying causes (or 'determinants') (Bennett 1991: 220) of convergence is likely to be significantly more difficult, but no less important. Early convergence studies tended to assume that policy outputs were strongly correlated with levels of technological and economic development. On this view, states following similar pathways of social and economic development would naturally gravitate towards common policies and policy instruments. We now realize that 'politics does matter' (Brickman *et al.* 1985: 302). However, if it 'matters', which aspects matter more than others? For Bennett (1991: 233), this is *the* analytical problem which scholars of policy convergence now need to get a better grip on.

The problem of demonstrating causality is not, of course, unique to policy convergence research – it complicates all forms of comparative political analysis (Peters 1998: 70). It is not simply a question of finding sufficient variation on *the* independent variable as suggested by Drezner (2005: 841) in his paper, but of working out what that variable might be and disentangling its effect from other ones.[1] Those who operate from a positivist perspective like Paul Sabatier (1999: 267–8) strongly believe that we should all 'think causal process'. In a similar vein, Peters (1998: 6) writes that 'findings [that] are excessively intuitive . . . do not necessarily contribute to political science.'

Several of the papers in this special issue certainly try to 'think causal process'. For example, in their paper, Holzinger and Knill usefully identify and unpack a number of underlying causes of convergence, which resonate powerfully with those identified by Bennett (1991) among others. To these, they also usefully add and explore the notion of 'independent problem-solving' arising from 'parallel problem pressures'. Holzinger and Knill (2005: 777) then go on to declare that their 'primary interest is to theoretically investigate the effects and operation of [these] single convergence mechanisms.' This would be a gargantuan task to complete even in an entire special issue, so sensibly they limit themselves to developing a number of hypotheses on the potential forms of interaction that *could* occur between possible causal mechanisms. To their credit, Lenschow *et al.* (2005: 808) not only develop testable hypotheses, but also empirically test them (although they acknowledge this is closer to a 'thought experiment' than formal deductive analysis). In a similar vein, Drezner modestly describes his own paper as a 'plausibility probe'. And in the papers by Marcussen (2005) and Albrecht and Arts (2005), the question of causality is explored, but the evidence offered is, I am sure they will agree, of a suggestive rather than a conclusive nature. To conclude, this special issue does underline the need for clarity in the definition of variables and it goes some (but not all) of the way towards testing them empirically. In that sense, the foundations have been successfully laid for more detailed exploration and analysis in the future.

HOOKING INTO ESTABLISHED DEBATES

In recent years, the centre of gravity within EU studies has shifted appreciably from what Caporaso (1996: 30) once described as an 'ontological phase', in which most analysts pondered the 'the nature of the beast', to a new one, in which internal policy processes and outcomes are increasingly the centre of attention. That established EU researchers such as Knill and his co-workers should choose to explore policy convergence in the EU is a further indication that the popularity of 'post ontological languages, conceptual frameworks and models' continues to grow (Radaelli 2000: 133).

The precise place of policy convergence in these older debates within EU studies is, at least on one level, rather intriguing as its roots lie squarely in the domain of comparative politics. There is a lively debate as to whether it is realistic to view the EU from this perspective (for a summary, see Rosamond (2000: 105–9). Given this, some EU scholars may be suspicious of policy convergence research. Any such suspicions are, in my view, very much misplaced. The papers in this special issue successfully demonstrate that studying policy convergence is capable of shedding new light on aspects of the EU that have not been explored as closely or as systematically before. If anything, the contributors greatly undersell their case for being taken more seriously by mainstream EU scholars. In his introduction Knill (2005: 765), notes that policy convergence is closely related to 'the booming research industry on globalization and Europeanization'. Fruitful links, for example, are already being made between these literatures (Dimitrova and Steunenberg 2000; Jordan and Liefferink 2004). These demonstrate empirically that EU involvement ('Europeanization') does not necessarily cause every aspect of national policy to converge. Some of the potential causes are, of course, usefully explored in the paper by Lenschow *et al.* (2005).

Europeanization research is, of course, not the only sub-area of EU scholarship that stands to be enriched by the addition of a convergence perspective. Without pretending to be exhaustive, other similarly 'booming industries' include the following:

- *Isomorphism and the EU*: there is a burgeoning literature which explores the extent to which (different aspects of) national and European public administration are converging (Knill 1998; Harmsen 1999; Lodge 2000; Kassim 2003). As yet, strong links have not been forged with the convergence literature.
- *The implementation of EU policy*: in recent years, EU scholars have begun to look at the implementation of policy more systematically and from new theoretical perspectives. As the implementation and convergence literatures both focus on policy outputs and outcomes, there is a rich potential for cross-over work.
- *Policy transfer in the EU*: the EU has been aptly described as 'a valuable laboratory for developing the concept of policy transfer' (Bulmer and Padgett 2004: 110). Diffusion and transfer are very intimately related processes, but the extent to which they genuinely lead to greater similarity in forms is very much the stock in trade of convergence scholars.
- *New modes of EU co-ordination:* as the EU seeks to develop and implement new modes of governance (Hodson and Maher 2001; Scott and Trubek 2002; Jordan and Schout 2006), an obvious question to ask is, do they actually produce the desired level of convergence 'on the ground'? Currently, this literature is more interested in the design and adoption of the new modes rather than their relative effectiveness.
- *European integration*: as the governance 'turn' in EU scholarship gathers pace, it is sometimes easy to forget that many of the issues raised by the older

integration theorists have not gone away. In particular, the hoary debate about whether integration follows a gradual and smooth course (as per neo-functionalism), or a more stepwise pattern (as per intergovernmentalism), is far from being resolved. In many ways, the policy convergence and implementation literatures may help us to arbitrate between these claims (Jordan 1997), because European integration is as much about what happens at the national level within member states, as at the EU level.

CONCLUSIONS

Time will eventually tell us whether policy convergence is another passing fad or a new integrating focus in EU studies. There are enough points of potential synergy hinted at in this special issue to be cautiously positive. Jeremy Richardson's decision to devote an entire issue of this journal to the theme of policy convergence amply demonstrates his own continuing commitment to bringing 'the ... debate about the EU ... into the mainstream of political inquiry' (Wallace 2000: 68). At the same time, the papers assembled here powerfully suggest that any interaction could be mutually beneficial, in the sense that the EU provides a highly dynamic context in which imported concepts (such as policy diffusion, transfer and convergence) can be further refined and extended.

I suspect that the contributors to this special issue are too modest to claim any more than that they have tried to raise the profile of policy convergence among EU scholars. I think that they have done considerably more than that. By clarifying important terms, identifying key variables and making a genuine attempt to tackle the vexed question of causality, they have taken large steps towards fashioning policy convergence into a coherent and cumulative focus of research, which I hope will eventually speak directly to those working in the mainstream of EU studies.

Address for correspondence: Andrew Jordan, School of Environmental Sciences, University of East Anglia, Norwich NR4 7TJ, UK. email: a.jordan@uea.ac.uk

ACKNOWLEDGEMENTS

I am indebted to Christoph Knill for his comments on this commentary. I retain full responsibility for any remaining omissions or misinterpretations. I am grateful to the ESRC (L216252013; M535255117) and the Leverhulme Trust for funding the writing of this paper.

NOTE

1 The urge to test for and demonstrate causality is by no means widely shared among policy scientists, as a recent symposium in the pages of this very journal revealed (Dudley *et al.* 2000) (for a more wide-ranging discussion of this theme, see Hay (2002)).

REFERENCES

Albrecht, J. and Arts, B. (2005) 'Climate policy convergence in Europe: an assessment based on National Communications to the UNFCCC', *Journal of European Public Policy* 12(5): 885–902.

Bennett, C. (1988) 'Different processes, one result: the convergence of data protection policy in Europe and the US', *Governance* 1(4): 415–41.

Bennett, C. (1991) 'Review article: What is policy convergence and what causes it?', *British Journal of Political Science* 21: 215–33.

Brickman, R., Jassanoff, S. and Ilgen, T. (1985) *Controlling Chemicals*, Ithaca: Cornell University Press.

Bulmer, S. and Padgett, S. (2004) 'Policy transfer in the European Union', *British Journal of Political Science* 35: 103–26.

Busch, P.-O. and Jörgens, H. (2005) 'The international sources of policy convergence: explaining the spread of environmental policy innovations', *Journal of European Public Policy* 12(5): 860–84.

Caporaso, J. (1996) 'The EU and forms of state', *Journal of Common Market Studies* 34(1): 29–52.

Dimitrova, A. and Steunenberg, B. (2000) 'The search for convergence of national policies in the European Union', *European Union Politics* 1(2): 201–26.

Drezner, D.W. (2005) 'Globalization, harmonization, and competition: the different pathways to policy convergence', *Journal of European Public Policy* 12(5): 841–59.

Dudley, G., Parsons, W., Radaelli, C.M. and Sabatier, P. (2000) 'Symposium: *Theories of the Policy Process*', *Journal of European Public Policy* 7(1): 122–40.

Ham, C. and Hill, M. (1993) *The Policy Process in the Modern Capitalist State*, 2nd edn, London: Harvester Wheatsheaf.

Harmsen, R. (1999) 'The Europeanization of national administrations', *Governance* 12(1): 81–113.

Hay, C. (2002) *Political Analysis*, Basingstoke: Palgrave.

Heichel, S., Pape, J. and Sommerer, T. (2005) 'Is there convergence in convergence research? An overview of empirical studies on policy convergence', *Journal of European Public Policy* 12(5): 817–40.

Hodson, D. and Maher, I. (2001) 'The open method as a new mode of governance', *Journal of Common Market Studies* 39(4): 719–46.

Holzinger, K. and Knill, C. (2005) 'Causes and conditions of cross-national policy convergence', *Journal of European Public Policy* 12(5): 775–96.

Howlett, M. (2000) 'Beyond legalism? Policy ideas, implementation styles and emulation-based convergence on Canadian and US environmental policy', *Journal of Public Policy* 20: 305–29.

John, P. (1998) *Analysing Public Policy*, London: Pinter.

Jordan, A.J. (1997) '"Overcoming the divide" between international relations and comparative politics approaches to the EC: what role for "postdecisional" politics?', *West European Politics* 20(4): 43–70.

Jordan, A.J. and Liefferink, D. (eds) (2004) *Environmental Policy in Europe: The Europeanization of National Environmental Policy*, London: Routledge.

Jordan, A. and Schout, A. (2006) *The Coordination of the European Union: Exploring the Capacities for Networked Governance*, Oxford: Oxford University Press (in press).

Kassim, H. (2003) 'The European administration: between Europeanization and domestication', in J. Hayward and A. Menon (eds), *Governing Europe*, Oxford: Oxford University Press.

Knill, C. (1998) 'European policies: the impact of national administrative traditions', *Journal of Public Policy* 18(1): 1–28.

Knill, C. (2005) 'Introduction: Cross-national policy convergence: concepts, approaches and explanatory factors', *Journal of European Public Policy* 12(5): 764–74.

Lenschow, A., Liefferink, D. and Veenman, S. (2005) 'When the birds sing. A framework for analysing domestic factors behind policy convergence', *Journal of European Public Policy* 12(5): 797–816.

Lodge, M. (2000) 'Isomorphism of national policies?', *West European Politics* 23(1): 89–107.

Marcussen, M. (2005) 'Central banks on the move', *Journal of European Public Policy* 12(5): 903–23.

Parsons, W. (1995) *Public Policy*, Aldershot: Edward Elgar.

Peters, B.G. (1998) *Comparative Politics: Theory and Methods*, Basingstoke: Macmillan.

Peterson, J. and Bomberg, E. (1999) *Decision-Making in the European Union*, Basingstoke: Palgrave.

Radaelli, C. (2000) 'Public policy comes of age', *Journal of European Public Policy* 7(1): 130–5.

Radaelli, C.M. (2005) 'Diffusion without convergence: how political context shapes the adoption of regulatory impact assessment', *Journal of European Public Policy* 12(5): 924–43.

Richardson, J.J. (ed.) (2001) *European Union: Power and Policy Making*, London: Routledge.

Rosamond, B. (2000) *Theories of European Integration*, Basingstoke: Palgrave.

Sabatier, P. (ed.) (1999) *Theories of the Policy Process*, Boulder: Westview Press.

Scott, J. and Trubek, D. (2002) 'Mind the gap: law and new approaches to governing in the European Union', *European Law Journal* 8(1): 1–18.

Unger, B. and van Waarden, F. (eds) (1995) *Convergence or Diversity?*, Aldershot: Avebury.

Wallace, H. (2000) 'Analysing and explaining policies', in H. Wallace and W. Wallace (eds), *Policy Making in the European Union (4e)*, Oxford: Oxford University Press.

Wiener, A. and Diez, T. (eds) (2004) *European Integration Theory*, Oxford: Oxford University Press.

Notes on contributors

Johan Albrecht is Assistant Professor, Department of General Economics, Ghent University, Belgium.

Bas Arts is Associate Professor, Department of Political Sciences of the Environment, Nijmegen School of Management, Radboud University Nijmegen, The Netherlands.

Per-Olof Busch is Research Associate in the Environmental Policy Research Centre at the Free University of Berlin, Germany.

Daniel W. Drezner is Assistant Professor of Political Science, University of Chicago, USA.

Stephan Heichel is Research Associate, Department of Politics and Management, University of Konstanz, Germany.

Katharina Holzinger is Professor in the Institute of Political Science, University of Hamburg, Germany.

Andrew Jordan is a Senior Research Associate at the ESRC's Centre for Social and Economic Research on the Global Environment at the University of East Anglia, UK.

Helge Jörgens is a Senior Research Associate at the German Advisory Council on the Environment, Berlin, Germany.

Christoph Knill is Professor of Political and Administrative Science at the University of Konstanz, Germany.

Andrea Lenschow is Assistant Professor of Political Science in the Faculty of Social Sciences, University of Osnabrück, Germany.

David Levi-Faur is Senior Research Associate in the School of Political Sciences, University of Haifa, Israel.

Duncan Liefferink is a Senior Research Associate in the Department of Environmental Policy Sciences at Radboud University Nijmegen, The Netherlands.

Martin Marcussen is an Associate Professor in Political Science, International Centre for Business and Politics, Copenhagen Business School, Denmark.

Jessica Pape is Research Associate, Department of Politics and Management, University of Konstanz, Germany.

Claudio M. Radaelli is Professor of Politics at the University of Exeter, UK.

Thomas Sommerer is Research Associate, Department of Political Science, University of Hamburg, Germany.

Sietske Veenman is Research Associate in the Department of Environmental Policy Sciences at Radboud University Nijmegen, The Netherlands.

Index

D

E

F

G

H

I

J

K

L

M

N

O

P

Q

R

S

T

U

V

W

For Product Safety Concerns and Information please contact our EU representative GPSR@taylorandfrancis.com
Taylor & Francis Verlag GmbH, Kaufingerstraße 24, 80331 München, Germany

www.ingramcontent.com/pod-product-compliance
Lightning Source LLC
Chambersburg PA
CBHW072137270326
41931CB00010B/1782

* 9 7 8 1 1 3 8 9 6 7 0 2 1 *